American Decades

U·X·L

2000·2009

Rebecca Valentine

Julie Mellors, Project Editor

U·X·L
A part of Gale, Cengage Learning

GALE
CENGAGE Learning·

Detroit • New York • San Francisco • New Haven, Conn • Waterville, Maine • London

GALE
CENGAGE Learning®

**U•X•L American Decades,
2000–2009**

Rebecca Valentine

Project Editor: Julie Mellors

Rights Acquisition and Management:
Sheila Spencer

Composition: Evi Abou-El-Seoud

Manufacturing: Rita Wimberley

Imaging: John Watkins

Product Design: Kristine Julien

For product information and technology assistance, contact us at
Gale Customer Support, 1-800-877-4253.
For permission to use material from this text or product, submit all requests online at **www.cengage.com/permissions.**
Further permissions questions can be emailed to
permissionrequest@cengage.com

Cover photograph reproduced by permission of © AP Images/Patrick Sison

Library of Congress Cataloging-in-Publication Data

U•X•L American decades
    p. cm.
Includes bibliographical references and index.
Contents: v. 1. 1900-1910 - - v. 2. 1910-1919 - - v. 3. 1920-1929 - - v. 4. 1930-1939 - - v. 5. 1940-1949 - - v. 6. 1950-1959 - - v. 7. 1960-1969 - - v. 8. 1970-1979 - - v. 9. 1980-1989 - - v. 10.1991-1999.
Summary: A ten-volume overview of the twentieth century which explores such topics as the arts, economy, education, government, politics, fashions, health, science, technology, and sports which characterize each decade.
    ISBN 0-7876-6454-5 (set : hardcover : alk. paper)
1. United States- -Civilization- -20th century- -Juvenile literature. 2. United States- -History- -20th century- -Juvenile literature. [1. United States- -Civilization- -20th century. 2. United States- -History- -20th century.] I. UXL (Firm) II. Title: UXL American decades. III. Title: American decades.
    E169.1.U88 2003
    973.91- -cd21
                                                                          2002010176

Gale
27500 Drake Rd.
Farmington Hills, MI 48331-3535

ISBN-13: 978-0-7876-6455-8 (Vol. 1)   ISBN-10: 0-7876-6455-3 (Vol. 1)
ISBN-13: 978-0-7876-6456-5 (Vol. 2)   ISBN-10: 0-7876-6456-1 (Vol. 2)
ISBN-13: 978-0-7876-6457-2 (Vol. 3)   ISBN-10: 0-7876-6457-X (Vol. 3)
ISBN-13: 978-0-7876-6458-9 (Vol. 4)   ISBN-10: 0-7876-6458-8 (Vol. 4)
ISBN-13: 978-0-7876-6459-6 (Vol. 5)   ISBN-10: 0-7876-6459-6 (Vol. 5)
ISBN-13: 978-0-7876-6460-2 (Vol. 6)   ISBN-10: 0-7876-6460-X (Vol. 6)
ISBN-13: 978-0-7876-6461-9 (Vol. 7)   ISBN-10: 0-7876-6461-8 (Vol. 7)
ISBN-13: 978-0-7876-6462-6 (Vol. 8)   ISBN-10: 0-7876-6462-6 (Vol. 8)
ISBN-13: 978-0-7876-6463-3 (Vol. 9)   ISBN-10: 0-7876-6463-4 (Vol. 9)
ISBN-13: 978-0-7876-6464-0 (Vol. 10)   ISBN-10: 0-7876-6464-2 (Vol. 10)
ISBN-13: 978-1-4144-9125-7 (Vol. 11)   ISBN-10: 1-4144-9125-5 (Vol. 11)

This title is also available as an e-book.
ISBN-13: 978-1-4144-9126-4 ISBN-10: 1-4144-9126-3
Contact your Gale, a part of Cengage Learning sales representative for ordering information.

Printed in Mexico
1 2 3 4 5 6 7 16 15 14 13 12

Contents

chapter four

Government, Politics, and Law 71

chapter seven **Science and Technology** . . . 149

Reader's Guide

U·X·L American Decades provides a broad overview of the major events and people that helped to shape American society throughout the twentieth century and the first decade of the twenty-first century. Each volume in this eleven-volume set chronicles a single decade and begins with an introduction to that decade and a timeline of major events in twentieth- and twenty-first century America. Following are eight chapters devoted to these categories of American endeavor:

- Arts and Entertainment
- Business and the Economy
- Education
- Government, Politics, and Law
- Lifestyles and Social Trends
- Medicine and Health
- Science and Technology
- Sports

These chapters are then divided into five sections:

Chronology: A timeline of significant events within the chapter's particular field.

Overview: A summary of the events and people detailed in that chapter.

Headline Makers: Short biographical accounts of key people and their achievements during the decade.

❖ **Topics in the News:** A series of short topical essays describing events and people within the chapter's theme.

☞ **For More Information:** A section that lists books and Web sites directing the student to further information about the events and people covered in the chapter.

OTHER FEATURES

Each volume of *U•X•L American Decades* contains more than eighty black-and-white photographs and illustrations that bring the events and people discussed to life and sidebar boxes that expand on items of high interest to readers. Concluding each volume is a general bibliography of books and Web sites that explore the particular decade in general and a thorough subject index that allows readers to easily locate the events, people, and places discussed throughout that volume of *U•X•L American Decades*.

COMMENTS AND SUGGESTIONS

We welcome your comments on *U•X•L American Decades* and suggestions for other history topics to consider. Please write: Editors, *U•X•L American Decades*, U•X•L, 27500 Drake Rd., Farmington Hills, MI 48331-3535; call toll-free: 1-800-877-4253; fax: 248-699-8097; or send e-mail via http://www.gale.cengage.com.

Chronology

2000 Nightly network news attracts fewer than 30 million regular viewers, down almost half since 1980. More people are turning to the Internet and cable news programs.

2000 **January 10** America Online agrees to buy Time Warner, America's largest traditional media company. The $165-billion deal makes this the biggest merger in the nation's history and proves that the Internet as a media tool is here to stay.

2000 **January 13** Legendary business mogul Bill Gates announces that he will step down from his position as CEO of Microsoft Corporation.

2000 **January 30** The St. Louis Rams win the National Football League (NFL) Super Bowl XXXIV, held in the Georgia Dome in Atlanta, by defeating the Tennessee Titans.

2000 **March 10** The NASDAQ industrial average reaches a high point of 5132.52 thanks to the growth of Internet business. Following this expansion, "dot-com" (Internet-based) companies rapidly experienced a decline in investment funding and profits that momentarily crippled the global economy.

2000 **April 19** Media mogul Oprah Winfrey debuts *O: The Oprah Magazine*.

2000 **April 22** Elián González, the young survivor of a tragic attempt to emigrate from Cuba to the United States in November 1999, is taken from his late mother's family in Miami. He is returned to Cuba to live with his father on June 28. The controversial decision to return González sparks tensions between Cuban immigrants and the federal government.

2000 **June** Google, an Internet technology company, indexes one billion Web pages for its search engine.

2000 **August 2** Kansas voters oust two conservative members of the state school board who had voted to remove any mention of evolution from the state curriculum.

2000 **August 12** Evander Holyfield becomes the first boxer in the sport's history to hold four heavyweight championship titles when he beats John Ruiz in twelve rounds by unanimous decision.

2000 **August 23** Richard Hatch wins one million dollars and the first season of the phenomenally successful television reality show *Survivor*. An estimated 51 million viewers tuned in to the season's final episode.

2000 **September 15** The 2000 Summer Olympic Games commence in Sydney, Australia. American track-and-field athlete Marion Jones becomes the only female to ever win five medals in that sport by earning three gold and two bronze medals. The U.S. Olympic squad takes home a total of ninety–two medals, thirty–seven of which are gold.

2000 **September 21** Barbara Walters extends her contract with *ABC News* and becomes the highest paid broadcast journalist in history. She receives $12 million annually.

2000 **October 12** Al Qaeda terrorists attack the USS *Cole* at port in Yemen, killing seventeen U.S. sailors.

2000 **December 12** In determining the outcome of the 2000 presidential election, the U.S. Supreme Court decides in favor of Bush, overturning the Florida Supreme Court's decision to continue the recount of disputed ballots in Florida. One day later, Gore concedes the election and George W. Bush is officially elected President of the United States.

2001 Toyota begins selling its hybrid-model, Prius, in the United States and immediately generates long wait lists, evidence of evolving interest in eco-consciousness and climate change.

2001 **January 15** *Wikipedia*, the free, volunteer-driven online encyclopedia site, debuts. Within ten years, it has over 18 million user-generated entries in 279 languages and is hailed by *The New York Times* as one of the ten most popular sites on the Internet.

2001   **February 14** The Kansas State Board of Education reverses its 1999 decision to remove the theory of evolution from the state's science curriculum.

2001   **February 18** Beloved National Association for Stock Car Auto Racing (NASCAR) driver Dale Earnhardt Sr. dies in an accident during the final lap of the Daytona 500.

2001   **April 8** Tiger Woods becomes the first golfer to hold all four of the sport's major titles at the same time when he wins his second Masters Golf Tournament.

2001   **May 14** The Supreme Court rules unanimously in *United States v. Oakland Cannabis Buyers' Cooperative* that marijuana cannot be legally used for medical purposes.

2001   **July 2** Fifty-nine-year-old Robert Tools receives the first fully implantable, battery-powered artificial heart, at Jewish Hospital in Louisville, Kentucky. The surgery is performed by Laman A. Gray Jr. and Robert D. Dowling.

2001   **September 11** Terrorists hijack four American airliners and initiate the worst terrorist attack on U.S. soil in history. Hundreds of people die.

2001   **September 24** The XM Satellite Radio service is launched, providing news, music, and other entertainment.

2001   **October 7** U.S. and British forces begin air strikes (Operation Enduring Freedom) in Afghanistan. Hours after U.S. forces strike, Osama bin Laden releases a video praising the terrorist attacks of September 11, though he does not take credit for them.

2001   **November 2** *United States v. Microsoft,* an antitrust lawsuit filed in an attempt to restrict the technology and electronics corporation's "uncompetitive" business practices, reaches a settlement. The case sets precedent for increased government intervention and regulation in the technology sector and largely shapes the decade's legal climate in regards to the new challenges and legal problems associated with the computer age.

2001   **November 10** Apple debuts the iPod, forever changing the music landscape. As happened to the 8-track tape, the cassette tape, and the vinyl album, CDs quickly become "old school."

2001 **November 29** Former Beatles member George Harrison dies after a long struggle with cancer.

2001 **December 2** Enron, a powerful energy company, files for bankruptcy. At the time the biggest in corporate history, Enron's bankruptcy costs investors more than $1 billion. Former CEO Kenneth Lay was convicted of accounting fraud and died soon after.

2002 The BlackBerry smart phone is introduced to the American market.

2002 Nearly 4,200 cases of West Nile virus infection are reported during the year; 284 people die from the disease.

2002 **January 1** The term "blogosphere" (first coined by Brad Graham in 1999) is popularized by William Quick when he uses it on his blog *Daily Pundit* to describe the increase in popularity of blogging.

2002 **January 8** The No Child Left Behind Act (NCLB), which mandates that schools have to perform to new federal standards or face a range of penalties, is signed into law by President George W. Bush.

2002 **January 11** The first twenty detainees arrive at the detainment facility established on the U.S. Naval Base in Guantanamo Bay, Cuba. Labeled "enemy combatants" by Defense Secretary Donald Rumsfeld, these prisoners have no rights under the Geneva Convention.

2002 **January 29** In an infamous State of the Union Address, Bush refers to Iraq, North Korea, and Iran as the "axis of evil."

2002 **February 8** The U.S. Olympic team wins thirty–four medals, ten of which are gold, at the XIX Winter Olympic Games in Salt Lake City, Utah.

2002 **February 21** The media releases a video depicting the death of *Wall Street Journal* reporter Daniel Pearl, who had traveled to Pakistan to investigate links between Richard Reid (the "Shoe-bomber") and al Qaeda.

2002 **April 11** The Walton Family Charitable Support Foundation, created by the family of Wal-Mart founder Sam Walton, donates $300 million to the University of Arkansas. It is the largest donation ever made to an American public university.

2002 **June 11** *American Idol* debuts. It becomes the only program to be ranked number one in the Nielsen Ratings for seven consecutive seasons.

2002 **July 21** Telecommunications company WorldCom files for bankruptcy, surpassing Enron as the largest corporation to fold. It is later revealed that the company's demise was the result of misrepresentative accounting practices, resulting in CEO Bernard Ebbers being sentenced to 25 years in prison.

2002 **August 30** Following lengthy deliberation, a last–minute agreement is reached between MLB officials and the players' union to avoid a labor strike for the remainder of the 2002 season. The bargain negotiated included player consent to mandatory testing for performance–enhancing drugs.

2002 **September 4** Kelly Clarkson wins the first season of *American Idol* with 58 percent of the vote.

2002 **October** Online auction retailer eBay purchases PayPal, a burgeoning Internet money transfer company, for $1.5 billion. PayPal will go on to claim the majority of all eBay transactions and become the primary provider of online shopping transactions.

2002 **November 25** The Department of Homeland Security is established.

2003 **February 1** The space shuttle Columbia disintegrates upon reentering the atmosphere above Texas at approximately 9:00 a.m. The entire crew, comprising of six Americans and Ilan Ramon, Israel's first astronaut, is killed in the accident.

2003 **February 5** Secretary of State Colin Powell addresses the United Nations to plead the U.S. case for an invasion in Iraq. Powell insists that evidence confirms biological and chemical weapons in Iraq.

2003 **March** The social networking site MySpace launches.

2003 **March 20** The United States and a coalition of forces invade Iraq.

2003 **April 3** *Washington Post* reporter Michael Kelly is the first journalist killed in Iraq.

2003 **May 1** Bush holds a press conference on the USS *Abraham Lincoln* declaring an end to major military operations in Iraq. He stands before a banner that reads "Mission Accomplished." As violence escalates in Iraq, Bush is criticized for declaring the end to what could be a much longer war. In 2009 the president admits that the banner was a "mistake."

2003 **June 3** While playing against the Tampa Bay Rays at Wrigley Field, Chicago Cubs power–hitter Sammy Sosa's bat shatters, revealing that it had cork inserted into the barrel. This violation of

MLB regulations casts doubt on the legitimacy of Sosa's recent 500th home run.

2003 **June 4** Celebrity homemaker Martha Stewart is indicted on charges of financial misconduct stemming from an insider trading scandal. In July she is sentenced to a five-month prison sentence and fined.

2003 **June 23** The Supreme Court rules that the University of Michigan's law school admissions policy, which considers race as a factor, is constitutional while its similar undergraduate system is not, in *Grutter v. Bollinger* and *Gratz v. Bollinger*, respectively.

2003 **June 28** New York City officials announce plans for Harvey Milk High School, the first public school aimed at protecting gay students from discrimination.

2003 **July 14** In his *Washington Post* column, Robert Novak exposes Valerie Plame as an undercover CIA operative. The scandal surrounding the leak of Plame's identity to Novak reaches the office of Vice President Dick Cheney.

2003 **September 3** A federal raid of a Bay Area Laboratory Co–operative (BALCO) office reveals rampant steroid abuse in professional sports. The subsequent investigation uncovers connections between the company and high-caliber athletes such as Barry Bonds, Bill Romanowski, and Marion Jones.

2003 **September 3** New York attorney general Eliot Spitzer announces fraud charges against hedge fund Canary Capital Partners LLC, alleging improper trading of mutual fund shares. The case initiates a wave of charges by Spitzer's office and the Securities and Exchange Commission against mutual-fund companies.

2003 **October 3** Roy Horn, one half of the entertaining duo known as Siegfried & Roy, is critically injured while performing with a tiger at The Mirage in Las Vegas. Bitten on the neck, Horn sustained major blood loss and eventually suffered a stroke and partial paralysis, thus ending his career and that of his partner.

2003 **December 8** Bush signs the Medicare Modernization bill into law, adding prescription benefits to the program, allowing for billions of dollars in subsidies to health-care and insurance providers, and opening up competition from private plans.

2003 **December 14** After months of eluding U.S. troops, Saddam Hussein is discovered in a bunker on a farm near the Iraqi city of Tikrit.

2004 **February** Mark Zuckerberg, at the time a sophomore at Harvard, launches Facebook, a social media site. Facebook goes on to become the most successful and ubiquitous social media platform, generating billions of dollars for its owners.

2004 **March 2** Former WorldCom Inc. chief Bernard Ebbers is charged with securities fraud, conspiracy, and false regulatory filings; he pleads not guilty. The company's former chief financial officer, Scott Sullivan, pleads guilty on the same day to securities fraud and agrees to cooperate with prosecutors. Ebbers is convicted on March 15, 2005.

2004 **April 19** Google makes its initial public offering (IPO), with shares priced at $85 apiece. Investors react enthusiastically, generating millions of dollars for Google, which develops into one of the most successful and innovative Internet-based businesses in history.

2004 **April 22** Patrick Daniel "Pat" Tillman, football star and Army Ranger, is killed in combat in Afghanistan. His death becomes an embarrassing scandal for the U.S. Army, when it is revealed that military officials covered up his death by friendly fire in order to avoid bad publicity. He is posthumously awarded the Silver Star citation for valor by Lt. Gen. Stanley McChrystal.

2004 **May** *New Yorker* investigative reporter Seymour Hersh publishes an article on abuses of prisoners of war by U.S. troops at Abu Ghraib in Iraq.

2004 **May 6** The popular sitcom *Friends* airs its final episode after enjoying a 10-season run.

2004 **June 5** Former president Ronald Reagan dies after deteriorating health due to Alzheimer's disease. His family publicly supports stem-cell research as an avenue for potential cures.

2004 **July 7** Federal prosecutors indict former Enron chief Kenneth Lay on charges including conspiracy and bank, securities, and wire fraud. He is convicted on May 15, 2005.

2004 **August 13** The opening ceremony of the 2004 Summer Olympics takes place in Athens, Greece, marking the beginning of a highly successful run for the United States; the American team would go on to earn 103 medals, 35 being gold.

2004 **October 8** Congress passes the Anabolic Steroid Control Act, which reclassifies some performance-enhancing drugs as controlled substances and stiffens penalties for companies trying to work around steroid laws.

2004 **November** The Mozilla Firefox web browser, an open source, free alternative to Internet Explorer, is released.

2004 **November 3** Bush beats Democrat John Kerry to become re-elected president.

2004 **November 4** Eleven states ban gay marriage in local elections. Voters in exit polls cite "moral values" as the most important issue on the ballot.

2004 **December 26** An earthquake with a magnitude of 9.1 on the moment magnitude scale (the third most powerful earthquake ever measured with a seismograph) occurs in the Indian Ocean. The resulting force produces a tsunami as powerful as it is unexpected, which causes destruction in fourteen countries and kills more than 230,000 people.

2005 Mega-celebrities Brad Pitt and Angelina Jolie work together on the set of *Mr. and Mrs. Smith* and become romantically involved. The media dubs them "Brangelina."

2005 The sixth volume in the beloved, best-selling *Harry Potter* series sets a new record for a first printing while the fourth movie in the series becomes the second highest-grossing film of the year.

2005 RedOctane and Harmonix Music Systems release Guitar Hero, a music video game that features the playing of a real guitar. A series of similar games follows, breathing new life into classic rock songs for a new generation.

2005 **January 5** While examining images of space taken in 2003, a team of astronomers discovers Eris, a planet (by the accepted, albeit broad, definition used in determining planethood prior to 2006) more massive than Pluto, which is later determined to be one of the most distant objects in the Solar System.

2005 **February** Three former PayPal employees collaborate to create YouTube, a video-sharing Web site.

2005 **March 31** After a lengthy court battle and a passionate political debate, Terri Schiavo dies in hospice care at the age of forty-one. Schiavo became the center of national media attention when her husband successfully petitioned to have her feeding tube removed. Her parents appealed the decision and attracted the support of prominent politicians. However, when the federal appeals were exhausted, Schiavo's feeding tube was removed and she died of dehydration.

2005 **May** The progressive news and blogging Web site Huffington Post debuts.

2005 **July 24** Cyclist Lance Armstrong wins his seventh consecutive Tour de France and announces his retirement.

2005 **August 29** Hurricane Katrina strikes the Gulf Coast, leaving 80 percent of New Orleans underwater and causing extensive damage in Gulfport and Biloxi, Mississippi, and Mobile, Alabama, while hobbling the Gulf's petrochemical, maritime cargo, fishing, sugarcane, rice, cotton, and tourism industries. Light sweet crude oil hits $71 per barrel on August 30 due to Gulf shortages. Congress approves $62 billion in emergency spending for hurricane relief on September 8. The cost to private insurers tops $40 billion.

2005 **September 28** A Texas grand jury indicts House Majority Leader Republican Tom DeLay on charges of criminal conspiracy relating to the scandal associated with powerful Washington lobbyist Jack Abramoff. DeLay announces his resignation from Congress on January 7, 2006.

2005 **October 31** After the death of Chief Justice William Rehnquist, John Glover Roberts Jr. becomes the seventeenth Chief Justice of the U.S. Supreme Court.

2006 President Bush signs a bill promoting awareness and funding of autism research.

2006 **May 8** Illusionist David Blaine attempts to break the world record for being submerged in water for nine minutes. He is rescued after being under water for seven minutes, eight seconds.

2006 **May 31** Former FBI associate director W. Mark Felt Sr. admits that he is "Deep Throat," the key informant to *Washington Post* reporters Bob Woodward and Carl Bernstein, whose investigative journalism uncovered the Watergate scandal.

2006 **June** Multibillionaire and esteemed businessman Warren Buffett pledges to donate the majority of his enormous fortune to charities, with most of it going to the Gates Foundation. Buffett, who gained his wealth with his company Berkshire Hathaway, began systematically dissolving his estate immediately.

2006 **July** The online instant-messaging and social site Twitter launches and becomes an almost instant sensation.

2006 **July 19** Bush vetoes the embryonic stem-cell research bill.

2006 **July 27** Floyd Landis, who had been announced as the winner of the Tour de France four days earlier, fails his obligatory drug test. He is forced to forfeit his win to Oscar Pereiro, only the second time in the race's history that the winner has been disqualified.

2006 **September 4** Steve Irwin, better known as the "Crocodile Hunter," is killed by a stingray barb on the Great Barrier Reef.

2006 **September 5** Katie Couric joins *CBS Evening News* as the first solo female evening news anchor. At the same time, the channel begins casting on the World Wide Web.

2006 **October** After 35 years as host, Bob Barker tapes his last episode of the popular game show, *The Price is Right*.

2006 **October 2** Charles Carl Roberts IV invades the Amish schoolhouse in Nickel Mines, Pennsylvania, with guns and restraints. After sending out all the boys and adults, he shoots the girls, killing five and wounding five. He then kills himself.

2006 **November 5** Saddam Hussein is sentenced to death and hanged for his crimes against humanity.

2006 **December 2** Nintendo's video game console, the Wii, debuts in the United States at a retail price of $249.99. It outsells both the Xbox 360 and the PlayStation 3 combined throughout the first six months of 2007.

2007 The Dow Jones Industrial Average, a stock market index used to measure the average performance of the American economy, closes above 13,000 (April 27) and 14,000 (May 5), both previously unreached marks. This sign of unprecedented economic achievement is misleading, however, as the market soon declines drastically.

2007 **January 7** Democrat Nancy Pelosi is elected the first female Speaker of the House.

2007 **January 9** Apple unveils the iPhone, which is made available to the public in June and instantly becomes the trendsetter in cellphone design and technology.

2007 **January 10** Bush announces an escalation of troop deployment in Iraq. Later known as the "surge," the increase of military personnel becomes a hotly contested foreign-policy decision for the White House.

2007   **April 10** *Jon and Kate Plus 8* airs on TLC. It features the Gosselin family, which includes parents Jon and Kate plus their eight children. During its seven-year run, it was one of the most popular reality television series. The Gosselins separated in 2009 and the show was revamped as *Kate Plus 8*.

2007   **June 1** Right-to-die advocate Dr. Jack Kevorkian, who was serving a 10-to-25-year sentence for a second-degree murder conviction in 1999 for assisting in a suicide, is released from prison on parole.

2007   **August 7** Barry Bonds hits his 756th home run, surpassing Hank Aaron to claim the major league career home run record.

2007   **August 27** U.S. attorney general Alberto R. Gonzales resigns amid accusations of perjury before Congress, related to his testimony about the improper or illegal use of the USA PATRIOT Act to expose information about citizens.

2007   **August 31** Karl Rove resigns from his position as White House deputy chief of staff.

2007   **October 5** Track star Marion Jones pleads guilty to lying to federal agents about her steroid use and forfeits all titles and race results dating back to September 2000, among them her five medals from the 2000 Summer Olympics.

2007   **November** The Writers Guild of America goes on strike, leaving Americans with a winter television season of repeats and reality shows.

2007   **November 19** Amazon releases the Kindle, an e-book reader, for $399. It sells out in five-and-a-half hours and remains out of stock for five months.

2007   **December 5** The Bush administration's abstinence-only sex education program's effectiveness is questioned when the birth rate for teens ages fifteen to nineteen rises 3 percent in 2006. It is the first time this statistic had risen since 1991.

2008   The four books of the *Twilight* series—fantasy romance novels with a vampire theme—are the best-selling novels of the year. Collectively, they spend more than 235 weeks on *The New York Times* best seller list. The first *Twilight* movie debuts in November and earns $175 million by mid-December.

2008   **January 14** Bush proposes a $145 billion stimulus package focused on tax breaks for consumers and businesses, in order to spur economic recovery in the face of increasing unemployment and home foreclosures.

2008   **March 12**   New York governor Eliot Spitzer resigns.

2008   **March 24**   The official death toll for American soldiers in Iraq reaches four thousand.

2008   **July**   Google indexes one trillion Web pages for its search engine.

2008   **July 5**   Venus Williams defeats her sister Serena to claim her fifth Wimbledon title.

2008   **August 16**   American swimmer Michael Phelps wins his eighth gold medal of the 2008 Summer Olympics, setting a new record for gold medals won by an individual at a single Olympics.

2008   **August 29**   Republican presidential nominee John McCain chooses Alaska governor Sarah Palin as his running mate. She is the first woman on a Republican presidential ticket and proves to be an energizing force within the party.

2008   **September**   As a result of massive losses incurred after the financial crash, banking company Lehman Bros. Holdings files for bankruptcy. The company's $613 billion debt makes it the biggest bankruptcy filing ever submitted in the country. Lehman Bros. Holding's collapse further damages the already-stricken American economy.

2008   **September 13**   *Saturday Night Live* comedian Tina Fey parodies Republican vice-presidential candidate Sarah Palin. The video becomes an instant sensation on YouTube.

2008   **October 3**   Bush signs the Emergency Economic Stabilization Act, a $700 billion bailout of the American financial system.

2008   **November 4**   Barack Obama becomes the first African American president of the United States.

2008   **November 10**   The White House announces it will increase the American International Group (AIG) bailout from $123 billion to $150 billion.

2009   **January 26**   Nadya Suleman (known derisively in the media as "Octomom"), an unemployed single mother, gives birth to eight children after fertility treatments (she already had six). She is accused of wishing to become famous, misusing fertility treatments, and wanting to "cash in" on the birth of her children.

2009   **March**   President Barack Obama overturns his predecessors stem-cell policy and allows the National Institutes of Health to fund research on embryonic stem cells beyond previous restrictions.

2009   **March 12**   Aging investment mogul Bernie Madoff pleads guilty to 11 federal felony charges, all stemming from his establishment and operation of a massive financial fraud. Madoff, whose elaborate scheme spanned decades and conned celebrities, universities, and other major financial entities, was sentenced to 150 years in prison.

2009   **May 19**   The musical comedy-drama show *Glee* debuts on Fox, sparking a nationwide phenomenon of "Gleeks" and merchandise related to the show.

2009   **June 1**   General Motors files for bankruptcy protection with $172.81 billion in debt and $82.29 billion in assets.

2009   **June 12**   By government order, all television shows shift from analog to digital broadcasting.

2009   **June 14**   The Los Angeles Lakers make their record–setting thirtieth appearance in the NBA finals, outperforming the Orlando Magic to earn their fourth championship of the decade.

2009   **June 25**   Mega-superstar and King of Pop Michael Jackson dies at the age of 50. Actress Farrah Fawcett, age 62, also dies.

2009   **July 24**   The federal government begins offering refund vouchers of up to $4,500 on trade-ins of older, low-fuel-efficiency automobiles. The initial $1 billion funding of the so-called Cash for Clunkers program runs out quickly, prompting Congress to pass a $2 billion extension.

2009   **August**   Sonia Sotomayor becomes the first Hispanic woman on the U.S. Supreme Court.

2009   **October 1**   Scientists announce the discovery of Ardi, a 4.4-million-year-old fossilized skeleton that is thought to be the closest genetic link between humans and chimpanzees.

2009   **November 4**   The New York Yankees defeat the Philadelphia Phillies four games to two in the World Series. The win earns the team its twenty–seventh championship title, making the Yankees the most successful professional sports franchise in American history.

2009   **November 13**   NASA announces the discovery of water on the Moon.

2009   **December 10** Obama is awarded the Nobel Peace Prize "for his extraordinary efforts to strengthen international diplomacy and cooperation between peoples."

2009   **December 11** Tiger Woods announces that he will be taking an indefinite leave from professional golf stemming from public marital conflicts and multiple accusations of infidelity.

2009   **December 18** The epic science fiction film *Avatar* premiers in the United States, ten years after its original release date. It becomes the highest-grossing film in North American cinematic history.

The 2000s: An Overview

The first decade of the twenty-first century was, even at its close, nameless. No nicknames, like in the 1920s (the "Roaring" Twenties), or the 1980s, which in hindsight are often referred to as the Reagan Years. The years 2000 to 2009 simply remain, by and large, the two thousands, a generally meaningless referral that accurately reflects the decade's tangled web of political, social, and cultural conflicts.

It was a decade marked by globalization, and technology made that globalization possible. The 2000s saw some of the most influential technological advancements since the age of Thomas Edison as the Internet, cellular phones, and mp3 players came to dominate the American lifestyle and change the way society interacted not only within the boundaries of the United States, but across the world. Staying connected became easier with the click of a mouse and the typing of a cell phone keyboard as social networking and texting became the methods with which to develop new relationships while nurturing old ones. Time zones, political divisions, and geographical distance no longer deterred or prevented communication, and the world's 6.8 billion people seemed more like neighbors than strangers as they signed on to FaceBook, YouTube, and Twitter.

Media and the way in which news was reported also contributed to the feeling of globalization throughout the decade. Due primarily to the advent of the Internet, media coverage was now available twenty-four hours a day, seven days a week, and events could be reported on in real time. As print publications tanked and disappeared, traditional television stations developed Weblogs (blogs) and online news magazines. The down side to this eternal news update was that anyone could now post reports, accurate or otherwise. The power of the world wide web also brought the two wars—one in Afghanistan, the other in Iraq—into the daily lives of Americans as journalists headed to the front lines with the troops; some paid for their tenacity with their lives. Likewise, the terrorist attack that took place on September 11, 2001, took on a highly personal meaning for all of America, as citizens watched footage of the event over and over again. Reporting on the tragedy was immediate and unceasing.

Technology impacted the entertainment industry at a level never before experienced. Mp3 players changed the music listener's world forever, allowing for a mobility that was previously nonexistent. Songs provided a background soundtrack for any and all activities as millions of Americans bought iPods and other devices and filled them with their favorite tunes, videos, and photos. But if the listener was impacted, the recording artist and music publishing industry were to an even greater degree. Just as tapes once replaced vinyl, and CDs replaced tapes, so the mp3 single replaced CDs, and musicians could now release their music, one song at a time. YouTube gave America entertainment for free, and both professional and amateur performers took advantage of this new global audience.

As America's youthful culture adapted fashion styles with names like Emo, Goth, Hipster and Scene while tuning in to 24/7 entertainment, society's economic sector rode to the peak of the wave and then crashed with a devastating *THUD*. The United States experienced economic recession in the early part of the decade before enjoying a boom in real estate. As lenders found new—and ethically questionable—strategies to loan money to potential homebuyers, the housing market peaked mid-decade, then collapsed by 2008. As the economy took a nosedive, unemployment rates soared and people were without homes. The 2000s claimed the highest rate of home foreclosures in a thirty-year-history.

Directly, but not solely, responsible for the economic decline was big business. These companies—some corporations, others lending firms—acted irresponsibly and out of greed, the results of which were the financial struggles not only of individuals, but of major industries such as automobile and airlines. When it became clear that these industries would fail, the government bailed them out with billions of dollars in aid. Meanwhile, corrupt business executives like Bernie Madoff, Kenneth Lay, and several others began serving prison terms for their misdeeds. Business giants such as Enron and WorldCom declared bankruptcy, and America was left not knowing who to trust.

The political arena offered no respite from the nation's economic woes. With three presidential elections, the decade was host to some of the most expensive, personally-directed campaigns in political history. Divisions between political parties deepened, and America turned into a country of them and us. George W. Bush took the United States to war not once but twice during his two terms in the White House. By 2008, the country was ready for a change, and the first African American president—Barack Obama—took office. History was made in politics in other ways, too, as the federal Supreme Court intervened in a presidential election for the first time and declared a winner when one of the most problematic elections ended in a recount.

Into this political, business, and economical predicament came a number of global natural disasters. The tsunami of 2004 was, in terms of damage and death, one of the worst disasters in world history. What began as an earthquake off the coast of Indonesia resulted in a tsunami in the Indian Ocean, and more than 230,000 people in fourteen countries lost their lives in the devastation. The world's generosity was remarkable, as more than $14 billion in humanitarian aid was donated. Mother Nature was not finished wreaking havoc, however, and in 2005, Hurricane Katrina slammed Louisiana and neighboring southern states, flooding New Orleans and killing more than 1,450 people in that state alone.

Whether natural or man-made, one disaster after another bombarded America in the 2000s, and by 2009, the country was exhausted, disheartened, and disenchanted. With troops still in Afghanistan and Iraq, money problems on both an individual and national basis, and people not willing to find common ground on personal issues such as moral values, the end of the decade provided hope that 2010 would bring better things.

Arts and Entertainment

2000 January 10 America Online agrees to buy Time Warner, the largest traditional media company in the United States. The $165-billion deal makes this the biggest merger in the nation's history and proves that the Internet as a media tool is here to stay.

2000 February 29 After 11 years of co-hosting with Regis Philbin, Kathie Lee Gifford announces she is leaving the popular morning talk show *Live with Regis and Kathie Lee.*

2000 August 23 Richard Hatch wins $1 million on the first season of the phenomenally successful television reality show *Survivor.* An estimated 51 million viewers tune in to the season's final episode.

2000 September 21 Barbara Walters extends her contract with ABC and becomes the highest-paid broadcast journalist in history. She receives $12 million annually.

2001 November 2 Pixar's movie *Monsters, Inc.* opens and takes in a studio record-breaking $63.5 million in its first weekend.

2001 November 10 Apple debuts the iPod, thus transforming the music landscape. As with the vinyl album, 8-track tape, and compact cassette tape, the compact disc, or CD, is quickly out of fashion.

2001 November 29 Former Beatles member George Harrison dies after a long struggle with cancer.

2002 January Famed fashion designer Yves Saint Laurent announces his retirement. During his career of over forty years, Saint Laurent made popular the beatnik style of the 1960s and the tailored pant suits of the 1970s.

2002 February 27 New recording artist Alicia Keys wins five Grammy awards.

2002 September 4 Kelly Clarkson wins the first season of *American Idol* with 58 percent of the vote.

2003 February 23 Singer Norah Jones wins five Grammy awards, taking home an award in every category for which she was nominated.

2003 August 28 Performers Britney Spears and Madonna shock the nation when they share a French kiss on the MTV Video Music Awards.

2003 October 3 Roy Horn, one half of the entertaining duo known as Siegfried & Roy, is critically injured while performing with a tiger at The Mirage in Las Vegas. Bitten on the neck, Horn sustains major blood loss and eventually suffers a stroke and partial paralysis, thus ending his career and that of his partner.

2004 Actor Mel Gibson produces *The Passion of the Christ,* a movie controversial for its portrayal of the life of Jesus. Gibson is accused of anti-Semitism, an accusation that recurs after his 2006 arrest for drunk driving during which he makes anti-Semitic statements.

2004 February 1 Janet Jackson and Justin Timberlake provide halftime entertainment at Super Bowl XXXVIII, during which a "wardrobe malfunction" causes Jackson's right breast to be exposed on live television.

2004 May 6 The popular sitcom *Friends* airs its final episode after enjoying a 10-season run.

2005 The sixth volume in the beloved bestselling *Harry Potter* series sets a new record for a first printing while the fourth movie in the series becomes the second-highest-grossing film of the year.

2005 February Three former PayPal employees collaborate to create YouTube, a video-sharing Web site.

2005 November 1 RedOctane and Harmonix Music Systems release *Guitar Hero,* a music video game that simulates the playing of a real guitar. A series of similar games follows, breathing new life into classic rock songs for a new generation.

2005 December 9 Ang Lee's romantic drama, *Brokeback Mountain,* is released to both praise and criticism, as the romantic and sexual relationship portrayed is between two cowboys in the American West.

2006 September 4 Australian Steve Irwin, well-known as the "Crocodile Hunter," is killed by a stingray barb on the Great Barrier Reef.

2006 October After 35 years as host, Bob Barker tapes his last episode of the popular game show *The Price Is Right.*

2006 December 2 Nintendo's video game console, the Wii, debuts in the United States at a retail price of $249.99. It outsells both the Xbox 360 and the PlayStation 3 combined during the first six months of 2007.

2007 April 10 *Jon and Kate Plus 8* airs on TLC. The popular reality television show features the Gosselin family, which includes parents Jon and Kate plus their eight children. The Gosselins separate in 2009, and the show is revamped as *Kate Plus 8.*

2007 November The Writers Guild of America goes on strike, leaving viewers with a winter television season of repeats and reality shows.

2008 The four books of the *Twilight* series—fantasy romance novels with a vampire theme—are the bestselling novels of the year. Collectively, the novels are on the *New York Times* bestseller list for over 235 weeks. The first *Twilight* movie debuts in

November and earns $175 million by mid-December.

2008 September 13 Comedienne and actress Tina Fey entertains many Americans with her television impersonation of vice-presidential hopeful and then-governor of Alaska, Sarah Palin.

2009 June 25 King of Pop Michael Jackson dies at the age of 50. Actress Farrah Fawcett, age 62, dies the same day.

2009 December 18 The epic science fiction film *Avatar* premiers in the United States, 10 years after its original release date. It becomes the highest-grossing film in North American cinematic history.

Everything old was new again in the arts and entertainment industries in the first decade of the twenty-first century. Classic literature subjects such as vampires and magic found their way into two of the decade's most popular book series, *Harry Potter* and *Twilight*. Those books, in turn, were adapted to film, as was the good-versus-evil-themed J. R. R. Tolkien series *The Lord of the Rings*. But retro was cool not only on the big screen. Television series such as *That 70s Show* and *Mad Men* gave younger viewers a front-row seat into yesteryear as it dramatized a world without cell phones, the Internet, or video games.

Nostalgia or the longing for what is past was affirmed by the first interactive music video games *Guitar Hero* and *Rock Band*. Young gamers across the United States were discovering songs by classic rock bands such as AC/DC, Styx, Journey, and Kiss as well as solo artists such as Jimi Hendrix, Sting, and Ozzy Osbourne. Many adults did not hesitate to pick up a guitar or sit down at the drums to play along with the younger generation, and family members enjoyed sharing a new favorite pastime.

The decade was not all about reminiscing, however. Reality shows such as *American Idol, Wipe Out,* and *Survivor* became instant hits as millions of viewers tuned in each week to watch ordinary individuals compete against one another for money and their 15 minutes of fame. Some reality TV focused on charitable activities and humanitarianism; other shows relied on drama and conflict to draw in viewers. Whatever the premise, reality television became an important part of U.S. entertainment in the first decade of the twenty-first century.

The music scene arguably realized the most drastic changes of all in this decade, thanks in large part to the introduction of the MPEG-2 audio layer III (mp3), particularly Apple's iPod. Illegal downloading of songs made a huge impact on the music industry and brought to the forefront the issue of copyrighting and residuals, the money those involved in creating songs or television programs get when their work is rebroadcast or distributed in a new way, also called royalties. Compact discs (CDs) soon joined the ranks of vinyl albums and 8-track tapes, occupying the ignored back racks of the few music stores still in business. The ability of consumers to purchase single tracks as opposed to entire CDs affected the way recording artists produced their music.

The video-streaming site YouTube greatly influenced the music industry, giving previously obscure musicians and private individuals a world-wide audience and the unprecedented opportunity to showcase their music—for free. But music was just part of the appeal of YouTube; all individuals were free to shoot a video about anything and upload it to the site. Consequently, YouTube became controversial for its uncensored content and was banned in various locations around the world.

Americans enjoyed serial films throughout the decade. Millions of movie-goers paid high ticket prices to watch Johnny Depp wearing eyeliner and acting the part of Jack Sparrow in several *Pirates of the Caribbean* movies. The *Harry Potter, Lord of the Rings,* and *Twilight* films were major box-office hits as well. Another trend in films was the three-dimensional (3D) effect, which viewers experienced in such films as *Avatar.*

In the years from 2000 through 2009 a number of celebrities died, including the great actors Paul Newman and Katharine Hepburn and *Peanuts* comic strip creator Charles Schulz. The world mourned the loss of Michael Jackson, the King of Pop and inventor of the "moonwalk," a dance step that became as much his trademark as his single studded glove. Farrah Fawcett, eternal poster girl of the 1970s and television star, died on the same day as Jackson.

Judd Apatow (1967–)   New York-born Judd Apatow is a film producer, director, and screenwriter best known for his character-driven comedy films. A stand-up comedian by age 17, Apatow dropped out of college and moved into an apartment with fellow comedian Adam Sandler. When Apatow failed to make it big as a performer himself, he turned to writing material for other performers. His early career was punctuated by short-lived projects, including two television series *Freaks and Geeks* (1999–2000) and *Undeclared* (2001–2003). The 2000s brought Apatow national acclaim as he wrote one box-office hit after another. Among his scriptwriting credits are *Anchorman: The Legend of Ron Burgundy* (2004), *The 40-Year-Old Virgin* (2005), and *Knocked Up* (2007). *(© AP Photo/Matt Sayles)*

Miley Cyrus (1992–)   Born Destiny Hope Cyrus on November 23, 1992, in Nashville, Tennessee, Miley Ray Cyrus became one of the most successful pop singer-songwriters in the United States in the 2000s. She gained fame as Miley Stewart/Hannah Montana on Disney Channel's sitcom *Hannah Montana*. The show debuted in 2006 and instantly became one of the top-rated series on cable television. That same year, Cyrus released her first single, which was the theme song to her show. By fall 2007, the teen star was touring North America to promote her two record albums, *Hannah Montana* and *Meet Miley Cyrus*. The later years of the decade saw Cyrus touring more even as she starred in several films and released more albums.
(© AP Images/Silvia Izquierdo)

Lady Gaga (1986–)   Born Stefani Joanne Angelina Germanotta, New York City native Lady Gaga released her debut album, *The Fame,* in 2008. The album sold more than fifteen million copies worldwide and earned her six Grammy Award nominations. She was the first recording artist in history to claim four number-one hits from a debut album and the only musician in the digital era to exceed the five million sales mark with her first two hits ("Just Dance" and "Poker Face"). Her second release, *The Fame Monster* (2009), produced two more chart-topping singles and sent her on her second world concert tour. Although Lady Gaga's music combines genres, she is mostly considered a pop music singer-songwriter and is known as much for her outlandish outfits and performance style as for her musical ability. *(© Steve Granitz/WireImage/Getty Images)*

Arianna Huffington (1950–)   Author and syndicated columnist Arianna Huffington began her career as a journalist for the *National Review*. In the early 1990s, Huffington supported her husband, Michael Huffington, a

Republican, in his political ambitions. Before the end of the decade, the now divorced Huffington acquired more liberal political views, and in 2004 she endorsed Democratic presidential candidate John Kerry. Huffington is widely known as the co-founder of the online news site *The Huffington Post*, which was launched on May 9, 2005, and covers various subjects, including U.S. politics, entertainment, and world events. Huffington placed twelfth on *Forbes*'s 2009 Most Influential Women in Media list. In 2010, the public radio program *Both Sides Now* debuted, which Huffington co-hosts. The program presents opposing sides to current political issues. *(© Jason Kempin/Getty Images)*

Michael Jackson (1957–2009) According to Guinness World Records, Michael Jackson was the most successful entertainer of all time. Born into a musical family, the man who would become known as the "King of Pop" began performing with his brothers as part of the group The Jackson 5. He was a pioneer of music and dance and of the music video, which he developed into an art form that helped promote his megahit singles "Beat It," "Billie Jean," and "Thriller." His 1982 album *Thriller* remained in the early 2000s the bestselling album of all time, and Jackson was inducted into the Rock and Roll Hall of Fame twice. His solo career garnered him 13 number-one singles, and by the time of his death in 2009, he had won hundreds of awards, making him the most highly awarded singer worldwide. Jackson's personal life generated much controversy, particularly regarding his eccentric and questionable behavior and for his ever-changing facial appearance. His death from cardiac arrest following an overdose of propofol was declared a homicide. *(© AP Photo/Koji Sasahara)*

Stephenie Meyer (1973–) Stay-at-home mother of three Stephenie Meyer had a dream on June 3, 2003. The characters in her dream were so vivid that she spent the next three months developing a plot concerning them. The result was the first in a series of young-adult, vampire-themed novels called *Twilight*. The book debuted in 2005 at fifth on the *New York Times* bestseller list and received numerous awards. The sequel, *New Moon*, was published in 2006 and sat at the top of the *New York Times* bestseller list for more than 25 weeks. *Eclipse*, the third novel in the series, appeared in 2007. What followed was *The Host* (2008), the author's first adult novel, and *Breaking Dawn* (2008), the fourth *Twilight* series novel. The latter sold 1.3 million copies within 24 hours of being released. Meyer's first novel was made into a 2008 blockbuster movie; the film debuted at number one at the box office. The next two books in the series also enjoyed great success in theaters throughout the world. *(© Jon Kopaloff/FilmMagic/Getty Images)*

Taylor Swift (1989–) Country and pop singer Taylor Swift grew up on a Christmas-tree farm in Reading, Pennsylvania, and began performing at the age of ten. Her self-titled debut album was released in 2006 and went multi-platinum. Her 2008 album *Fearless* won the recording artist four Grammy awards, including Album of the Year. By the end of 2008, her two albums boasted combined sales of four million copies. Swift was named Artist of the Year by *Billboard Magazine* in 2009. That same year, Swift won the MTV Video Music Award for Best Female Video for her single "You Belong With Me." Swift showed her staying power as she accepted the Entertainer of the Year Award from the Country Music Association, the youngest artist ever to win that honor. *(© Jon Kopaloff/FilmMagic/Getty Images)*

Kanye West (1977–) Georgia-born rapper, singer, and record producer Kanye West began his career working with local artists in his adopted city of Chicago. In 2001, West moved to New York to focus on music as a full-time career. That same year, rapper Jay-Z hired West to produce songs for his sixth studio album. Soon, West was working with other big-name stars. In 2002, he cut his own demo and landed a deal with Jay-Z's record label, Roc-a-Fella Records, thus beginning his own recording career. West released his debut album, *The College Dropout* in 2004 and earned himself a Best Rap Album Grammy Award. From that point on, the rapper released consistently top-selling albums and collected one music industry award after another. His personal life made headlines almost as often as his music achievements did. In 2006, West declared "George Bush doesn't care about black people." In 2009, West publicly embarrassed himself when he interrupted fellow recording artist Taylor Swift as she accepted her MTV Video Music Award for Best Female Video of the year. *(© AP Photo/Frank Micelotta/ PictureGroup)*

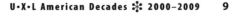

◆ ◆ *Topics in the News*
◆ ◆

❖ FILMS: AMERICANS' ESCAPE

The first decade of the twenty-first century was a difficult time economically. Unemployment was at its worst since the Great Depression (1929–41), and many people struggled just to pay their bills. Prices for houses fell sharply in the middle of the decade, causing many homeowners to owe more on their mortgages than their houses were now worth in the depressed housing market. Unemployment increased as the national economy slowed. Millions of middle- and lower-class Americans in the 2000s faced unexpected financial problems. They needed a way to escape their daily concerns, and popular entertainment provided temporary distractions.

Various kinds of movies provided escape. The most popular movies of the decade were serial in nature; viewers knew at the end of the first movie that there would be one or two sequels. Young magician Harry Potter, the protagonist of seven books by British author J. K. Rowling, was adapted to the screen in eight movies. The first debuted in 2001 and the final one in 2011. The series made more money than any other in film history. Even before the release of the final movie, the series had grossed $6.3 billion worldwide.

Another book-to-film success was the adaptation of J. R. R. Tolkien's 1950s trilogy, *The Lord of the Rings*. Situated in the fantasy world known as Middle Earth, the epic explores classic themes such as good-versus-evil and social class conflict. The films, released in 2001, 2002, and 2003 respectively, became the highest-grossing film trilogy in the world, earning $3 billion in movie ticket sales alone. The popular *Pirates of the Caribbean* series, starring Johnny Depp in four films released between 2003 and 2011, grossed more than $3.6 billion worldwide. It is the only series to include two movies that have exceeded $1 billion in ticket sales. A Disney franchise, the series will be complete with two more film releases.

Comic book characters inspired filmmakers throughout the decade. Batman is the hero in *The Dark Knight*, the highest-grossing film of 2008. Other superhero movies are 2002's *Spider-Man* and its two sequels, several X-Men movies, and a couple films featuring the Fantastic Four. Not one year passed in the decade without a new superhero movie release.

Not surprisingly, comedy was big in the 2000s, particularly the character-driven films written and/or produced by Judd Apatow. Among his box-office hits are *Anchorman: The Legend of Ron Burgundy* (2004), *Talladega Nights: The Ballad of Ricky Bobby* (2006), *Superbad* (2007),

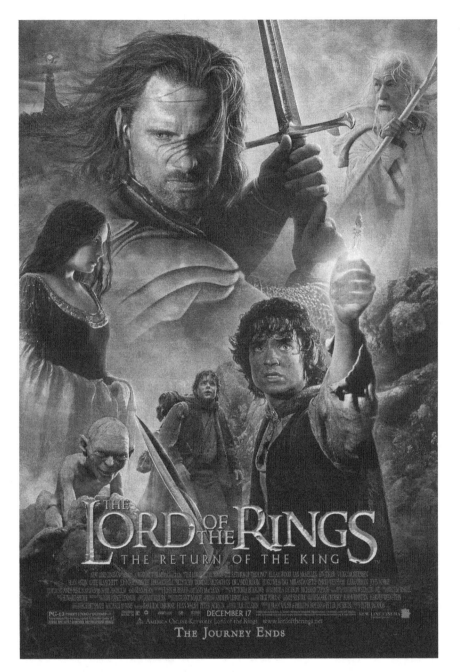

The three *Lord of the Rings* movies became the highest-grossing trilogy in the world following the release of the final movie in 2003. © *New Line Cinema/ The Kobal Collection/The Picture Desk, Inc.*

Forgetting Sarah Marshall (2008), *Step Brothers* (2008), *Year One* (2009), and *Funny People* (2009). Apatow used certain actors repeatedly in these films, namely, Seth Rogen, Will Ferrell, Steve Carrell, and Russell Brand. Other hit comedies of the decade are 2007's *Juno*, the *Scary Movie* series of

Highest-Grossing Films of the 2000s

Year	Title
2000	*Mission: Impossible II*
2001	*Harry Potter and the Sorcerer's Stone*
2002	*The Lord of the Rings: The Two Towers*
2003	*The Lord of the Rings: The Return of the King*
2004	*Shrek 2*
2005	*Harry Potter and the Goblet of Fire*
2006	*Pirates of the Caribbean: Dead Man's Chest*
2007	*Pirates of the Caribbean: At World's End*
2008	*The Dark Knight*
2009	*Avatar*

four films (2000–06, with a fifth film scheduled for release in 2012), and *I Love You, Man* (2009).

Filmmakers experimented with 3-dimensional (3D) filming techniques to entertain and engage moviegoers. Earlier in the decade, giant-screen IMAX theaters used 3D in movies such as *The Polar Express* (2003) and found that audiences liked the experience and were willing to pay more to enjoy the novelty. As a result, 3D was used frequently throughout the 2000s, for example, in *Chicken Little* (2005, the first Disney film to be shot in 3D), 2009's blockbuster hit *Avatar*, and many other family films.

Never the most popular genre at the Academy Award ceremonies, documentaries in the 2000s were particularly high quality. Among the notable films were *Bowling for Columbine* (2002), a commentary on gun use in the United States; *Supersize Me* (2004), an investigation of the effect of fast-food consumption on health and weight; *An Inconvenient Truth* (2006), Al Gore's presentation on the causes and potential effects of global climate change; and *Jesus Camp* (2006), film coverage without narrative interpretation of a fundamentalist Christian children's summer camp.

❖ TELEVISION HITS

The quality of television, in both the writing and the acting, was high in the first decade of the new millennium—so much so, that many

considered the first decade a new golden age of TV. Broadcast television maintained a fast-paced level of drama with weekly serials such as *The West Wing, Grey's Anatomy, 24, Lost,* and *CSI: Crime Scene Investigation.* Cable television did its part with *The Sopranos, Big Love, Six Feet Under,* and *Mad Men.*

As was true of films, comedy was popular in the 2000s, and there were many choices: *30 Rock, Arrested Development, How I Met Your Mother, Family Guy, The Office,* and *The Big Bang Theory.* Cable TV offered humor on a darker level with *Nurse Jackie* and *Pushing Daisies,* but it also drew the laughs with lighter fare such as *Curb Your Enthusiasm.*

Relatively new to the 2000s was reality TV, programs that filmed private individuals as they engaged in various activities or stunts, often in hopes of gaining money and instant celebrity status. These programs presented apparently unscripted stories about individuals, not actors, in various candid situations reacting spontaneously and often emotionally. Although this type of programming appeared during the twentieth century in such programs as *Candid Camera* and *America's Funniest Home Videos,* reality television did not become widely popular until the 2000s.

The first cast of *Survivor* is pictured in 2000. The popular television show ushered in a new era of reality television program-ming in the first decade of the twenty-first century. © *CBS Photo Archive/Getty Images*

Most-Watched Broadcast TV Shows of the 2000s

Year	Title
2000	*Survivor: The Australian Outback*
2001	*Friends*
2002	*CSI: Crime Scene Investigation*
2003	*American Idol*
2004	*American Idol*
2005	*American Idol*
2006	*American Idol*
2007	*American Idol*
2008	*American Idol*
2009	*American Idol*

It is human nature to want to watch other people, to gaze into their lives, to laugh at their mistakes and cheer them on when the going gets tough. Reality TV offers the chance to do all of that and more. First seen in the United States in 2000, the early reality show *Survivor* gained a wide viewing audience and is credited with beginning the reality TV revolution. Before the end of the decade, many Americans were watching the good (*Extreme Makeover: Home Edition*), the bad (*Jersey Shore* and *Temptation Island*), and the questionable (*The Apprentice, Fear Factor,* and *Wife Swap*). But no other reality show attracted as many viewers as *American Idol*. The show premiered in 2002 and dominated the ratings as the number-one most-watched show each of the following years for the remainder of the decade.

❖ OLD GUYS AND NEW GALS: MILLENNIUM MUSIC

American Idol helped change not only the television landscape, but the face of music. Aspiring singers from even the most remote parts of the country now had an opportunity to step into the spotlight and gain national attention. Similarly influential in the new millennium's music scene were the interactive music video games *Rock Band* and *Guitar Hero*. Made for various game systems, these games employ drum pads, guitars, and microphones so that gamers can play along with the band and be judged on accuracy and skill. Millions of gamers heard the music offered

along with these games, causing classic rock bands such as Aerosmith, Journey, Metallica, and Heart to enjoy a revival as a new generation discovered their sound. These bands began touring the United States again, often together with other classic rock bands, playing for people of various ages. Keen audience interest encouraged the release of new music from these old bands as well as re-releases of long-ago hits.

Every decade has its stand-out entertainers, those whose names are linked permanently with a particular type of music, a fashion style, or a particular incident or behavior. Among these entertainers is Stefani Joanne Angelina Germanotta, whose stage name is Lady Gaga. Lady Gaga was just 22 when in 2008 her debut studio album, *The Fame,* shot her into superstardom with the hit singles "Just Dance" and "Poker Face." Credited with impressive songwriting and singing ability, Lady Gaga is also known for her outlandish outfits and her unique performing style. With bleached hair and dramatic makeup, Gaga often conveys an androgynous (having both male and female characteristics) image. She is considered an icon in the gay community and has publicly stated that her megahit "Poker Face" was written about her bisexuality (inclination to

Joe Perry (left) and Steven Tyler of the rock band Aerosmith celebrate at the launch of Aerosmith Guitar Hero on June 27, 2008. The popularity of the Guitar Hero video game also brought new popularity to the classic bands featured in the game. © Kevin Mazur/WireImage/Getty Images

To Tune or Not to Tune

O ne of the most controversial aspects of the 2000s music scene was the rise in popularity of Auto-Tune, an audio processor that corrects pitch in vocal and instrumental performances. If a singer is off-key or an instrument out of tune, Auto-Tune can correct it. The first singer to publicly use Auto-Tune was Cher, when she recorded "Believe" in 1998. Although Auto-Tune enjoyed popularity for a brief time after that, it was mostly not used until rapper T-Pain revived its use in the middle of the decade.

Many musicians view the use of Auto-Tune as an ethical issue. These musicians believe that if performers are good at what they do, they should not need to use the processor. If performers are not good at what they do, they should be doing something else. Some musicians, including the group Death Cab for Cutie, Reba McEntire, and Vince Gill, refuse to use the technology, whereas others, such as Jay-Z, acknowledge its usefulness in some situations but not as a gimmick to be relied upon for performance quality.

have either a female or male sexual partner). Gaga has won hundreds of awards for her music and has used some of her considerable income for humanitarian causes.

The past may have belonged to rock and disco, but the 2000s claimed hip-hop as its main form. Prominent and prolific mainstream hip-hop artists include Kanye West, Lil Wayne, Missy Elliott, 50 Cent, Eminem, and The Black Eyed Peas. Another genre or type of music to move to the forefront was alternative or indie rock, which includes garage rock, post-punk, and new wave. Bands that fall into this category and which enjoyed success in the 2000s include the White Stripes, the Stokes, MGMT, and the Kings of Leon.

Nu metal bands, a subcategory of heavy metal, such as Korn, Linkin Park, Slipknot, Disturbed, and Evanescence brought a new type of heavy metal to the mainstream airwaves. Pop-punk music gained popularity through bands such as Green Day, Weezer, Blink-182, and Good Charlotte. But Emo music in the 2000s seemed to appeal to a much wider audience than it had in previous decades as bands such as My Chemical Romance, Fall Out Boy, and Panic at the Disco enjoyed newfound popularity.

Top Singles of the 2000s

Year	Title	Artist
2000	"Breathe"	Faith Hill
2001	"Hanging by a Moment"	Lifehouse
2002	"How You Remind Me"	Nickelback
2003	"In Da Club"	50 Cent
2004	"Yeah!"	Usher, Lil John, and Ludacris
2005	"We Belong Together"	Mariah Carey
2006	"Bad Day"	Daniel Powter
2007	"Irreplaceable"	Beyonce
2008	"Low"	Flo Rlda and T-Pain
2009	"Boom Boom Pow"	The Black Eyed Peas

The genre that never goes completely out of style is pop, and the first decade of the twenty-first century was no exception. Without a doubt, Britney Spears and Christina Aguilera led the pop music movement in the new millennium, though boy bands such as Backstreet Boys continued to churn out hit after hit in the early years of the decade. The latter years were taken over by the Jonas Brothers. Girl bands such as Destiny's Child had their moments in the spotlight, too, but they never were as popular or successful as their male counterparts.

The crossover pop-rock artists enjoyed a successful decade, with 17-year-old Avril Lavigne leading the way with her 2002 debut album, *Let Go*. The album went four times platinum, and by 2009, Lavigne had sold more than 16 million copies around the world. Before the end of the decade, she had released two more chart-busting albums. Other successful pop-rock entertainers are Pink, Miley Cyrus, Katy Perry, Taylor Swift, and Jennifer Lopez.

The adult music scene welcomed crossover artists Coldplay, Norah Jones, Alicia Keys, and Colbie Caillat, along with veteran recording artists such as Sheryl Crow, Celine Dion, and Phil Stewart. The country music industry embraced *American Idol* winner Carrie Underwood as one of its own, and Underwood joined veteran performers Faith Hill, Tim McGraw, and Keith Urban on the stage and airwaves. Taylor Swift built an early

Top Fiction of the 2000s

Year	Title	Author
2000	The Brethren	John Grisham
2001	Desecration	Jerry B. Jenkins and Tim LaHaye
2002	The Summons	John Grisham
2003	The Da Vinci Code	Dan Brown
2004	The Da Vinci Code	Dan Brown
2005	The Broker	John Grisham
2006	For One More Day	Mitch Albom
2007	A Thousand Splendid Suns	Khaled Hosseini
2008	When Will There Be Good News?	Kate Atkinson
2009	The Lost Symbol	Dan Brown

career on a country-pop sound, and her music won awards in both the pop and country industries.

❖ THE CHANGING LITERARY SCENE

In 2007, Amazon introduced Kindle, the first e-book reader, which changed the book publishing and reading industry. Following the introduction of Kindle, other e-book readers came on the market, and sales were impressive from the start. By mid-2008, experts predicted Amazon would sell $750 million in Kindles by 2010.

E-readers are not for everyone. Those readers who enjoy holding a real book and turning physical pages are less likely to enjoy e-readers. But for people who travel a lot and do not want to carry heavy books, and for readers whose eyesight is strained even with large-print books, the e-reader is a valuable tool. Within four years of launching the Kindle, e-book sales on Amazon surpassed the Web site's sale of print editions.

Whether they preferred reading the old-fashioned way or embraced the new technology, readers chose Dan Brown's novels *The Da Vinci Code* and *The Lost Symbol* and works by favorite 1990s lawyer-turned-author John Grisham. Many Americans enjoyed Nicholas Sparks, who penned 11 novels and one work of nonfiction during the decade. Six of those novels were

A Decade of Celebrity Deaths

THE ARTS LOST MANY NOTABLE PEOPLE IN THE 2000s:

Year	Celebrities
2000	Cartoonist Charles Schulz, actor Sir John Gielgud, actor Walter Matthau
2001	Author Anne Morrow Lindbergh, actor Jack Lemmon, actor Anthony Quinn
2002	Fashion designer Bill Blass, actor Richard Harris, conductor Evgeny Svetlanov
2003	Cartoonist William Steig, pianist Rosalyn Tureck, actor Gregory Peck, actress Katharine Hepburn, filmmaker Elia Kazan
2004	Photographer Richard Avedon, author Alistair Cooke, actor Christopher Reeve, philosopher Jacques Derrida, actress Fay Wray, actor Marlon Brando
2005	Comedian Richard Pryor, television host Johnny Carson, author Hunter S. Thompson, actor Ossie Davis
2006	Author Peter Benchley, composer Gyorgy Ligeti, dancer Katherine Dunham, actor Jack Palance, filmmaker Robert Altman
2007	Fashion designer Liz Claiborne, author Kurt Vonnegut Jr., tenor Luciano Pavarotti, soprano Beverly Sills, filmmaker Ingmar Bergman
2008	Actor Heath Ledger, actor Paul Newman, author-artist Tasha Tudor, fashion designer Yves Saint Laurent, actor Charlton Heston
2009	Artist Andrew Wyeth, choreographer Merce Cunningham, composer Lukas Foss, actor David Carradine, actress Natasha Richardson, actor Patrick Swayze

adapted for the big screen, among them *Message in a Bottle*, *The Notebook*, and *The Last Song*.

The 2000s saw resurgence in the popularity of young-adult literature, primarily in the fantasy and science-fiction genres. Leading in this group was Stephenie Meyer's bestselling *Twilight* series. By the end of the decade, three of her four novels had been made into movies, all of them blockbuster hits. J. K. Rowling's *Harry Potter* series was another success, with her seven novels also being adapted to film.

A number of influential writers died during the decade, including the Beat Generation's Ken Kesey (2001), author of *One Flew Over the Cuckoo's Nest*; feminist writer Susan Sontag (2004); Pulitzer-Prize winner Saul Bellow (2005); playwright Arthur Miller (2005), who wrote *Death of a Salesman*; William Styron (2006), who wrote *Sophie's Choice*; Michael Crichton (2008), the creator of the Jurassic Park series; social commentator Studs Terkel (2008); and John Updike (2009), novelist, essayist, and literary critic.

For More Information

BOOKS

Batchelor, Bob. *The 2000s (American Popular Culture Through History)*. Santa Barbara, CA: Greenwood, 2008.

Pomerance, Murray, ed. *Shining in Shadows: Movie Stars of the 2000s (Star Decades)*. Piscataway, NJ: Rutgers University Press, 2011.

Whitburn, Joel. *Billboard Hot 100 Charts: The 2000s*. Menomonee Falls, WI: Record Research, 2011.

PERIODICALS

"Bestselling Books of the Year, 1996–2007." *Publishers Weekly* (March 24, 2008). This article can be found online at http://www.publishersweekly.com/pw/by-topic/industry-news/publishing-and-marketing/article/2110-bestselling-books-of-the-year-1996-2007.html (accessed on June 29, 2011).

Capps, Robert. "Writer-Director (and Geek God) Judd Apatow Invites You Into His Mind Test." *Wired* 15, no. 6 (May 23, 2007). This article can be found online at http://www.wired.com/entertainment/hollywood/magazine/15-06/ff_apatow (accessed on June 26, 2011).

WEB SITES

"About Arianna." *Arianna Online.* http://ariannaonline.huffingtonpost.com/about/index.php (accessed on June 26, 2011).

"Bio." *The Official Website of Stephenie Meyer.* http://www.stepheniemeyer.com/bio.html (accessed on June 26, 2011).

"Biography & Profile of Taylor Swift." *Taylor Swift Biography.* http://taylorswiftbiography.net/news/biography-profile-of-taylor-swift/ (accessed on June 26, 2011).

"Celebrity Central/Top 25 Celebs: Miley Cyrus." *People.com.* http://www.people.com/people/miley_cyrus/biography (accessed on June 26, 2011).

"Kanye West Biography." *Biography.* http://www.biography.com/articles/Kanye-West-362922 (accessed on June 26, 2011).

Kincaid, Jason. "That Was Fast: Amazon's Kindle Ebook Sales Surpass Print (It Only Took Four Years)." *TC*. May 19, 2011. http://techcrunch.com/2011/05/19/that-was-fast-amazons-kindle-ebook-sales-surpass-print-it-only-took-four-years/ (accessed on June 30, 2011).

"Michael Jackson Biography." *Rock & Roll Hall of Fame*. http://rockhall.com/inductees/michael-jackson/bio/ (accessed on June 26, 2011).

"Music Charts." *Billboard.com*. http://www.billboard.com/#/charts (accessed on June 29, 2011).

"Nielsen Ratings/Historic/Network Television by Season/2000s." *The TV IV*. http://tviv.org/Nielsen_Ratings/Historic/Network_Television_by_Season/2000s (accessed on June 29, 2011).

Nilsen, Richard. "Decade in Review: Entertainment." *azcentral.com*. November 25, 2009. http://www.azcentral.com/review/2009/ent/articles/2009/11/25/20091125notable-art-deaths.html (accessed June 30, 2011).

chapter two # *Business and the Economy*

2000 January 13 Legendary business mogul Bill Gates announces that he will step down from his position as CEO of Microsoft Corporation.

2000 March 10 The NASDAQ industrial average reaches a high point of 5,132.52, thanks to the growth of Internet business. Following this expansion, "dot-com" (Internet-based) companies rapidly experience a decline in investment funding and profits, which momentarily cripples the global economy.

2001 September 11 Hijacked planes are crashed in New York City; in Arlington County, Virginia; and in rural Pennsylvania. Subsequently all international flights are cancelled, and the resulting panic causes the temporary closure of all major U.S. stock exchanges.

2001 November 2 *United States v. Microsoft,* an antitrust lawsuit filed in an attempt to restrict the technology and electronics corporation's "uncompetitive" business practices, reaches a settlement. The case sets precedent for increased government intervention and regulation in the technology sector and largely shapes the decade's legal climate in regards to the new challenges and legal problems associated with the computer age.

2001 November 10 Apple, Inc. releases its iPod portable media player. The device is capable of synchronizing with a home computer's digital music library. The iPod goes on to become one of the most successful innovations in the personal electronics industry.

2001 December 2 Enron, a powerful energy company, files for bankruptcy. At the time the biggest in corporate history, Enron's bankruptcy cost investors more than $1 billion. Former CEO Ken Lay is later convicted of accounting fraud and dies soon after.

2001 December 28 President George W. Bush grants official normal-trade status to China, effective January 1, 2002. The resulting surge in economic activity is beneficial to China and the United States.

2002 July 21 Telecommunications company WorldCom files for bankruptcy, surpassing Enron as the largest corporation to fold. It is later revealed that the company had inflated its earnings, resulting in CEO Bernard Ebbers being sentenced to 25 years in prison.

2003 April 28 Ten of the nation's biggest investment banks reach a settlement with the Securities and Exchange Commission, National Association of Securities Dealers, and the New York Stock Exchange to avoid prosecution over tainted research reports.

2004 February Mark Zuckerberg, at the time a sophomore at Harvard, launches Facebook, a social media site. Facebook goes on to become the most successful and ubiquitous social media platform, generating billions of dollars for its owners.

2004 April 19 Google makes its initial public offering (IPO), with shares priced at $85 apiece. Investors react enthusiastically, generating millions of dollars for Google, which develops into one of the most successful and innovative Internet-based businesses in history.

2005 June 23 In a highly criticized landmark opinion, the Supreme Court rules in *Kelo v. City of New London* that the city was justified in invoking eminent domain rights to private property in order for private contractors to develop a tract of land. This decision broadly expands the power of local governments to seize private property for "urban development" purposes.

2005 August 29 Hurricane Katrina strikes the Gulf Coast, leaving 80 percent of New Orleans underwater and causing extensive damage in Gulfport and Biloxi, Mississippi, and Mobile, Alabama, while hobbling the Gulf's petrochemical, maritime cargo, fishing, sugarcane, rice, cotton, and tourism industries. Light sweet crude oil hits $71 per barrel on August 30 due to Gulf shortages. Congress approves $62 billion in emergency spending for hurricane relief on September 8. The cost to private insurers tops $40 billion.

2006 January 24 Ford Motor Company announces plans to cut up to thirty thousand jobs over six years and close as many as fourteen factories.

2007 The Dow Jones Industrial Average, a stock market index used to measure the average performance of the U.S. economy, closes above 13,000 (April 27) and 14,000 (May 5), both previously unreached marks. This sign of unprecedented economic achievement is misleading, however, as the market soon declines drastically.

2007 October 30 Merrill Lynch & Co. chief E. Stanley O'Neal announces his resignation less than a week after the company's disclosure of an $8.4 billion write-down on bad subprime mortgage investments. He is succeeded on November 14 by New York Stock Exchange chief John A. Thain.

2007 December 19 Morgan Stanley & Co. discloses a $9.4 billion write-down of subprime mortgage assets.

2008 September As a result of massive losses incurred after the financial crash, banking company Lehman Bros. Holdings files for bankruptcy. The company's debt of over $6 billion makes it the biggest bankruptcy filing ever submitted in the country. Lehman Bros. Holding's collapse further damages the already-stricken U.S. economy.

2008 September 29 The Dow Jones Industrial Average closes at 10,365.45—777 points fewer than the day's high point, a record single-day loss—as stockbrokers reflexively sell their assets. The panic is a reaction to a decision made by Congress to strike down the proposed $700 billion federal "bailout plan," which many economists felt was crucial to continued U.S. economic functioning.

2008 October 3 The economic stimulus plan, colloquially called the "bailout," is passed by the House of Representatives and signed into law by President Barack Obama. The plan was issued as an emergency measure in an attempt to correct the steady decline of the U.S. financial system, which had been devastated by the subprime mortgage crisis. The stimulus package gave $700 billion to banks so that they could continue to function, albeit with a tarnished reputation and reduced public trust.

2008 November 23 Citigroup finalizes its rescue plan with the Treasury Department, Federal Reserve, and FDIC, providing for the government to invest $20 billion in the bank and to partially guarantee more than $300 billion in assets.

2008 November 25 The Federal Reserve and the Treasury Department announce an $800 billion program to thaw frozen credit markets—$600 billion allocated to buying debt from Fannie Mae, Freddie Mac, and other mortgage financiers and $200 million to encourage investors to buy securities tied to car and student loans and other forms of consumer credit.

2009 March 12 Aging investment mogul Bernie Madoff pleads guilty to eleven federal felony charges, all stemming from his establishment and operation of a massive financial fraud. Madoff, whose elaborate scheme spanned decades and conned celebrities, universities, and other major financial entities, is sentenced to 150 years in prison.

2009 April 30 Chrysler files for bankruptcy protection after creditors reject a White House-brokered restructuring plan.

2009 June 1 GM files for bankruptcy protection with $172.81 billion in debt and $82.29 billion in assets.

2009 October 16 Raj Rajaratnam, founder of the Galleon Group financial group, is arrested by the FBI in connection with his involvement with an insider trading enterprise. Following a shocking exposure of extensive, deliberate conspiracy to trade on material, non-public information for upwards of $50 million in illegal profits, Rajaratnam is found guilty on fourteen federal charges and assigned a prison sentence.

The first decade of the twenty-first century was a period of deep uncertainty, rapid innovation, and constant fluctuation for the U.S. economy. The collapse of the dot-com stock market bubble in the first months of the new millennium set a tone of unease that would pervade the atmosphere of American business throughout the 2000s as investors, analysts, and academics struggled to understand the cause and nature of the market's behavior. Amid the clamor of overzealous real estate investors, confusing and contradictory market predictions from economists, credit scarcity, assorted fraudulent schemes, inexplicably fluctuating Dow levels, and an overall devaluation of the economy, only the most stolid of law-abiding investors made profits. Corporations and financial firms, whose reckless lending and spending practices played a major role in the national economy's tumult, were conversely safe from harm, as many were determined by the government to be "too big to fail" and given billions of dollars in financial assistance.

As businesses in many unrelated industries, such as automobile manufacturing and airline operations, began to falter and stumble under the pressure of the declining national economy, every entity implicit in the decline resorted to pointing fingers, denying responsibility for the intensifying recession: Mortgagers and consumers were blamed for irresponsible credit use and overspending; investors were blamed for speculating on stocks and overvaluing asset-backed securities; lenders were blamed for offering absurdly hazardous loans, disguising the risks associated with sub-prime lending, and paying out exorbitant executive compensation; manufacturers were blamed for producing poor products and ignoring consumer desires; organized workers were blamed for demanding uncompetitive wages and benefits; and the federal government was blamed for not being diligent in its market regulation duties and, conversely, for providing too much assistance to troubled companies and indebted credit-users.

This culture of hostility became widespread in the world of U.S. business, with public indignation building with the seemingly endless procession of lying executives, corporate trickery, fraudulent schemes, governmental mismanagement, and the illegal financial activities of high-profile figures. As the decade drew to a close, the U.S. economy had devolved into an angry brawl between its various components, while unemployment, poverty, and homelessness afflicted the working class, whose concerns went unheard until the entire nation was in a major recession. Although unable to determine what factors were mostly responsible for the market's erratic behavior, the federal government attempted to manage the recession, authorizing stimulus and bailout packages and rescuing several major corporations from assured insolvency. Those injured by the market's steep drop were critical of this government intervention, however; they argued that the government should have given the money to financially troubled individuals rather than pump the money into a system that was obviously flawed.

Fortunately, not every economic development to take place during the 2000s was negative. Several Internet-based companies that had managed to weather the dot-com burst and subsequent bust developed into unique, radical operations that laid the framework for future companies. In addition, certain industry newcomers, whose population saw rapid growth during the mid-2000s, were straightaway provided with the skills, concepts, and tools required to establish and operate a profitable Internet business; thus, they avoided the follies of their 1990s predecessors. These new companies innovated in previously unconsidered ways and established an Internet economy that was as varied and diverse as the interests of its consumers. Many Internet-based businesses—some learned veterans and others ambitious, talented upstarts—experienced unprecedented success during the 2000s.

As Internet business grew, so too did the technology sector, particularly the consumer electronics portion. Personal electronics manufacturers capitalized on the Internet's prominence by releasing a slew of Internet-capable devices. Also of note was the propagation of small, portable devices such as cellular telephones, personal organizers, and digital music players. While these emerging industries grew throughout the 2000s, they presented unfamiliar legal problems, which led to several important, precedent-setting court rulings in cases such as *United States v. Microsoft*.

Ben Bernanke (1953–)   Ben Bernanke was one of the decade's most respected and distinguished economists. Not only an intellectual but also an effective decision maker with an expert understanding of the market, Bernanke served remarkably as a member of the Board of Governors of the Federal Reserve System from 2002 to 2005, chairman for the Council of Economic Advisors from 2005 to 2006, and chairman of the Federal Reserve from 2006 through the rest of the decade. Bernanke came from humble origins in South Carolina to attend Harvard University and then the Massachusetts Institute of Technology (MIT), from which he obtained a PhD in economics. In 2002 he was appointed to the Board of Governors of the Federal Reserve, a position from which he delivered his economic philosophy, later dubbed the "Bernanke Doctrine." In accordance with this doctrine, Bernanke was instrumental in helping deliver the U.S. financial system from the recession of the late 2000s. Although some have criticized his interventionist approach, there is little doubt that Bernanke's studied intelligence played a large role in shaping the economic climate of the 2000s. *(© Chip Somodevilla/Getty Images)*

Sergey Brin (1973–) and Larry Page (1973–)   Sergey Brin and Larry Page established the Internet search engine Google. As a result of their dedication and vision, Google ranks as one of the most innovative and influential businesses to develop during the decade. The partners gained Internet industry notoriety for their proprietary search engine service. In 1998, after two years of operating the Google search engine from the Stanford Web site, Brin and Page established Google Inc., having already secured enough investment capital to get their startup running. The operation and continued development of the Google search engine was the primary focus of the company during its early days, which the founders managed to capitalize on by selling online advertising space, allowing them to offer their search services for free. On August 19, 2004, Google made its initial public offering (IPO). Using the money generated from external investors, Google made several strategic acquisitions (most notably YouTube, the leading Internet video hosting site) and expansions, gradually broadening its focus from its Internet search engine to email services, social networking, and the ambitious Google Earth map project. The company continues to lead its field as the most successful and widely respected provider of free online services, and its founders continue to experience Internet-industry fame. *(© AP Photo/Ben Margot)*

Alan Greenspan (1926–)   Alan Greenspan is a controversial figure in U.S. economic policy theory, claiming many ardent supporters and detractors for his fervent free-market conservatism. He has served in both the public and private sectors over the course of his career, having obtained a PhD in economics from New York University and subsequently holding a variety of high-profile corporate positions before accepting the appointment of chairman of the Federal Reserve from President Ronald Reagan. Greenspan held this position from his nomination in 1987 until he was replaced in 2005. While in charge of the Fed's operation and thus the U.S. monetary policy, Greenspan expressed views that often differed from those of his colleagues and many mainstream economists, although the policies that reflected his beliefs in noninterfering government regulation of the market are credited with maintaining the stability of the U.S. economy through the tumultuous 1990s. His views were partially refuted by the crash of the housing market and resultant economic collapse, prompting Greenspan to acknowledge that the government might be justified in engaging the market more directly to influence its success and stability. This statement, made before Congress, is widely credited with justifying increased economic regulation in the United States. *(© AP Photo/J. Scott Applewhite)*

Bernard Madoff (1938–)   After obtaining a bachelor's degree in political science from Hofstra University in 1960, Bernard Madoff founded his own investment firm, Bernard L. Madoff Investment Securities, in which he worked for his entire career. Although part of this company was a legitimate investment firm, its true purpose was far more sinister: From its inception, Madoff used the funds entrusted to his business to conduct one of the largest financial frauds in history. The wealth management arm of his business was used to con investors out of their money in what is known as a Ponzi scheme. A Ponzi scheme is a type of systematic investment fraud in which investors are given false return reports, and the funds given back as profit redemptions are actually just investment funds contributed by other investors or themselves. As with all Ponzi schemes, this type of run on redemptions took place following the 2008 mortgage crisis, which led to a distressed Madoff confiding in his sons that he owed several billion dollars to investors that he could not afford to pay and that his business was a fraud. His sons reported him to federal authorities, and the following investigation revealed an extensive and elaborate scheme that had conned investors out of a reported $18 billion. *(© AP Photo/Louis Lanzano)*

Rupert Murdoch (1931–)   Rupert Murdoch was, during the 2000s, one of the few remaining "old school" business magnates, whose vast media empire made up one of the most valuable personal fortunes in the world. Murdoch himself became an enormously influential figure in the global business world. He established his vast media holdings by purchasing small or failing news and entertainment publications, broadcasters, and producers at low cost and converting them into a cheaply produced, widely disseminated, and profitable media network. This modern version of the nineteenth-century empire business model allowed Murdoch to establish a powerful position in the Australian, British, and U.S. news markets over the course of five decades. Murdoch capitalized on sensationalist reporting and is largely cited as having pioneered the modern tabloid journal. He used his amassed wealth to found many innovative and successful businesses, notably British satellite television network Sky Television (later changed to BSkyB) and the Fox television network. By the 2000s, Murdoch had consolidated his various holdings under the banner of News Corporation, which was one of the most influential business empires in the world. *(© AP Photo/Evan Agostini)*

Eliot Spitzer (1959–)   Eliot Spitzer graduated from Princeton University and then from Harvard Law School, after which he worked as a lawyer with the Manhattan District Attorney combating organized crime. He was highly successful in that role, famously exposing Mafia operations and eliminating their operations in the city. After a stint at a legal firm, Spitzer revealed his ambition to hold public office. After losing his first campaign as a Democratic contender for the office of New York State attorney general, Spitzer recouped and claimed the position in 1996, serving as an enthusiastic supporter of consumer protection and business regulation. He was reelected and, in 2003, he experienced a surge in popularity as he exposed large-scale corporate fraud taking place within Canary Capital Partners and then launched a large anti-fraud campaign that exposed corruption within several hedge fund firms. Spitzer campaigned for the office of governor of New York in 2004, and soundly defeated his competition to earn the seat. However, he only held the governorship briefly. In March 2008, federal investigators revealed that Spitzer had employed the services of a prostitute, and ensuing revelations regarding the extent of his prostitution habit led to calls for his impeachment (special removal from office). Rather than suffer further embarrassment, Spitzer resigned and apologized for his misdeeds. *(© Bill Clark/Roll Call/Getty Images)*

Martha Stewart (1941–)   Martha Stewart is a rare example of a corporate criminal who managed to maintain composure, financial solvency, and public sympathy despite her misdeeds. Born Martha Kostyra in New Jersey, Stewart learned domestic skills when she was young, which she combined with her business prowess to establish herself as a branded personality through various ventures, such as her cookbook series, television shows, magazine, and home decoration lines. In September 1997, Stewart consolidated ownership of all the properties that carried her brand under the umbrella company Martha Stewart Living Omnimedia, which made its highly successful initial public offering in

1999. By the 2000s, Stewart was a household name and a successful businesswoman, with considerable personal worth and good rapport with the American public. In 2003 Stewart was charged with fraud offenses, and in 2004, she was found guilty of obstruction of justice and conspiracy following a trial that revealed Stewart's involvement with insider trading. Subsequently, Stewart paid a fine and served five months in prison, after which she was put on a probationary, supervised release. She continued to work with her company, although more as a promoter and creative consultant than as a corporate head and continued to expand her brand through the decade. *(© Ben Hider/Getty Images)*

Donald Trump (1946–) Regarded with puzzled fascination or profound distaste, Donald Trump is an enigmatic figure in U.S. business. Both cunning and boisterous, Trump was a highly public personality during the 2000s, and his assorted ventures and media appearances gained him begrudging acceptance from many Americans. He received a bachelor's degree in economics from the Wharton School of the University of Pennsylvania and immediately gained employment under his father, successful entrepreneur and real estate magnate Fred Trump. After acquiring his father's company in 1971 and renaming it The Trump Organization, Trump was brazen and bold, accruing prestigious and valuable properties such as the Taj Mahal Casino in Atlantic City, and several commercial structures that he named after himself. The recession of the early 1980s led to financial uncertainty and mounting debt for Trump, who was forced to file for business bankruptcy and relinquish a significant portion of his property holdings. He recovered quickly, and by 2003, he was hosting his own reality television show, *The Apprentice.* He continued to pursue public acknowledgment throughout the 2000s but ultimately came to represent an exaggerated caricature of U.S. business culture. *(© Steve Granitz/WireImage)*

❖ BURSTING BUBBLES

"Market bubble" is a term used by economists to describe a situation in which an asset or commodity of any sort—examples range from flowers to real estate properties—is traded (bought and sold) at prices much higher than its actual, utility-based equilibrium price. This phenomenon is called a bubble because prices are inflated without any actual value being added to the traded good, leading to unsustainable, vulnerable investments that can fall in value as suddenly as a bubble can burst. Market bubbles arise for a variety of reasons, involving a complex and unpredictable combination of factors, all influenced by the irrational, calculating, or greedy tendencies of speculating investors. Commodity bubbles, which involve irrationally inflated trading prices for a specific tangible good such as uranium (2005–07) or rhodium (2008), are relatively common and generally endurable by the domestic economy, with some noteworthy exceptions. Other bubbles, such as the "dot-com" bubble of the late 1990s, are characterized by enormous overvaluation of shares in businesses in a specific industry, and are generally more damaging to the national economy.

The economic landscape of the 2000s was heavily influenced by the bursting of two over-inflated market bubbles. A market bubble is said to have burst when, having inflated in price dramatically, a traded asset is so overvalued that nobody is willing to buy it at the requested price; the resulting rapid devaluation (loss of value) of the traded asset from its inflated price to its actual, value-based equilibrium price often produces a recession on a national scale as billions of dollars are lost by those who have invested and by related or involved industries. The first of the decade's fated bubbles, the dot-com bubble, was the product of over-eager investors detecting opportunity in an emerging industry; the second, known as the housing bubble, was a more complex affair, involving not only the overvaluation of a specific commodity (houses) but also the near-collapse of the financial industry.

The Dot-Com Bubble

The Internet developed quickly during the early 1990s, which prompted the development of the first round of fully developed, well-planned Internet businesses. Many of the companies started during this initial boom, such as Google, Yahoo!, Amazon, and eBay, went on to shape the face of Internet business during the 2000s. Others, however, attracted hopeful but uninformed investors by using dubious business models and vague new "e-commerce" language without ever producing profitable results. These companies rode a wave of stock market optimism resultant from the quick success and financial gains made by more legitimate and thoughtful businesses, attracting huge investments. Investors were unaware of the hazards of dot-com businesses because, thanks to the increased public availability of the Internet and corresponding explosion in profitability, purchasing shares of Internet businesses seemed like a totally right decision. Because of these factors, combined with low interest rates and a misguided sense of insulation from harm among investors, almost every Internet business enjoyed rapid expansion during the late 1990s. Stock prices soared to unsustainable levels, with now-unknown companies such as Freeinternet.com, Think Tools AG, and InfoSpace fetching billions of dollars in stock revenue while reporting no profits.

Not surprisingly, the dot-com bubble soon burst under the growing strain of overvalued stocks. Investors, whose money was often leveraged (backed) by banks, lost billions as misguided Internet companies collapsed after spending all of their investment funding without earning returns. On March 10, 2000, at the height of the bubble's expansion phase, the Nasdaq Composite stock market index, which tracks the stock market for the technology sector, closed at a record high of 5,048.62. Amid the jubilation of investors, the bubble burst, and the national economy was sent into decline, reaching free-fall by early 2001. Technology speculators were devastated, and many Internet businesses went bankrupt. The effect was amplified as it spread through the stock market, culminating in a minor recession that set a bleak stage for the rest of the 2000s. Not everything was dreary, however; those Internet startups that were capable of weathering the financial tumult were rewarded for their survival with greater market share and business experience.

The Housing Bubble

Perhaps one of the few positive results of the dot-com bubble was its effect on the collective investment culture in the United States. Having only recently recovered from the setback of the dot-com bubble, American investors were better steeled to withstand the impact of the housing bubble, which grew to bloated proportions through the early 2000s only to peak in 2006 and collapse soon after. Although technically a commodity bubble, the factors involved in the development of the housing bubble were highly complex and not entirely understood even by the economics community.

The simplest explanation of the housing bubble is that, as the price of real estate properties, particularly homes, rose to unprecedented heights during the 2000s, many of them were traded and valued in excess of their actual worth. As the situation worsened, many properties went unsold because owners expected much higher returns than were affordable or sustainable by the market. Investors were oblivious to the overvaluation of real estate properties for a variety of reasons. Economists and government officials argued that housing prices were at levels consistent with market factors. Plus, banks were eager to finance hefty property acquisitions, often with favorable mortgage rates. Finally, investment experts talked about a fundamental demand for housing that was supposed to exempt the housing market from the regular rules of economics.

Unfortunately, the follies of housing speculation were exposed in 2006, when prices on houses began falling dramatically due to natural market correction. Property owners, who had been enticed into amassing land holdings by low interest rates and tax exemptions on homes, lost billions of dollars as the market value of their properties fell sharply. Thousands of lavish houses, constructed by optimistic developers in reaction to once-rising house prices, sat vacant and unsold. Banks were forced to raise mortgage rates, causing thousands of families to leave their houses because they were only able to afford their homes under the buyer-friendly terms of the expanding bubble. Others ended up owing more on their mortgage than their property was now worth, resulting in a net loss on their home investments. Owing the bank more on a house than the house is now worth is called being "upside down" in a mortgage.

When faced with mounting evidence of a burst bubble in the U.S. housing market, government agencies sought to remedy the situation by raising interest rates, instituting stricter mortgage regulation and oversight policies, and contributing hundreds of billions of dollars in loans to financial institutions put at risk by falling housing values. President George W. Bush also authorized corrective policies that aided indebted mortgagers by allowing them to avoid foreclosure. Despite such action, housing values continued to fall from 2006 through the end of the decade.

❖ THE SUBPRIME MORTGAGE CRISIS

The most far-reaching result of the housing bubble was its instigation of the "subprime mortgage crisis," a term used to describe the decline in value of securities (a traded representation of value ownership) backed by subprime mortgage debt. Subprime mortgages are those in which a lending institution, usually a bank, funds a loan for a house to a person who would not ordinarily meet the credit requirements for such a loan. These loans were initially authorized to allow financially disadvantaged citizens, such as low-income individuals and those with poor credit history, to buy a house.

The subprime mortgage crisis that erupted after the housing bubble burst in 2006 sent thousands of homes into foreclosure across the country as homeowners could no longer afford their mortgage payments. © Justin Sullivan/Getty Images

As the housing market was flourishing during the early 2000s, banks enthusiastically relaxed their lending standards, qualifying millions for home ownership who otherwise would not have been able to afford it. Between 2004 and 2006, subprime mortgages grew to account for around 20 percent of all mortgage loans. Many banks were happy to grant such high-risk loans because of government encouragement (in the form of lender-friendly monetary and fiscal policies and a culture of permissiveness) and because these loan agreements were immensely profitable to those banks. These banks compensated for the risk of such loans by offering them with high interest rates.

Lending institutions developed several tricks to make their risky practices appear more secure. Those house buyers who were receiving subprime mortgage financing were often persuaded to sign adjustable-rate mortgages, in which the interest rate on their loans was initially small but would increase gradually over time. This practice often resulted in what was called "predatory lending" scenarios in which lenders granted loans with the expectation that the recipient would have to renegotiate the rates, generating easy profit for the bank. Banks combined prime and subprime mortgages into asset-backed securities (ownership of debt backed by collateral—in this case, houses). Doing so pulled in many investors with deceptively high expected return rates (thanks to the inclusion of prime mortgages, which are generally secure and predictable), in turn providing banks with more money to offer more loans.

When the housing bubble burst in early 2006, interest rates on home loans rose rapidly. Those people with subprime loans, who had agreed to adjustable-rate mortgages, saw their monthly mortgage payment skyrocket. Many other people assumed high-interest mortgages because they believed that housing prices would continue to rise at the same rate they had for the first half of the 2000s. Assuming their prediction for the future was correct, they could then renegotiate for more favorable terms when their house was valued higher. However, that constant rise in house prices did not happen, and many were unable to afford their loans and were forced to default (unable to pay as agreed), costing the banks, and by extension those who had purchased asset-backed securities, billions of dollars. Panic set in as thousands of Americans were forced out of their homes in foreclosures, while prospective home buyers who would ordinarily have qualified found it difficult to obtain loans. Foreclosure is an action by the mortgage lender when the buyer does not make payments as agreed; the mortgage lender takes back the property and sells it to someone else, generally at a much reduced price. Losses incurred by large financial institutions as a result of the subprime mortgage crisis led directly to the greater financial crisis of the late 2000s.

❖ ECONOMIC FAILURE

In the face of mounting losses, the U.S. financial industry—the various banks, credit unions, and investment groups involved in the national economy—struggled to maintain operation. As the effects of the subprime mortgage crisis spread, major financial institutions began reporting massive failures. The Dow Jones Industrial Average, an index used to track and measure the performance of major components of the U.S. stock market, plummeted from a record-high position in October 2006, steadily declining through the end of the decade. The ready availability of credit throughout the early 2000s had produced an enormous amount of consumer debt, which greatly reduced investment availability and general spending power. Public frustration was largely directed toward the banks that had issued such credit, and their executives were accused of being greedy and irresponsible. The situation was further intensified as major banks, struggling to recuperate from subprime mortgage losses, had to turn to the government for protection against complete collapse.

The federal government was willing to assist the faltering banks, in part because its own lax policies and previous decades of deregulation had enabled the looming economic meltdown to occur. The primary corrective measure taken to assist the ailing financial system was the passage of the Emergency Economic Stabilization Act of 2008, which was enacted October 3, 2008. The law, publicly referred to as the "bailout bill," allocated $700 billion to the rescue and resuscitation of troubled financial institutions. Although this move was enough to save many banks from assured failure, industry giants such as Lehman Brothers and Washington Mutual were still forced to file for bankruptcy. Having decided that monitoring and regulation would be the best ways to prevent further economic distress, in 2008, the government acquired control over Fannie Mae and Freddie Mac, two of the nation's most active mortgage associations. Other attempts to rectify the financial crisis included the passage of the Economic Recovery Act of 2008, which sought to make mortgages more widely available and secure, and the American Recovery and Reinvestment Act of 2009, an economic stimulus package designed to alleviate growing unemployment and maintain economic progress by providing $787 billion for various projects.

❖ COLLAPSE OF THE AUTOMOTIVE INDUSTRY

Another contributing factor in the development of stock market depreciation of the late 2000s was the near-collapse of the U.S. automotive industry. Traditionally among the manufacturing sector's largest employers and money-earners, by 2008 the U.S. automobile companies were losing a lot of money and market share. Several factors contributed to the automotive industry's problems. One factor was collective bargaining agreements had forced manufacturers to pay its employees higher wages and provide larger benefits packages than their competitors paid. Also, many consumers had come to prefer the fuel efficiency and reliability of foreign-made cars to the large, expensive models sold by the "Big Three" American automobile manufacturers: Chrysler, Ford Motor Company, and General Motors. To make matters worse, export sales declined for these three companies. Compounding the problem was the scarcity of credit with which to purchase cars after the financial crisis had taken hold of the economy.

By early 2009, the Big Three had lost so much money that these companies appealed to the federal government for assistance. Mismanagement and poor business caused both Chrysler and General Motors to file for bankruptcy and subsequently to be granted massive financial assistance packages from the government, while Ford managed to survive by extending its credit line and scaling back production. Chrysler and GM emerged from their predicaments in decent financial health after receiving billions of dollars in "bailouts" given to them by the government, and all three gradually recovered through the end of the decade. By restructuring and focusing on producing fuel-efficient and more affordable cars, the automotive industry continued to propel the U.S. economy, but it did so at a reduced level.

❖ BANKRUPTCIES

In addition to the collapse of financial and automotive corporations, the 2000s saw an assortment of large, seemingly secure businesses failing and filing for bankruptcy. During the 2000s more than a dozen major U.S. airlines, under financial duress from rising oil prices and post-9/11 industry changes, sought bankruptcy or government-sponsored debt restructuring. Most of these airlines, such as Delta and Frontier, endured their brief periods of uncertainty and continued operation. Others, such as ATA and Skybus, had such unmanageable debt that they had to cease operation altogether.

Early in the decade, significant public attention was directed towards WorldCom, at the time a leader in the telecommunications industry, when its fraudulent accounting practices were exposed. Concerned about the company's declining stock value, WorldCom executives had deliberately disguised its losses in an attempt to attract continued investment. The fraud was discovered in early 2002, followed shortly by the resignation or termination of several high-ranking employees involved in the scandal. Chief executive officer (CEO) Bernard Ebbers and chief financial officer (CFO) Scott Sullivan, the perpetrators of the fraud, were tried, convicted, and sentenced to prison terms for their involvement in the conspiracy. Stock in the company fell drastically, and it was forced to file for bankruptcy in July 2002. At the time of the filing, WorldCom's bankruptcy was the largest in U.S. corporate history.

At the same time as the WorldCom failure, Enron Corporation, one of the nation's largest and most powerful energy companies, experienced a similar implosion. Like WorldCom, Enron was found to have hidden millions of dollars in debt from investors. Enron executives hid the debt by resorting to illegal accounting practices. The company distorted profit reports and resorted to complicated financial entities known as "special purpose entities" to hide its mounting debt. The mechanics of the conspiracy and the extent of senior corporate involvement were exposed in court, resulting in felony convictions for former CFO Andrew Fastow,

Stadium employees remove letters from one of the Enron Field signs in Houston, Texas, on March 21, 2002. The Houston Astros paid $2.1 million to get back the naming rights to their stadium after Enron's bankruptcy. © *James Nielsen/Getty Images*

former CEO Jeffrey Skilling, and founder Kenneth Lay, all of whom received felony prison sentences for directing the fraud.

Shareholders, many of whom were company employees, were devastated as Enron's stock value fell to a small fraction of its original value, amounting to approximately $74 billion in total losses. The company was left with no option but to file for bankruptcy, accounting for $63.4 billion in assets. This and other large corporate bankruptcies paved the way for the rest of the decade's various business failures, as well as contributing to a growing public dissatisfaction with and distrust of "big business" that would only intensify as the decade wore on.

❖ INSIDER TRADING SCANDALS

Another reason for mainstream Americans' growing distaste for corporate business was a string of misdeeds committed by high-level corporate figures. One of the first offenders of the decade was Martha Stewart (1941–), the respected and well-liked homemaking mogul and founder of Martha Stewart Living Omnimedia. Stewart, a celebrated personality, businesswoman, designer, writer, and television host, was a popular figure during the 2000s, and her cookbooks and homemaking merchandise were enjoyed by millions of Americans. It came as a shock, then, when in 2002, it was revealed that Stewart had been involved in insider trading. Insider trading is an illegal practice in which a company insider gives inside (not available to the general public) information to an outside investor so that the investor can profit by making investments based on the information. In this case, Stewart had received a tip from her stockbroker in December 2001 regarding an expected drop in the value of ImClone stock following an unfavorable Food and Drug Administration (FDA) decision. Acting on her broker's advice, Stewart sold the entirety of her holding in the biopharmaceutical company and, as predicted, avoided a large loss.

Unfortunately for Stewart, the U.S. Securities and Exchange Commission (SEC) was aware of Stewart's illegal activity, and she was investigated during the following year. In June 2003, Stewart was charged with several felonies and made to stand trial in January 2004. Two months later, she was convicted of obstructing justice and lying to investigators and given a five-month prison sentence, a considerable fine, and a period of supervised release. Upon her release, Stewart resumed her business activity and continued to expand her business empire, although an agreement with the SEC prohibited her from holding executive positions with her own or any other publicly traded company. Stewart continued to serve as a creative advisor to her company through the end of the decade.

The next insider trading operation to be uncovered hugely exceeded Stewart's mishap. Although banker Raj Rajaratnam was guilty of the same offense as Stewart, his investment scheme was a more harmful affair from which he profited immensely. Whereas Stewart's insider trading resulted from opportunism and loss avoidance instinct, Rajaratnam had intentionally obtained and acted upon non-public information to illegally generate an estimated $20 million in profits over an extended period (2003–09). Rajaratnam's Galleon Group, a leading hedge fund, was abandoned by investors and shut down soon after Rajaratnam was arrested in October 2009. (A hedge fund is an investing group that speculates with its investments in order to make money.) Investigators determined that Rajaratnam, one of the wealthiest men in the world, had used contacts in the technology and financial industries to get insider information about expected changes in stock values, which served as the basis for his investments. Evidence of Rajaratnam's criminal activity was gathered by federal authorities as recorded phone conversations obtained via wiretap in an organized crackdown on insider trading. A federal jury found

Rajaratnam guilty on fourteen counts of securities fraud and conspiracy in May 2011 and sentenced him to eleven years in prison.

Insider trading is a frequent occurrence in the United States and most other countries because it is a fairly easy, low-hazard way for investors to "beat the market," earning almost guaranteed profits without substantial risk of being discovered; insider trading is practically impossible to detect if it only involves small transactions. Like those before (and likely after) it, the 2000s decade had a host of low-profile, largely insignificant insider trading convictions in addition to the widely reported cases, and probably even more insider trading schemes that were never detected.

❖ BERNIE MADOFF

Even by the standards of Americans living in the 2000s, to whom scandal, corruption, and white-collar crime were unremarkable and commonplace parts of the economy, the incredible scale and duration of Bernard "Bernie" Madoff's (1938–) financial deceit distinguishes it as an extraordinary work of financial trickery. Using his investment firm, Bernard L. Madoff Investment Securities, Madoff conducted a massive, prolonged investment fraud that lasted from the early 1990s until his scam was exposed in December 2008. Madoff had used the wealth management arm of his business to orchestrate the fraud while the majority of the company engaged in standard, completely legal investment banking.

Madoff's operation was modeled after a classic Ponzi scheme. A Ponzi scheme is a type of systematic investment fraud in which investors are given false investment reports and in which funds returned to investors as profit redemptions are actually just funds contributed by other investors or themselves. Ponzi schemes are successful because they can often claim unrealistically high investment returns, attracting naive and inexperienced investors less likely to develop suspicions; the high rates can be maintained for an extended period so long as new investors are continually acquired and provided the fraudster does not embezzle (steal) too much money from investors. Such a system requires continued reinvestment of its victims' funds and constant expansion of customer volume. If too many investors want to draw out money at the same time, money embezzled by the fraudulent individuals—in this case Madoff and, as some sources allege, his family and several business partners—is not available and cannot be paid to the investor. Investors cannot be allowed to withdraw their fictional profits because that would expose the fraud.

Madoff's lie began to be exposed when a large number of investors wanted access to their money in response to the 2008 market collapse and attempted to withdraw the total (falsified) balances of their investments. With the reality of his predicament closing in around him and little hope for salvation, a distressed Madoff confided in his sons that he owed several billion dollars to investors that he could not hope to pay and that his business was a fraud. His sons reported him to federal authorities on December 10, 2008. The next day Madoff was arrested by the FBI on a security fraud charge, to which he acknowledged guilt and then willingly surrendered himself to their custody. The following investigation revealed a large and elaborate scheme that had conned investors out of a reported $18 billion.

Madoff stood trial on March 12, 2009. He pleaded guilty on eleven charges, all related to his admitted fraud, and was sentenced to 150 years in prison and fined $170 million. Leading up to the date of his incarceration, Madoff remained an enigmatic figure. By the end of the 2000s, Madoff stood as a symbol of all that was wrong with the financial system—one man who was able to indiscriminately defraud charities, banks, religious institutions, and wealthy individuals over the course of more than fifteen years without any government regulation at all. The greatest irony of Madoff's operation is that he had submitted to repeated SEC misconduct investigations, at least one of which was specifically intended to determine if his business was a veiled Ponzi scheme. Throughout the 1990s and much of the 2000s his fraud was not revealed.

❖ MERGERS

A merger is the combination of two separately owned corporations into a single, consolidated entity. After two companies merge, they are legally considered the same entity and thus operate under the same management, name, and policies. Acquisitions are mergers in which one corporation aggressively seeks to consolidate with or buy out another, regardless of the desires of the target corporation. Of course, these explanations are simplistic; very few mergers are straightforward as the U.S. corporate system has invented a variety of complex ways in which businesses can merge, each producing a different final combination. The tumultuous market of the 2000s led many corporations to perform mergers for a variety of reasons. These mergers had various results.

Several mergers took place within the financial industry during the decade. In 2000, J. P. Morgan & Co. Incorporated and The Chase Manhattan Group merged to form J. P. Morgan Chase & Co., a super-bank and one of the world's largest corporations. As banks and financial

Microsoft Cannot Be Trusted

"Monopoly" is a term used to describe a situation in which a single entity controls the supply of a given product or service. The U.S. government has a vested interest in preventing the development of monopolies. In the domestic marketplace, monopolies reduce or eliminate free competition in the economy and the delicate balance of supply and demand. Laws, policies, attitudes, and business practices that oppose monopolies are described as "anti-trust."

In 1998, Microsoft Corporation, a leading technology and computing corporation, was faced with a civil suit filed by the United States Department of Justice (DOJ) and the attorney generals of twenty states. Prosecutors alleged (charged) that Microsoft, a leading producer and supplier of personal computers, had gained monopolistic control over the personal computer market. Furthermore, they asserted that Microsoft had abused its monopoly over the computer market by selling Microsoft Windows computer operating systems preinstalled with Microsoft's Internet Explorer web browser software. Because the majority of computers bought and sold in the United States at the time were Microsoft personal computers, and most Microsoft computers ran Windows, and every copy of Windows included a free copy of Internet Explorer, the prosecution argued that Microsoft was using its control over the market to prevent consumers from buying or installing other browsers.

Hearings for *United States v. Microsoft* began on May 18, 1998. Microsoft's only defense against characterizations of the company as monopolistic was to explain that companies are typically allowed to give away free merchandise with the sale of a more expensive item. Microsoft executives also defended the practice of including Internet Explorer with Windows operating systems by explaining that it makes it much easier to use a computer if the programs consumers want to use are already installed on it when they first purchase their computer. Regardless of Microsoft's actual stance regarding aggressive monopolism, the company was ruled to be in violation of the Sherman Anti-Trust Act, and, on April 3, 2000, the presiding judge decided that Microsoft had to be split in half so as to eliminate its monopolistic grasp of the technology industry. Microsoft appealed the ruling and had it revoked, but in exchange was forced to agree to share proprietary code with its competitors.

institutions emerged from the 2008 market crash in different circumstances, the corporations that were still competitive eagerly bought out their struggling competitors. For example, in 2008, J. P. Morgan Chase acquired responsibility for the operation of the struggling Washington Mutual banking system. Similarly, Bank of America jumped at the opportunity to rescue Merrill Lynch (at a cost of $50 billion), one of its largest competitors prior to the subprime mortgage crisis, which inflicted massive losses.

Non-bank mergers also took place during the 2000s, including the consolidation of the Dutch and British energy companies Royal Dutch and Shell Group to form the huge Royal Dutch Shell corporation. Sporting goods and apparel brands Adidas and Reebok merged in 2006 when Adidas purchased its competitor for $3.4 billion, allowing a better, collectivized market share position from which the two brands could attempt to usurp Nike. In 2003, Pfizer Inc., a major pharmaceutical corporation, acquired Pharmacia Corporation, another major pharmaceutical corporation, for $55 billion. Many other businesses engaged in buying, selling, and combining with their rivals. Sometimes, two businesses with little in common would merge with optimistic zeal, only to realize too late that they had little to offer one another, as seemed to be the case when dialup Internet service provider America Online Inc. merged with Time Warner to form a bumbling media giant that did not make much money.

❖ APPLE DOMINATES THE TECHNOLOGY INDUSTRY

The 2000s were a spectacular period for the American technology industry, particularly for those involved in the consumer electronics sector. Rapid technological advances coupled with steady progress in business operation techniques, new marketing tactics, and improved product design resulted in a decade dominated by emergent technology and financial success for designers, engineers, and administrators.

During the 2000s, Apple Corporation was consistently ranked among the most successful, inspired, and recognizable companies on the planet. The company was founded in 1977 by a pair of enterprising young visionaries, Stephen Wozniak (1950–) and Steve Jobs (1955–2011), whose intense interests in and skills with personal computer technology led them to experiment with and improve upon the technology constantly. In the 1980s, Apple supplanted IBM as the primary personal computer company in the United States. In 1985, Jobs was fired from his position at Apple for largely political reasons (such as disagreements with shareholders and other executives). His passion for computer technology was not hampered,

Customers wait in line outside the Apple retail store in Chicago, Illinois, for a chance to buy a copy of Apple computer's O.S. 10.4 "Tiger" operating system on April 29, 2005. Apple inspired passionate customer loyalty with its innovative, user-friendly products in the first decade of the twenty-first century. © Scott Olson/Getty Images

however; Jobs immediately founded another computer company called NeXT, which focused primarily on the operating systems of personal computers and purchased a digital animation studio that would go on to become the legendary Pixar Studio.

Apple lost its reputation as a cutting-edge technology company during the early 1990s, only to recover it by purchasing NeXT in 1996 and reinstating Jobs as head of Apple a year later. As Apple's leader, Jobs carefully shifted the company's production lines and product designs, emphasizing slick, simple appearances and correspondingly simple-to-use technology. In orienting the entire company's focus towards specific metrics and adopting a uniform aesthetic for all products, Jobs successfully established what has since come to be referred to as the "Apple cult," a large group of consumers dedicated to only buying products with the Apple brand.

Apple's grasp on the hearts and wallets of American citizens was cemented when, in 2001, Jobs unveiled the iPod, a personal digital music player. The device was a blockbuster, selling millions of units over the decade and establishing Apple as the most sought-after and hip purveyor of technology. Consumers clamored to purchase every upgraded version of the iPod, gladly paying a premium for the Apple brand name itself. Jobs, always a clever businessman, began increasing the rate at which new iPods and related devices were released, implementing a planned system in which annual upgrades were released with incremental improvement and added features over years. The iPhone, released in 2007, attracted fervor and devotion from members of the Apple cult, who waited eagerly for each improved version of the smartphone. By the end of the decade, Apple had essentially cornered the market on personal digital media players and consumer computers. The true brilliance of Steve Jobs, it would appear, was his ability to market the Apple brand—smooth, shiny, sleek, slender, and simple—over its actual products.

❖ THE BUSINESS OF THE INTERNET

The culture of Internet business progressed a great deal during the 2000s. It moved from the self-delusional, unfounded optimism that had so painfully characterized the first round of Internet-based businesses, or "dot-coms," to a legitimate, carefully planned industry like any other, with the added excitement of exploration. Some experienced and successful remnants of the first round of Internet business, such as online auction host eBay and online discount retailer Amazon.com, refined their corners of the market and enjoyed the profitability they established during the first round of Internet business startups. Other energetic young ventures such as Facebook and Twitter spent the decade inventing and refining new ways for Internet-based businesses to turn a profit.

Internet industry giant Google was among the first to pursue creative options about how to generate profit. Having only just emerged from the debris of the dot-com bubble, the fledgling company sought to make its search engine free to users but still profitable. In 2002, the company reworked its AdWords advertising platform so that advertisers paid to host ads by the clicks received on the ads rather than just paying Google a certain rate to host the ad. As a result, Google revenues soared to $439 million. Following the company's impressive initial public offering (IPO), Google was left with huge investment sums. A public offering is a company's decision to sell stock in order to raise money. Google used the money it raised from selling stock towards research and development on innovative and perpetually free-to-user projects. It developed Google Earth, Maps, Books, Documents, Email, and even social networking sites. Google continued to build wealth throughout the 2000s by offering simple, useful tools at a cost only to advertisers and through varied business ventures, investments, and technological research.

Warren Buffett

W arren Buffet (1930–) is one of the recent century's most famous and successful Americans. Buffet was born in Omaha, Nebraska, and obtained a bachelor's degree in business administration, followed by a master's in economics from Columbia Business School. After college, Buffet, who had expressed an interest in finance and business from an early age, navigated the investment industry expertly and generated significant returns for the firms that employed him. Buffet's notorious frugality compelled him to invest the majority of his income in new businesses and the stock market, which rapidly expanded his wealth. By 1962, Buffet had accumulated over $1 million from his various business ventures. In 1965, Buffet acquired Berkshire Hathaway, a holding company (one that serves solely to exchange stocks in other businesses for profit), and effected institutional reforms. The banker continued to amass wealth, becoming a billionaire on May 29, 1990. In 2006, Buffet made the unprecedented move of committing 85 percent of his assets to various philanthropic institutions, the primary recipient being the Bill and Melinda Gates Foundation. In 2008, Buffet surpassed Bill Gates as the world's richest man, with an estimated $62 billion in personal wealth. The economist became widely respected for his political, academic, and business-related theories and continued as of 2009 to be one of the most influential businessmen in the United States.

The aforementioned Amazon.com and eBay Internet-based commercial sites profited from the Internet using wildly dissimilar business models, both of which were successful. Amazon.com established itself as the world's largest online retailer and acts the part, doing as much as it can to sell its products through advertisements, easy browsing, and suggested purchases because it relies on the actual transference of goods and money to turn a profit. By contrast, eBay offers the convenience, novelty, and affordability of online auctions combined with unavoidable payments to the company, either as a percentage of a sale or as a percentage of payments made with specific types of payment, such as PayPal, to generate profits. Both companies were highly successful during the 2000s decade because they employed industry-, market-, and company-specific business models that suit them well.

As the Internet developed culturally throughout the 2000s, many imaginative, creative, and successful business strategies were developed to earn profits for a specific business or type of business. Social networking sites such as Facebook and MySpace began selling advertising space and the personal information of their users in order to turn a profit while still making the service free to users, a system that raised concerns over privacy rights. Near the decade's end, many artists, webcomic writers, video game developers, and musicians had adopted what is known as a "pay what you want" system, in which the consumer is allowed to decide the actual value of a creative work or product. This model was widely used during the late 2000s as many creative types tried to find ways of getting paid for their work, with some actually making a good profit.

 For More Information

....

BOOKS

Auletta, Ken. *Googled: The End of the World as We Know It.* New York: Penguin, 2009.

Cassidy, John. *Dot.com: How America Lost Its Mind and Money in the Internet Era.* New York: Harper, 2003.

Lloyd, Allen. *Being Martha: The Inside Story of Martha Stewart and Her Amazing Life.* Hoboken, NJ: Wiley, 2006.

Lowenstein, Roger. *While America Aged.* New York: Penguin, 2008.

Masters, Brooke A. *Spoiling for a Fight: The Rise of Eliot Spitzer.* New York: Times Books, 2007.

McLean, Bethany, and Peter Elkind. *The Smartest Guys in the Room: The Amazing Rise and Scandalous Fall of Enron.* London: Portfolio, 2004.

Sorkin, Aaron Ross. *Too Big to Fail: The Inside Story of How Wall Street and Washington Fought to Save the Financial System from Crisis—and Themselves.* New York: Penguin, 2009.

WEB SITES

"Failed Bank List." *Federal Deposit Insurance Corporation.* http://www.fdic.gov/bank/individual/failed/banklist.html (accessed on October 5, 2011).

Lanman, Scott. "Greenspan Concedes to 'Flaw' in His Market Ideology (Update2)." *Bloomberg,* October 23, 2008. http://www.bloomberg.com/apps/news?pid=newsarchive&sid=ah5qh9Up4rIg (accessed on October 5, 2011).

Lattman, Peter, and Azam Ahmed. "Galleon's Rajaratnam Found Guilty." *The New York Times,* May 11, 2011. http://dealbook.nytimes.com/2011/05/11/rajaratnam-found-guilty/ (accessed on October 5, 2011).

Business and the Economy

....

FOR MORE INFORMATION

"The Madoff Scam: Meet The Liquidator." *CBS News,* June 20, 2010. http://www.cbsnews.com/stories/2009/09/24/60minutes/main5339719.shtml?tag=current-VideoInfo;segmentUtilities (accessed on October 5, 2011).

"Monthly Average Data and Charts (1972–2006)." *Kitco.* http://www.kitco.com/charts/historicalrhodium.html (accessed on October 5, 2011).

"The State of the Nation's Housing 2006." Joint Center for Housing Studies of Harvard University. http://www.jchs.harvard.edu/publications/markets/son2006/son2006.pdf (accessed on October 1, 2011).

"The State of the Nation's Housing 2008." Joint Center for Housing Studies of Harvard University. http://www.jchs.harvard.edu/publications/markets/son2008/son2008.pdf (accessed on October 5, 2011).

"Top Ten Business Mergers/Acquisitions of the Decade." *Pbleepd,* January 3, 2010. http://www.pbleepd.com/business/top-10-business-mergersacquisitions-of-the-decade-part-1/ (accessed on October 5, 2011).

"The 2000s in Review: 20 Most Memorable Business Events of the Decade." *New York Daily News,* December 23, 2009. http://www.nydailynews.com/money/toplists/top_25_most_memorable_business_moments_of_the_decade/top_25_most_memorable_business_moments_of_the_decade.html (accessed on October 5, 2011).

"*United States v. Microsoft* Current Case." United States Department of Justice. http://www.justice.gov/atr/cases/ms_index.htm (accessed on October 5, 2011).

Education

2000 February 29   A six-year-old boy in Mount Morris Township, Michigan, shoots and kills his classmate at their elementary school.

2000 May 8   The Philadelphia school board adopts a policy that requires all public-school students to wear a uniform to class, becoming the first major city school system to pass such a law.

2000 August 2   Kansas voters oust two conservative members of the state school board who had voted to remove any mention of evolution from the state science curriculum.

2000 September 11   California enacts a plan to help needy students attend college in which high-school students with good grades and financial need receive free tuition at public institutions or $10,000 a year toward tuition at a private school.

2001 February 14   The Kansas State Board of Education reverses its 1999 decision to remove the theory of evolution from the state's science curriculum.

2001 May 16   Fourteen-year-old Nathaniel Brazill is convicted of second-degree murder and sentenced to 28 years in prison for shooting a teacher at Lake Worth Middle School in Florida.

2002 January 8   The No Child Left Behind Act (NCLB), which mandates that schools have to meet new federal standards or face a range of penalties, is signed into law by President George W. Bush.

2002 April 11   The Walton Family Charitable Support Foundation, created by the family of Wal-Mart founder Sam Walton, donates $300 million to the University of Arkansas. It is the largest donation ever made to a public U.S. university.

2002 June 26   A federal appeals court in San Francisco rules that requiring students to recite the Pledge of Allegiance is unconstitutional because it includes the phrase "under God."

2003 June 23   The Supreme Court rules that University of Michigan's law school admissions policy, which considers race as a factor, is constitutional while its similar undergraduate system is not, in *Grutter v. Bollinger* and *Gratz v. Bollinger,* respectively.

2003 June 28   New York City officials announce plans for Harvey Milk High School, the first public school aimed at protecting gay students from discrimination.

2004 May 17   President George W. Bush and his presidential election opponent, Democratic senator John Kerry of Massachusetts, attend ceremonies in Topeka, Kansas, honoring the fiftieth anniversary of *Brown v. Board of Education,* the Supreme Court ruling making school segregation illegal.

2004 **August 17** A survey conducted by the National Assessment of Educational Progress finds that the test scores of charter-school students are considerably lower than those of students in public schools.

2005 **January 7** Conservative radio host Armstrong Williams admits that he accepted payments from the Department of Education to say favorable things about the Bush administration's education reform. Williams also admits an open-door policy with members of the administration that allowed them to come on his program whenever they chose.

2005 **December 7** The Supreme Court rules that the government may hold a person's Social Security benefits in order to collect unpaid student loans.

2006 **May 3** The three largest soft-drink companies in the United States announce that they will remove sugary drinks such as soda and iced tea from cafeterias and vending machines in schools, replacing soft drinks with water, milk, and fruit juice.

2006 **August 21** The Virginia Tech campus is closed and classes are canceled as police search for William

C. Morva, suspected in the murder of a security guard and a police officer. Officials arrest and charge Morva a day and a half later. He is sentenced to receive the death penalty.

2006 **October 2** Charles Carl Roberts IV invades the Amish schoolhouse in Nickel Mines, Pennsylvania, with guns and restraints. After sending out all the boys and adults, he shoots the girls, killing five and wounding five. He then kills himself.

2007 **February 11** Harvard University announces that historian Drew Gilpin Faust will become the first female president in the school's 371-year history.

2007 **April 11** Don Imus's popular radio show and television simulcasts are canceled after public outrage over racist comments Imus made about the Rutgers University women's basketball team. Imus later issues an apology.

2007 **August 8** Barbara R. Morgan, a former teacher from Idaho, is aboard the space shuttle *Endeavour* as it lifts off. Morgan was the backup to Christa McAuliffe, the teacher who died in the 1986 *Challenger* explosion.

2007 **December 5** The Bush administration's abstinence-only sex education program's effectiveness is questioned when the birth rate for teens ages fifteen to nineteen rises 3 percent in 2006. It is the first time this statistic rose since 1991.

2008 April 25   Students across the United States participate in the thirteenth annual Day of Silence, which protests the silencing of homosexual students by harassment, bullying, and intimidation.

2008 September 25   An effigy of presidential nominee Barack Obama is found hanging from a tree on the campus of George Fox University in Newburg, Oregon.

2009 April 26   The federal government declares the swine flu outbreak a public-health emergency after confirming twenty cases in the United States. Schools across the country close in an attempt to isolate those who have been infected.

2009 October 20   Richard Herman, chancellor of the University of Illinois at Urbana-Champaign, resigns as a result of an admissions scandal in which certain students were given preferential treatment.

When people consider the state of education in the United States in the first decade of the twenty-first century, one phrase stands out from all the rest: No Child Left Behind. Enacted in early 2001, the new law held schools— and teachers—to a new level of accountability, measurable by standardized tests and assessments. Those schools that failed to meet the revised standards were penalized. Controversy over the law erupted upon its introduction as a bill, for although accountability of schools was considered a positive requirement, the funding necessary to meet the new require- ments was inadequate. Schools across the nation struggled under the new legislation, and it was met with fierce opposition from administrators, teachers, and parents.

Directly related to the public-school reform was the education gap between white and minority students. Most schools that failed under the No Child Left Behind Act were inner-city schools, populated primarily with minority and at-risk students. Opponents of the new law pointed out that these particular schools needed assistance, not punishment. But the race issue was not relegated to K-12 public schools. Colleges and universities came under fire in the 2000s for taking into consideration race as a factor for admissions applicants. A landmark Supreme Court case, *Grutter v. Bollinger*, 539 U.S. 306 (2003), upheld the right of universities to allot admissions slots based on the minority race of its applicants. Rather than being resolved, the issue of race remained controversial on campuses across the nation.

Schools from the elementary level through college began the decade with increased security measures in place in an effort to prevent another school massacre similar to what occurred at Columbine High School in Colorado. In 1999, two Columbine students went on a shooting spree that resulted in 13 deaths and 21 injuries. The tragedy shocked Americans and raised school-safety awareness. Even with preventive measures in place, violence in U.S. schools made headlines repeatedly across the decade. A gunman in rural Pennsylvania fatally shot five girls and wounded five more in a one-room Amish schoolhouse in 2006. Thirty-two people were murdered and 25 injured on the campus of Virginia Tech before the gunman killed himself in 2007. In educational settings everywhere, it was a decade of fear and anxiety.

The economic recession of the first decade of the twenty-first century took a heavy toll on education as budgets and funding were cut, reducing or eliminating altogether arts, music, foreign languages, and other elective programs in thousands of school districts across the nation. Although federal stimulus packages were passed to help those schools in need, the decade ended in controversy as schools and students continued to struggle.

As cries of reform became more intense, the focus widened to include not only funding but curriculum. Theories such as global warming and intelligent design found their way into classrooms, causing controversy among educators and parents alike. At the same time, the government encouraged—through generous grants—school districts to implement sex-education programs that teach only abstinence as opposed to comprehensive courses that educate students about risky behaviors, social responsibility, and birth control.

Online and distance learning at the college level and beyond gained in popularity as millions of Americans pursued degrees from their own homes. As tuition at traditional colleges and universities increased, more people turned to this affordable alternative.

Headline Makers

Laura Bush (1946–) Laura Bush was the first lady of the United States from 2001 to 2009. Having graduated college with a bachelor's degree in education, Bush took a job teaching second grade before earning her master's degree in library science. Once she became first lady, Bush announced that she would focus on education and early childhood development with an emphasis on reading. In partnership with the Library of Congress, the first lady launched the annual National Book Festival, an event that features authors, illustrators, poets, and other child-centered attractions. In 2006, Bush hosted a Conference on Global Literacy. Bush has been the recipient of numerous awards honoring her education reform and literacy efforts. *(© AP Images/Peter Kramer/NBC NewsWire)*

Henry Louis Gates (1950–) Dr. Henry Louis Gates Jr., an African American scholar and literary critic, is well known in academic circles. A self-described literary historian, Gates has taught at Harvard, Yale, Cornell, and Duke universities. He has published numerous works of literary criticism and used his significant influence to promote education reform. Gates's approach to such reform includes expanding black studies programs at the college level and including an enhanced, in-depth study of the works of authors from around the world. Though he is both revered and criticized for his vocal support and promotion of his ideologies, Gates was synonymous with the best in African American studies and multicultural education in the new millennium. *(© AP Images/ Stephan Savoia)*

Michelle Rhee (1959–) Michelle Rhee had no experience running a school when she was named chancellor of education in Washington, D.C., in 2007. That appointment made her responsible for 144 schools and a total of 46,000 students. Rhee was running a non-profit organization called the New Teacher Project, which assisted schools in recruiting effective teachers. Rhee was not a popular choice for the job, and she became even more controversial when, in her first year, she closed 23 schools, fired 36 principals, and cut more than one hundred office jobs. She eventually fired 241 teachers and put another 737 school employees on notice. Although Rhee improved the struggling schools of the U.S. capital, she remained in the shadow of possible scandal and controversy when test scores were questioned for their accuracy. Rhee resigned in October 2010 from her position and subsequently founded StudentsFirst, a non-profit committed to education reform. *(© Andrew Harrer/Bloomberg/Getty Images)*

Margaret Spellings (1957–) Margaret Spellings served as secretary of education from 2005 to 2009 during the George W. Bush administration. Prior to that position, she was the president's domestic policy adviser. She focused on education reform as a leading supporter of the controversial No Child Left Behind Act, a law designed to help children reach grade-level proficiency in math and reading by 2014. She was the first mother of school-age children to serve as secretary of education, and was generally well respected in Congress as a capable and ethical leader. After serving her country in these high-profile positions, Spellings founded Margaret Spellings & Company, a public policy and consulting firm. *(© AP Images/Dennis Cook)*

❖ NO CHILD LEFT BEHIND

Officially titled the Elementary and Secondary Education Act, the 2001 law known as No Child Left Behind (NCLB) was supported by Republicans and Democrats alike. This reform law is based on the idea that individual outcomes in education can be improved through establishing high standards, focusing on objective exit exams, and establishing minimum acceptable performance goals. There is no national achievement standard dictated by NCLB; instead, each state develops tests and assessments in the basic skills of reading, writing, and math. The results of these standardized tests determine how much federal funding each school receives. The overall goal of NCLB is to hold schools and their teachers accountable for students' learning as measured by test performance.

Unfortunately, NCLB caused numerous problems. It thrust standardized testing into the spotlight, and opponents of the law claimed that too many teachers sacrificed comprehensive teaching in order to "teach to the test," meaning they taught lessons that provided information needed to do well on the required standardized tests but not more than that. So while students might score well on the tests, thereby earning their school better funding, their overall knowledge of any subject and their ability to think independently about that subject were lacking. Their broader understanding of the subject seemed actually to be inferior to what it might have been prior to NCLB.

School administration and staff complained that there was insufficient funding to implement NCLB, making success all the more unlikely. Educators argued that even if funding is plentiful, the law's goal of having all students test at grade level is unrealistic, given many variables that exist among schools and among various student populations and individual students. Opponents also pointed out that the emphasis on NCLB and its requirements force many schools to cut back or eliminate the elective classes in art, music, and sports, for example, including curriculum specifically designed for gifted and talented individuals.

As states struggled to conform to NCLB, educators and parents across the nation became more vocal in their opposition to the law. Near the end of the decade, President Barack Obama reformed the law by providing more federal funding and diluting some of its more punitive aspects.

New York City teachers protest budget cuts in 2003. Declining tax revenue resulted in an economic crisis in public schools across the country in the first decade of the twenty-first century. © *Bill Turnbull/NY Daily News Archive/Getty Images*

❖ BUDGET CUTS AND SCHOOL CLOSINGS

The economic recession of the latter years of the decade put a strain on every facet of U.S. society, including education. As schools lost funding due to declining tax revenues, thousands of schools from preschool through high school closed and millions of educators lost their jobs. Education secretary Arne Duncan called the situation "brutal." Duncan was not being an alarmist when he told Washington reporters, "This is a real emergency. What we're trying to avert is an education catastrophe."

In response to the economic crisis, the Obama administration passed the American Recovery and Reinvestment Act of 2009, also known as the Stimulus or Recovery Act. Designed to give the economy a boost and encourage consumer confidence, $100 billion of the roughly $787 billion designated in the act went to education. Local school districts received $53.6 billion to use for repairs and updates as well as to help stave off layoffs and cutbacks, while another $13 billion was earmarked for low-income students. The rest of the money was divided among other areas of perceived need, including childcare services, classroom technology, and teacher salary increases.

❖ TWENTY-FIRST CENTURY CLASSROOM TECHNOLOGY

While much of the focus of the first decade of the twenty-first century was on reform and budget, technology continued to progress with little fanfare. Schools fortunate enough to have good funding incorporated the latest advancements in their daily learning routines.

Traditional green and black chalkboards were being replaced by the now-familiar dry-erase boards at the beginning of the decade; by the end of the decade the dry-erase boards were being supplemented by Promethean Boards, interactive whiteboards that harness the power of a computer with front projection. Teachers used images, video, and audio to turn their lecture halls into interactive classrooms. The cost of Promethean Boards relegated them to the wish-lists of many educators, but that did not prevent teachers from using more readily accessible technology in their classrooms.

Many classes and extracurricular programs developed Web sites or blogs, and high-school teachers across the country finished the decade using the Internet as a tool for student assessment, homework, and even

A math teacher at a New York City school uses a computer projection board in his classroom. Schools that could afford technology introduced it into the classroom in greater measure during the early 2000s. © *Chris Hondros/Getty Images*

21st Century Skills

School districts have the right to choose their curriculums, as long as they meet or exceed all state standards. One such curriculum is 21st Century Skills, which gained momentum in the first decade of the century. The underlying perspective of 21st Century Skills is that traditional public schooling is 150 years old; it was developed in the nineteenth century and needs to be updated if students are to keep pace in an increasingly global economy and technology. Although the United States is no longer strictly an industrial society, traditional curriculums lagged behind the advent of information technology.

21st Century Skills maintains the core subjects at its foundation, but it incorporates life and career skills, learning and innovation skills, and information, media literacy, and technology skills. All of these are approached from a perspective of twenty-first century themes, with an eye to what is applicable and important in the 2000s. The curriculum takes into consideration and encourages professional development, up-to-date learning environments, and standards and assessments.

teaching. Students could connect to a site affiliated with a particular class, listen to and observe the lesson, and then complete the homework, turning it in to the teacher with the click of a mouse. One of the advantages to such a tool is that students can replay any part of the lesson as often as necessary in order to learn the information; it also allows students to complete the assignment in segments as well as stop and start as needed. Still other teachers used mp3s as tools in the classroom. Even traditional print textbooks were largely replaced by online versions of the books and supplemented by learning sites and online periodicals.

❖ WHEN SHOULD RACE MATTER?

Affirmative action is a policy initiated in the 1960s and adopted by schools, businesses, and other organizations to increase the presence of women and minorities in places from which they have historically been absent. It is a controversial policy because it often results in preferential selection, which can mean selection based on race, gender, or ethnicity.

Backlash against affirmative action began in the 1990s as several Supreme Court decisions banned universities from considering race in admissions standards. As a direct result, minority enrollment significantly declined. For example, when the state of Texas banned affirmative action policies in 1996, the number of African American students enrolled at University of Texas Law School dropped from 38 to four.

In 1995, Jennifer Gratz applied to the University of Michigan College of Literature, Science, and the Arts (LSA) with a grade point average (GPA) of 3.8 and an ACT score of 25 (out of a possible 36). Two years later, Patrick Hamacher applied to the college as well. He had a GPA of 3.3 and an ACT score of 28. Neither Gratz nor Hamacher was accepted by the university, which receives approximately 13,500 applications each year to the LSA and admits about 3,950 annually.

Both students were contacted by the Center for Individual Rights, a non-profit public interest law firm based in Washington, D.C. The center filed a lawsuit on behalf of Gratz and Hamacher in October 1997, alleging violation of the petitioners' Fourteenth Amendment rights, specifically the equal protection clause that prohibits racial discrimination.

The university used a 150-point scale to rank its applicants. In order to receive guaranteed admission, an applicant was required to achieve at least 100 points. Individuals belonging to minority groups—including Hispanics, Native Americans, and African Americans—were given an extra 20 points. The number of points was significant, given that a perfect SAT score was worth 12 points. Gratz and Hamacher are white; they received no points for their racial identity.

University of Michigan administrators admitted to using race as a factor in making admissions choices in the interest of creating a racially diverse student body. They also revealed a policy that admits nearly every qualified applicant if he or she is African American, Hispanic, or Native American and thus belongs to a group that is underrepresented on campus.

As the policy was written, then, race was not evaluated equally along with other factors such as grades, extracurricular activities, and interviews. It was, instead, given more emphasis because inclusion in one of three racial minorities alone automatically ensured the applicant's acceptance into the school.

In *Gratz v. Bollinger,* 539 U.S. 244 (2003), the High Court determined that the policy violates the Fourteenth Amendment's equal protection clause by a 6–3 vote. Justice William H. Rehnquist's majority opinion explained that while creating cultural diversity is a compelling interest, the university's policy of automatically giving 20 points (or one-fifth of the minimum requirements) to every applicant who falls into one of three racial categories is not narrowly tailored. Race, he judged, in the school's admission process had become a decisive factor.

In its companion case, *Grutter v. Bollinger*, 539 U.S. 306 (2003), the school was being sued by an applicant on the same grounds. In this case, the Court found in favor of the University of Michigan's Law School, which uses race as a factor in determining admission to the program. Its policy, according to Justice O'Connor, was narrowly tailored to the extent that it took race into consideration when attempting to cultivate a diverse student body, but race was not the overriding concern.

Affirmative action as it had been applied for four decades clearly earned the disapproval of courts and voters alike. By the end of the 2000s, a reformed version of the policy was developing, one based more on economic need than on race and gender.

❖ IMPORTANCE OF READING

The National Assessment of Educational Progress, which publishes "The Nation's Report Card," reported that two out of five American students could not read in 2005. In 2006 *USA Today* journalist William J. Moloney reported that "Among first-year college students, one-quarter require remediation for literacy deficiencies." It was an educational crisis that resisted resolution.

The situation was even more grave considering it was happening in the early years of the No Child Left Behind law, which was designed specifically to bring students up to grade level in the core skills of reading, writing, and math. The United States was getting desperate to improve its students' overall education quality. The response to the crisis was the development of reading initiatives at local, state, and national levels. Concerned citizens groups joined government programs to improve reading; retail giant Target hosted the Target Early Childhood Reading Grants, and the National Endowment for the Arts developed The Big Read. Monies from these organizations and others offered grants and scholarships to schools, book clubs, and other literacy-minded groups.

A 2009 literacy study published by the National Center for Education Statistics revealed that an estimated 32 million American adults— approximately one in seven—struggled with literacy to the point where they could read nothing more challenging than a child's picture book. Literacy continued to be a national concern into the second decade of the century.

Laura Bush promotes reading in a Washington, D.C., school on October 15, 2001. The First Lady focused on literacy during her husband's two terms in office. © *Paul J. Richards/ AFP/Getty Images*

❖ WHAT TO TEACH?

Reading was not the only cause for concern during the 2000s. In the classroom, two different subjects generated intense debate: sex education and evolution.

Sex education was part of many school health and wellness curriculums in the 2000s, and it was typically approached in one of two ways.

A comprehensive sex education curriculum focused on sexual health awareness, pregnancy and disease prevention, and understanding of risky behaviors as opposed to prudent choices. Abstinence-only curriculums promoted celibacy until marriage as the only right choice and depended upon a morality-based argument.

During the George W. Bush administration (2001–09), the federal government awarded in excess of $1 billion to funding abstinence-only programs in schools. The purpose of the program was to promote abstinence for its social and health advantages. By 2002, more than one-third of high schools implemented an abstinence-only curriculum. At the time, the Center for Disease Control and Prevention reported that 60 percent of high school seniors admitted to being sexually active.

Toward the end of the decade, several studies concluded that abstinence-only curriculums were ineffective in convincing teens to abstain from sexual activity. Furthermore, the General Accounting Office determined that most abstinence-only programs were not scientifically based or reviewed and relied instead on outdated information. Several national and state polls showed that the majority of parents were in favor of comprehensive sex education, and in 2009 President Barack Obama eliminated nearly all federal funding for abstinence-only programs.

Evolution, long a controversial topic in school and beyond, found itself in the spotlight again in the early 2000s, when debate arose over how to teach it in science classes. Some people argued that if evolution is taught in school then its opposing theory, called intelligent design, should be taught with it.

The debate entered a court of law in Pennsylvania in 2005. In *Tammy Kitzmiller, et al. v. Dover Area School District, et al.*, a U.S. district court held that the requirement to teach intelligent design in a public school science class violates First Amendment protection of the separation of church and state. The judge asserted that intelligent design is a form of creationism, a theory with clear theological implications.

❖ ALTERNATIVES TO TRADITIONAL PUBLIC SCHOOLS

The outcry for reform of traditional public schools also contributed to the growth of alternatives to public-school education: charter schools and homeschooling. State legislatures had begun passing charter legislation in the 1990s, and as of 2004, 39 states had launched approximately 2,700 charter schools. By 2009, that number had increased to 4,988. These schools run independently of the public school system and design their own programs and curriculum while still adhering to federal laws such as

No Child Left Behind. The cornerstones of a charter school are innovation, choice, and community/parent involvement. Charter schools are significantly smaller than traditional public schools and are likely to enroll low-income children but fewer special-needs students. According to the Department of Education, charters served more minorities and fewer whites than traditional public schools, and more than half of them met state performance standards.

Homeschooling was not a new movement in the 2000s, but it gained in popularity during the decade at a rate of 7 to 12 percent yearly. Homeschooling means children are taught at home, or, more accurately, in places other than school. Some children are homeschooled in groups in churches and recreation centers or other places where small groups can gather. There is no one specific curriculum, and there is even a style or method called un-schooling, in which children determine what they learn and how and when they learn it based on their individual interests and talents.

Once thought to be the education choice of religiously strict families, homeschooling became the choice for many families who were frustrated

More parents decided to teach their children at home rather than enroll them in public school during the first decade of the twenty-first century. © *wavebreakmedia ltd/ ShutterStock.com* with the traditional public school system for various reasons. Home-schooling was a viable option for students who place at either end of the learning spectrum as well, either those with special needs or those with special gifts and talents. In January 2007 the PBS program *Religion & Ethics* presented a segment on homeschooling. In it, it was estimated that "well over a million" children in the United States were being homeschooled, with minimal government oversight and regulation in some states.

Though appreciated by increasing numbers, homeschooling had its detractors. One frequent criticism is that parents may not be qualified to teach children, especially those with special needs. However, according to a 2006 article written by Brian D. Ray, "The home-educated typically score 15 to 30 percentile points above public-school students on standardized academic achievement tests."

❖ HIGHER LEARNING, FROM A DISTANCE

As tuition rates increased almost annually at traditional four-year colleges, more and more students opted to go to community colleges in the 2000s. According to a 2009 article by Richard Fry, "The share of 18- to 24-year-olds attending college in the United States hit an all-time high in October 2008, driven by a recession-era surge in enrollments at community colleges."

Fry, with information from a Pew Research Center analysis of data released by the U.S. Census Bureau, reported that 39.6 percent of that population (just under 11.5 million people) was enrolled in either a two- or four-year college. Both statistics were at their highest level ever. In October 2007, about 3.1 million adults were attending community college. One year later that figure had jumped to 3.4 million.

Labor market demands were such that diplomas from four-year colleges were not necessary, as careers in information technology and medical fields could be achieved with a two-year diploma. That trend was assisted by the fact that more and more high-school graduates were choosing to fulfill their basic first- and second-year college requirements at a less expensive community college rather than doing so at a more expensive four-year institution.

Community college was not the only popular choice in the 2000s. College enrollment numbers at traditional universities also increased, and those institutions could not accommodate the large numbers of students. Where once these brick-and-mortar buildings were expected to accommodate only the traditional-age student, they now had both recent high-school graduates and nontraditional students such as parents wanting to finish that last year of school to complete their degree.

Increased student populations in the early 2000s, coupled with the fact that many students have other family and work responsibilities, caused administrators and faculty to create curricula designed to be both flexible and convenient. Distance or online education programs developed to fit campus limitations and students' needs. As the 2000s progressed, more institutions began to offer degrees based on such programs, and industry experts predicted that the number of traditional college campuses would decline.

The Sloan Consortium published a study called *Learning on Demand: Online Education in the United States*, which indicated that in 2008, 80 percent of all online and distance learning classes were taken by undergraduates, while 14 percent were graduate students. The balance were students seeking certification.

 For More Information

BOOKS

Bonk, Curtis J. *The World Is Open: How Web Technology Is Revolutionizing Education.* Hoboken, NJ: Jossey-Bass, 2011.

Ravitch, Diane. *The Death and Life of the Great American School System: How Testing and Choice Are Undermining Education.* Jackson, TN: Basic Books, 2010.

WEB SITES

"ESEA Reauthorization: A Blueprint for Reform." *U.S. Department of Education.* Last modified May 26, 2011. http://www2.ed.gov/policy/elsec/leg/blueprint/index.html (accessed on July 20, 2011).

Fry, Richard. "College Enrollment Hits All-Time High, Fueled by Community College Surge." *Pew Research Center.* October 29, 2009. http://pewsocial-trends.org/2009/10/29/college-enrollment-hits-all-time-high-fueled-by-community-college-surge/ (accessed on July 20, 2011).

Gibson, Ken. "Reading Crisis in America." *SearchWarp.* April 17, 2006. http://searchwarp.com/swa57357.htm (accessed on July 20, 2011).

"Henry Louis Gates Jr." *The New York Times.* http://www.nytimes.com/ref/opinion/henrylouisgatesjr-bio.html (accessed on July 20, 2011).

Mara. "Enrollment in Online Classes on the Rise." *Financial Aid Finder.* February 15, 2010. http://www.financialaidfinder.com/enrollment-in-online-classes-on-the-rise.html (accessed on July 20, 2011).

Moloney, William J. "To Find the Answer to Our Illiteracy Crisis, Americans Must Look Within." *USA Today*. August 16, 2006. http://www.usatoday.com/news/opinion/editorials/2006-08-16-illiteracy_x.htm (accessed on July 20, 2011).

"National Charter School and Enrollment Statistics 2010." *The Center for Education Reform*. October 2010. http://www.edreform.com/_upload/CER_charter_numbers.pdf (accessed on July 20, 2011).

Ray, Brian D. "Research Facts on Homeschooling." *Exploring Homeschooling*. July 10, 2006. http://www.exploringhomeschooling.com/ResearchFactson Homeschooling.aspx (accessed on July 20, 2011).

Toppo, Greg. "Literacy Study: 1 in 7 U.S. Adults are Unable to Read This Story." *USA Today*. January 8, 2009. http://www.usatoday.com/news/education/2009-01-08-adult-literacy_N.htm (accessed on July 20, 2011).

"What Are 21st Century Skills?" *Smartbean*. November 15, 2009. http://www.thesmartbean.com/magazine/21st-century-skills-magazine/what-are-21st-century-skills/ (accessed on July 20, 2011).

Government, Politics, and Law

2000 April 22 Elián González, the young survivor of a tragic attempt to emigrate from Cuba to the United States in November 1999, is taken from his late mother's family in Miami. He is returned to Cuba to live with his father on June 28. The controversial decision to return González sparks tensions between Cuban immigrants and the federal government.

2000 October 12 Al Qaeda terrorists attack the USS *Cole* at port in Yemen, killing seventeen U.S. sailors.

2000 November 7 In the presidential election between Democrat Al Gore and Republican George W. Bush, the popular vote goes to Gore but the electoral college tally is too close to call. A recount is ordered when Bush is found to have a lead of fewer than two thousand votes.

2000 December 12 The U.S. Supreme Court decides in favor of Bush, overturning the Florida Supreme Court's decision to continue the recount of disputed ballots in Florida. One day later, Gore concedes the election, and George W. Bush is officially elected president of the United States.

2001 September 11 Terrorists hijack four U.S. commercial airplanes and initiate the worst terrorist attack on U.S. soil in history. More than two thousand people die.

2001 October 7 U.S. and British forces begin air strikes (Operation Enduring Freedom) in Afghanistan. Hours after U.S. forces strike, Osama bin Laden releases a video praising the terrorist attacks of September 11, though he does not take credit for them.

2001 October 26 In direct response to the 9/11 terrorist attacks, President Bush signs into law the USA PATRIOT Act, which expands the ability of law enforcement agencies to investigate private citizens in a number of ways, including surveying private communication.

2002 January 11 The first twenty detainees arrive at the detainment facility established on the U.S. Naval Base in Guantánamo Bay, Cuba. Labeled "enemy combatants" by Defense Secretary Donald Rumsfeld, these prisoners have no rights under the Geneva Convention.

2003 February 5 Secretary of State Colin Powell addresses the United Nations to plead the U.S. case for an invasion in Iraq. Powell insists that evidence confirms biological and chemical weapons in Iraq. Later it is revealed Powell was given a Bush administration text for the speech without reliable documentation.

2003 March 20 The United States and a coalition of forces invade Iraq.

2003 April 1 Private First Class Jessica Lynch is rescued by U.S. Special Forces from a hospital in Iraq. Members of the Iraqi military had taken Lynch after nine of her fellow soldiers were killed in an ambush. Her rescue is videotaped by a military cameraman and edited footage is released to the media, portraying Lynch as a heroic prisoner of war. However, Lynch later testifies that she had not fought back when captured, and she accuses the Pentagon of fabricating a story for war propaganda.

2003 December 14 After months of eluding U.S. troops, Saddam Hussein is discovered in a bunker on a farm near the Iraqi city of Tikrit.

2004 April *New Yorker* journalist Seymour M. Hersh publishes an article revealing abuse of prisoners at Abu Ghraib. Seventeen soldiers in Iraq are removed from duty for mistreating Iraqi prisoners after photographs of sexual, physical, and emotional abuse emerge.

2004 November 3 Bush beats Democrat John Kerry to win re-election as president.

2005 August 29 Hurricane Katrina strikes New Orleans. The storm and its aftermath devastates coastal regions in Louisiana, Mississippi, Alabama, and the panhandle of Florida, killing approximately 1,833 people and displacing hundreds of thousands. The Bush administration is severely criticized for alleged tardiness and ineptitude in responding to the catastrophe.

2005 September 28 A Texas grand jury indicts House Majority Leader Republican Tom DeLay on charges of criminal conspiracy relating to the scandal associated with powerful Washington lobbyist Jack Abramoff. DeLay announces his resignation from Congress on January 7, 2006.

2006 May 3 Zacarias Moussaoui is sentenced to life in prison by a federal jury for conspiring to kill U.S. citizens in the September 11 terrorist attacks. He denies involvement, claiming that he belonged to a separate al Qaeda cell.

2006 May 25 Kenneth Lay and Jeffrey Skilling, former Enron executives, are convicted of securities and wire fraud.

2006 July 19 Bush vetoes the embryonic stem-cell research bill.

2006 December 30 Saddam Hussein is sentenced to death and hanged in Baghdad for his crimes against humanity.

2007 January 7 Democrat Nancy Pelosi is elected the first female Speaker of the House.

2007 January 10   Bush announces an escalation of troop deployment in Iraq. Later known as the "surge," the increase of military personnel becomes a hotly contested foreign-policy decision for the White House.

2008 August 29   Republican presidential nominee John McCain chooses Alaska governor Sarah Palin as his running mate. She is the first woman on a Republican presidential ticket.

2008 September 15   Lehman Brothers files for bankruptcy, becoming the largest bankruptcy filing in U.S. history to date.

2008 September 29   The Dow Jones industrial average drops nearly 800 points, the biggest single-day point loss in stock market history. The loss marks the beginning of a long and damaging economic recession in the United States.

2008 October 3   Bush signs the Emergency Economic Stabilization Act, a $700 billion bailout of the U.S. financial system.

2008 November 4   Barack Obama becomes the first African American to be elected president of the United States.

2008 December 19   Bush announces a $17.4 billion auto-industry rescue, with $13.4 billion in emergency loans to prevent General Motors and Chrysler from collapsing.

2009 August 6   Sonia Sotomayor becomes the first Hispanic woman on the U.S. Supreme Court.

The 2000s were the most economically challenging and politically charged since the 1930s. The decade was marked by milestones, none of them good: terrorism and tragedy, war overseas and conflict at home in a nation divided, and economic collapse and renewed levels of distrust and doubt. Three controversial presidential elections, twisted acts of terrorism and two simultaneous wars, political scandals, corporate greed, and natural disasters all rocked the country and those who led it, and the United States no longer could claim being the world's superpower as the nation's reputation became tarnished and tainted. Former allies questioned U.S. motivations and intentions, and what was once considered strength was now looked upon as bullying. Within the country, political chasms deepened as the trend shifted to the right of center, and leaders looked to fewer regulations and more tax cuts. What began as economic concern spiraled into recession as unemployment rates rose, the housing market collapsed, and Wall Street scandals dominated the headlines.

Rarely in history has the division between Republicans and Democrats been as deep and wide as it was in this decade. Beginning with the 2000 election, in which one candidate won the popular vote but the other won the election, Americans looked to their leaders with a sense of distrust and disrespect as one issue after another forced these two political camps further and further apart. The politicians themselves focused on the hot-button issues of the decade: same-sex marriage, immigration, healthcare reform, role of government, and the right to die. As living leaders struggled to keep the nation moving forward, the country mourned the deaths of some of the most high-profile and influential politicians ever to serve.

The terrorist events of September 11, 2001, changed the course of the United States in a span of moments as planes crashed, buildings were destroyed, and thousands of citizens were killed. The U.S. response to these attacks was to wage war, a so-called war on terrorism that would result in more lives lost as thousands of international troops crossed the seas to combat enemies known and unknown in Afghanistan and Iraq. Saddam Hussein and Osama bin Ladin evaded capture for a while, outwitting U.S. intelligence and affecting the United States in far-reaching ways both big and small.

There were prices to pay for the war. Americans were shamed to discover the torture tactics employed and encouraged by the U.S. military as photos of such behavior from Abu Ghraib prison were released by the media. Journalist Daniel Pearl, who went to Pakistan to investigate links between Richard Reid (the "Shoe Bomber") and al Qaeda, was kidnapped and murdered. As military action continued, so did the loss of life of civilians, including other journalists and contractors, and military personnel.

The wartime economy gave way to recession as corporate scandals destroyed both companies and individuals. Giants Enron and WorldCom were toppled by bankruptcy, and their highest-level executives imprisoned for their greed and deceit. After a period of unprecedented growth, the housing market collapsed just as unemployment rates soared, and millions of Americans lost their homes and jobs. It was a vicious cycle that no amount of financial bail-out or organizational restructuring could salvage. Toward the end of the decade, Americans faced an unstable economy at home and in countries elsewhere in the world.

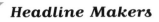
George W. Bush (1946–) Republican George W. Bush was the forty-third president of the United States and served from 2001 to 2009 with Vice President Dick Cheney. Before the 2000 election, Bush served six years as governor of Texas. Bush's presidency was marked with controversy and national crises, including the September 11, 2001 terrorist attacks; the war in Afghanistan; and the 2003 invasion of Iraq, which marked the beginning of a war that would last longer than many Americans anticipated. Among the major acts the president signed into law are the No Child Left Behind Act, the PATRIOT Act, the Partial-Birth Abortion Ban Act, and several sweeping tax cuts. His tax cuts, in particular, are credited with putting into motion fifty-two consecutive months of job creation, a feat never before achieved. Bush also reformed Medicare by adding a prescription drug benefit. Throughout his eight-year presidency, he was criticized for his public-speaking foibles, which came to be known as Bushisms. His response to the human rights violations perpetrated by U.S. soldiers at Abu Ghraib prison in 2004 and the devastation of Hurricane Katrina in 2005 incited anger and sharp criticism from many Americans and international critics. *(© AP Photo/The White House, Eric Draper)*

Hillary Rodham Clinton (1947–) Democrat Hillary Rodham Clinton was once known primarily as the wife of Bill Clinton, the forty-second president of the United States. Even as First Lady, Clinton was a powerful political figure as she focused on healthcare reform as well as several child-centered initiatives. During the White House years (1993–2001), she traveled to seventy-nine countries, a fact that made her the most mobile First Lady in history. Clinton made history twice with her next political move: as the only First Lady ever to run for public office and as the first woman to represent the state of New York in the U.S. Senate from 2001 to 2009. She entered the 2008 presidential nomination race and won more primaries and delegates than any other female candidate in U.S. history before losing to Barack Obama. Clinton accepted Obama's nomination for the position of secretary of state. She became the only former First Lady to serve in the United States Cabinet. By late 2009, Clinton was number seventeen on *Forbes*'s list of the World's Most Powerful People. *(© AP Photo/Tim Roske)*

W. Mark Felt (1913–2008) On May 31, 2005, *The Washington Post* confirmed that W. Mark Felt, one of the Federal Bureau of Investigation's highest ranking officials, was the legendary Deep Throat, the secret source whose information contributed to the newspaper's Pulitzer Prize–winning coverage of the 1970s Watergate scandal. That coverage was the impetus for the historic resignation of President Richard M. Nixon on August 9, 1974.

Speculation of Felt's role as Deep Throat was rampant in Washington for more than three decades. Felt denied being Deep Throat, but a family member revealed his identity to *Vanity Fair* magazine. Felt had joined the FBI in 1942 and, by the 1970s, had been appointed assistant director. He held this position until his retirement. Felt died in 2008 at the age of ninety-five. *(© AP Photo)*

John McCain (1936–) John McCain made headlines in the 2000s for his role as the Republican presidential candidate in the 2008 campaign. He had a long and distinguished political career prior to that, which began with his election to the U.S. House of Representatives in 1982. Four years later, he was elected to the U.S. Senate, where he fought for reform of Washington's political system with a focus on the handling of taxpayer funds and special-interest loopholes. In 1999, McCain announced his candidacy for the 2000 presidential election, but George W. Bush won the Republican nomination. In 2001, the presidential hopeful spoke out against the Bush administration on several key issues. McCain branded himself a "maverick" throughout his presidential campaign in an effort to convince Americans he would do whatever it took to get a job done, whether that required his following party lines or breaking from them. *(© AP Photo/Carolyn Kaster)*

Barack Obama (1961–) Democrat Barack Obama was inaugurated as the forty-fourth president of the United States in 2009. The first African American to be elected U.S. president, Obama ran on a platform of change and hope. Prior to his presidency, he served for six years (1997–2004) as Illinois state senator. From 2005 to 2008, Obama served in the U.S. Senate. As president, Obama passed a $787 billion stimulus bill to promote economic growth and made loans to the auto industry while increasing regulation of Wall Street. While committing 21,000 more troops to Afghanistan, the president publicly set August 2010 as the withdrawal date of troops in Iraq. He gave foreign policy a total makeover as he and Secretary of State Hillary Clinton focused efforts on repairing and strengthening relationships across the globe. In recognition of what he had achieved in a short time, Obama was awarded the 2009 Nobel Peace Prize. He was not without his detractors, however, as critics allege his failure to deliver on campaign promises of major healthcare reform, the closing of Guantánamo Bay prison, and improved economic conditions. *(© AP Photo/Obama Transition Office, Pete Souza)*

Sandra Day O'Connor (1930–) Nominated by President Ronald Reagan in 1981, Sandra Day O'Connor was criticized by both conservatives and liberals. The former doubted her effectiveness because of her lack of experience, whereas the latter decried her unwillingness to support feminist issues. Her nomination was a fulfillment of a campaign promise Reagan had made to put a woman on the U.S. Supreme Court. Her appointment was confirmed by a unanimous Senate, and she began what would be a remarkable twenty-five-year tenure as a Supreme Court justice. Although her voting record was primarily conservative, O'Connor tended to approach each court case on an individual basis. As such, she was often the judge to cast a tie-breaking vote. One of the issues closely associated with O'Connor was abortion. Her voting record indicated she was in favor of a woman's right to choose, but only with certain restrictions in place. When she retired in 2006 to care for her ailing husband, she did so having earned a reputation as a moderate, fair judge whose ability to tailor her judgments to serve practical solutions on a case-by-case basis allowed her to have great influence on the Court. *(© AP Photo/Tina Fineberg)*

Sarah Palin (1964–)   Although she served as the ninth governor of Alaska from December 2006 to July 2009, Republican Sarah Palin was most famous in the decade as John McCain's running mate in the 2008 presidential election. Palin took the United States by storm when McCain announced his choice. Few people had ever heard of her, and her political experience was not extensive in any way, which led to much speculation as to why McCain chose her to be his running mate. Palin, the first Republican female to run for vice president, became the target of criticism for her campaign spending. The Republican National Committee reported that she spent $150,000 on clothes, hair styling, and makeup. Palin also was the subject of one of the most famous parodies in television history. *Saturday Night Live* comedian Tina Fey, who resembles Palin, performed a skit on live television in which she satirized the governor. After the failed vice presidential run, Palin resigned from her position as governor and began writing a memoir and touring the country as a public speaker. She indicated the possibility of a presidential run in the next election but later said she did not intend to be a candidate. *(© AP Photo/Al Grillo)*

Colin Powell (1937–)   Born in Harlem, New York, to Jamaican immigrants, Colin Powell grew up to become one of the most distinguished statesmen of the twentieth- and twenty-first centuries. He first served in the White House under President Richard Nixon. Powell was appointed chairman of the Joint Chiefs of Staff under President George H. W. Bush in the early 1990s. At that time, Powell gained national notoriety for his leadership of Desert Shield and Desert Storm, operations which successfully expelled Iraq from its tiny neighbor, Kuwait. Powell was appointed secretary of state by the elder Bush's son, George W. Bush, in 2001, becoming the first African American to hold such a high position in federal government. Although in favor of sending troops to Afghanistan, Powell reportedly disagreed with initiating war in Iraq. Even so, he addressed the United Nations Security Council, claiming to have evidence

that Iraq possessed weapons of mass destruction (WMDs). Powell's statements were influential in convincing the U.S. Congress to support military involvement in Iraq. Some of the evidence was later proven to be false, and Powell was criticized. He resigned from his position shortly after Bush's re-election in 2004 and surprised many when he publicly endorsed Democrat Barack Obama for president in 2008. *(© AP Photo/Haraz N. Ghanbari)*

Topics in the News

❖ ELECTION 2000: BUSH V. GORE

Despite a sex scandal and the subsequent impeachment trial, Democrat Bill Clinton left his two-term presidency with a 65 percent approval rating, higher than any other post–World War II president. His legacy included a strong economy and a federal budget surplus. Many Americans were feeling secure at the time of the 2000 presidential election.

The candidates were Republican George W. Bush and Democrat Al Gore. Bush had been the governor of Texas since January 1995; Gore had been Clinton's vice president. Both men had years of political experience. Bush appealed to the conservative Christian factions. Gore, though distancing himself from the Clinton administration so as not to be affiliated with the president's personal scandal, relied on Clinton's popularity to an extent to bolster his own.

Bush's campaign was marred by media revelations of his past drug and alcohol abuse and plagued by his own social and speaking gaffes. One low point came when, during a Labor Day event in Illinois, the presidential hopeful referred to a reporter as a "major league asshole," unaware that his microphone was on. Gore's staff seized the moment and used his opponent's mistake against him. The vice president's campaign was not without challenges as he worked to counter the public's image of him as rather wooden and unemotional. Compared with Clinton's charismatic personality, Gore appeared to fall short. Yet he had been one of the most active vice presidents in U.S. history, and he had a chance to show that when, on October 12, 2000, a terrorist bomb killed seventeen U.S. sailors aboard the USS *Cole* in Yemen. While Bush's response was to defend his lack of foreign-policy experience, Gore addressed the event publicly, promising that the terrorists would not go unpunished.

The election itself was one of the most controversial and problematic in U.S. history. As the nation's polls closed, it was impossible to determine a clear victor in many states. Citizens had to wait more than a month to learn that Bush had won the election. The reasons for the delay were numerous: Ballot-counting issues had been reported in various counties as had illegally cast votes. Then Florida announced that it had possibly miscounted votes. Americans were left with a Democratic candidate who had clearly won the popular vote and a Republican candidate who had won slightly more electoral votes. This situation meant that Florida's results were more important than ever, because Florida was worth twenty-five electoral votes. If Gore took that state, he would win the election. Bush was in the same position.

Presidential Elections: The Issues

E very election has its own set of issues, which the candidates debate. Some of the issues of the 2000s were common to all three elections. For example, budget and economy were high on the list for candidates in 2000, 2004, and 2008. Likewise, tax and government reform were key topics. But each election also had its unique key issues, influenced by the times and the circumstances of the day.

Specific to the Bush-Gore campaigns was free trade, gun control, defense, and social security. For the 2004 election, Bush and Kerry debated terrorism, moral or "family" values, and foreign policy. The 2008 election revolved around healthcare reform, moral values (with a focus on same-sex marriage), immigration, energy, several medical issues, foreign policy, and the war in Iraq.

Most news networks announced Gore as the winner in Florida and thus the president-elect. But it soon became clear, as Florida votes were tallied, that the media had spoken too soon, and it appeared that Bush had won Florida. With a margin of victory of less than 0.5 percent of the total votes cast in Florida, a recount by machine was required according to state law. This recount gave Bush an even narrower victory than initially thought, and so Gore requested a recount in specific counties. Florida's secretary of state approved the recount, but then a number of counties missed the recount deadline of November 14. Harris extended the deadline to November 26, and Bush was declared the forty-third president of the United States. Concerned that a basic miscount had changed the outcome of the election, the Florida Supreme Court ordered a recount.

Bush was not in favor of a recount for fear his victory might slip through his hands, so he appealed to the U.S. Supreme Court. The Court agreed to hear the case on December 11. Both sides cited their rights under the Fourteenth Amendment of the U.S. Constitution, and the Court ultimately decided, in a 5–4 decision, that a valid recount could not be completed by the mandatory deadline of December 12, and Bush was declared the winner.

This election left Americans deeply divided and resentful. Those who voted for Gore and running mate Joe Lieberman had difficulty accepting

Bush as president because of questions surrounding the legitimacy of his victory. Politically, the country had been divided into Red (Republican) and Blue (Democrat) states by the media. In this way, Bush began serving his term, with Vice President Dick Cheney by his side, under a cloud of controversy.

❖ THE 9/11 TERRORIST ATTACKS

President Bush was a mere nine months into his term when, on the morning of September 11, 2001, a series of four coordinated terrorist attacks were launched on the United States. In New York City, hijackers crashed American Airlines Flight 11 and United Airlines Flight 175 into Towers One and Two of the World Trade Center, killing and injuring thousands of people in the towers and in the immediate area. Shortly afterward, American Airlines Flight 77 crashed into the Pentagon in Arlington, Virginia. In a rural area near Shanksville, Pennsylvania, United Airlines Flight 93 crashed into a field as passengers tried to overwhelm the hijackers and prevent the plane from reaching its intended target, assumed to be a major building in Washington, D.C. Altogether, the official death toll as of 2009 was 2,975 (not including the nineteen hijackers) and more than six thousand injured.

A second plane crashes into the World Trade Center on September 11, 2001. Terrorists hijacked four commercial planes that morning: two hit the World Trade Center, a third hit the Pentagon, and the fourth crashed in Pennsylvania. © *Seth McCallister/AFP/Getty Images*

Daniel Pearl

Four months after the 9/11 events, *Wall Street Journal* reporter Daniel Pearl was kidnapped while in Pakistan on assignment. Pearl was a particularly valuable target for the terrorists as both a prominent reporter and a Jewish American. His kidnappers claimed he was a spy, and sent a list of demands to the U.S. government that included the release of Pakistani prisoners jailed on suspicion of terrorism and the withdrawal of the U.S. presence from Pakistan.

For weeks, Americans awaited word of Pearl's fate. On February 21, 2002, the FBI and Pakistani officials received a videotape showing Pearl's execution at the hands of his captors. Within a month, four suspects were arrested for his murder; they were convicted in July 2002. Pearl's wife Mariane, who had been pregnant with their first child at the time of his death, wrote a memoir of Pearl's life titled *A Mighty Heart* (2003) that was later turned into a movie starring Angelina Jolie and Dan Futterman.

As the world watched media coverage of these events and their aftermath, life in the United States seemed changed forever. Many international leaders joined Bush in condemning the attacks, and many people across the globe sympathized with Americans. The tragedy, which became known simply as 9/11, set the U.S. government on a defensive and self-protective course. Many citizens criticized federal agencies that failed to protect the country. As reports were released and victims accounted for, the impact on New York City was clearly the worst of the three sites. More than two thousand World Trade Center employees and hundreds of rescue workers lost their lives, and more than four hundred thousand New Yorkers were eventually diagnosed with post-traumatic stress disorder (PTSD), symptoms of which include depression, anxiety, flashbacks, nightmares, emotional avoidance, and hyperarousal.

After the terrorist attacks, many Americans became more visible and vocal in expressing their patriotism. Recruitment numbers for the armed forces went up. Retailers reported increases in their sales of the national flag, and immediately following the attacks, Major League Baseball required that "God Bless America" be sung at every game for the remainder of the season. Sometimes, it even replaced the traditional "Take Me Out to the Ballgame."

Four days after the attacks, Bush declared a war on terrorism, specifically on the Islamic fundamentalist group al-Qaeda. He declared the terrorist network and its leader, Osama bin Laden, was responsible for the attacks. Bin Laden had long been on several international "wanted" lists but had managed to elude capture. Along with Bin Laden, Bush targeted the Taliban, another fundamentalist group. The Taliban operated out of Afghanistan and was rumored to be protecting bin Laden. As he addressed Congress on September 20, Bush sent out a warning to other nations: "You are either with us or with the terrorists." His speech that day received more than twenty standing ovations, but many Americans criticized it for being simplistic and antagonistic.

❖ INVASION OF AFGHANISTAN

The Taliban refused Bush's demands that they hand over bin Laden, so the administration sought to build a global coalition to help the United States fight terrorism. Many industrialized nations provided assistance of one kind or another, and on October 7, 2001, Operation Enduring Freedom began. U.S. and British forces initiated air strikes in Afghanistan.

Just days after the invasion, the White House announced what became known as the Bush Doctrine, a policy that demanded the world choose sides in the conflict. The president warned that those countries choosing not to support the United States may face military consequences. The doctrine identified seven countries that sponsored terrorism, and three of them—Iraq, Iran, and North Korea—were labeled by the president as the "axis of evil." It was a label that brought Bush intense criticism for its assumption that the three countries were acting in some type of conspiracy. In fact, Iran and Iraq had been at war with each other in the 1980s, under virtually the same leadership as they had in 2002 (the time of Bush's declaration).

U.S. and British forces successfully toppled the Taliban regime from power in a matter of weeks, though the Taliban mounted a campaign of violence that targeted the coalition and their Afghani allies for the remainder of the decade. The violence increased significantly after the United States handed control of the mission in Afghanistan to NATO in 2006. The U.S.-supported democratic government led by Hamid Karzai struggled to make progress in key areas such as the economy, education, and health in the war-torn country. By the end of the decade, the war in Afghanistan was on the verge of supplanting the Vietnam War as America's longest war. The number of U.S. and coalition forces killed in Afghanistan was more than 2700 as of 2011; a *USA Today* poll showed that 42% of

PATRIOT Act

The USA PATRIOT Act became law on October 26, 2001, just over a month after 9/11. The law was in direct response to the terrorist attacks and drastically reduced restrictions on law enforcement's right to investigate the private lives of individuals. The title of the law is an acronym for Uniting and Strengthening by Providing Appropriate Tools Required to Intercept and Obstruct Terrorism.

Though many of the law's provisions were intended to expire or at least relax beginning in December 2005, reauthorization of the bill occurred in July 2005, with changes made by both the Senate and the House. The final revised PATRIOT Act passed Congress and was signed into law in 2006. Critics denounced the law on the grounds that it ignores civil liberty laws that have been in place for years and are guaranteed through the U.S. Constitution.

Americans believed the Afghan war was a "mistake" in 2009 versus only 9% in 2001.

❖ THE WAR IN IRAQ

Afghanistan was not the only target of the Bush administration following the 9/11 attacks. Bush also believed that Saddam Hussein, dictator of Iraq, posed a threat to U.S. national security. He needed evidence to support this belief in order to make a convincing case to declare war on Iraq. National Security Advisor Condoleezza Rice and Vice President Dick Cheney worked to compile the evidence the president needed, specifically that Hussein was manufacturing and stockpiling weapons of mass destruction (WMDs)—biological, chemical, and nuclear weapons. The evidence was allegedly found, and Bush used it to win the support of Congress. Convincing the public and the United Nations (UN) Security Council that another war was the answer to this perceived threat, however, was not so easy.

Hussein was, by all accounts, a cruel dictator whose background included a list of human rights abuses. Even so, that fact did not mean he was producing and storing WMDs or was a real threat to the United States.

Reason for War: Speculation

Although President Bush's official reason for waging war on Iraq was to protect U.S. national security against WMDs, other reasons were given along the way.

In 2005, Bush responded to growing antiwar protests with a new reason for the war, saying he was protecting Iraq's oil fields from falling under the control of terrorists. All along, Bush asserted the link between Hussein and al-Qaeda, and yet those links were discredited by reputable intelligence agencies not long after the March invasion. There was no evidence found to suggest operational ties between Iraq and the terrorist organization.

There was widespread speculation that Bush's determination was actually a personal desire for revenge. Bush's father, George H. W. Bush, was in office during the Persian Gulf War (1990–91), in which thirty-four nations, led by the United States, attacked Iraq in response to its invasion of Kuwait. Although Iraq left Kuwait, Hussein remained in power.

ABC News pointed out the personal nature of the conflict in the president's mind and quoted Bush as saying, "There's no doubt he [Hussein] can't stand us. After all, this is a guy that tried to kill my dad at one time." Although not everyone believed the war was prompted by a vendetta, it was an idea that the media explored. *Salon* reporter Gary Kamiya wrote: "Bush wanted his Iraq war to be a lofty Shakespearean history. He got a vicious, corpse-strewn revenge tragedy."

He had, in 1998, expelled UN weapons inspectors from Iraq. He had been in possession of WMDs at least from the 1980s. But when the UN Security Council passed Resolution 1441, which demanded that Iraq permit inspectors into the country, Hussein denied the existence of WMDs and complied with the demand. Those UN inspectors found no evidence of WMDs during their search in 2002 and reported as much. Bush still refused to back down from his position that Iraq was a security threat, and he sent Secretary of State Colin Powell to another UN council meeting in hopes of having a second resolution passed, one that would legalize his intent to wage war. Powell asserted that intelligence operations had verified that Iraq was indeed stockpiling anthrax and building biological weapons labs. Powell further claimed that Hussein had ties to al-Qaeda.

The Birth of Homeland Security

The year 2003 saw not only the start of war in Iraq, but also the birth of a new governmental agency: the U.S. Department of Homeland Security (DHS). The DHS merged 22 governmental agencies such as the Federal Emergency Management Agency, the Immigration and Naturalization Service, the Coast Guard, and the Transportations Security Administration into a single department. The purpose of the agency is to protect the country through various means—emergency preparedness and response, intelligence activities, border security, cybersecurity, counterterrorism, and transportation security, among others.

The agency came under criticism for being ineffective and wasteful. In 2008, the *Washington Post* reported that the DHS oversaw $15 billion in failed contracts in its first five years of existence. The department's poor disaster management in New Orleans following the devastation of Hurricane Katrina in 2005 likewise drew heavy criticism.

The UN had contradicting evidence to Powell's claims, and there was much opposition to Bush among council members. Sensing defeat, Bush withdrew his request for a second resolution. To his thinking, the United States had ample evidence of Iraq's potential threat, and Resolution 1441 was written in such a way as to permit his ordering an invasion of the country.

On March 20, 2003, Bush and Tony Blair, prime minister of Great Britain, sent their coalition forces to Iraq, thus beginning the Iraq War, also known as Operation Iraqi Freedom. In early 2004, official reports from the CIA were released indicating that Bush's evidence was false. Even before the end of the decade, it became common knowledge that no WMDs had been found in Iraq.

Just weeks after the March 20 invasion, troops reached Baghdad and effectively dismantled Iraqi troops. Bush publicly declared victory for the United States in a famous speech aboard the aircraft carrier USS *Abraham Lincoln* with a banner reading "Mission Accomplished" behind him on May 1, 2003. It was a premature declaration, as time would tell.

Coalition forces had taken control of Iraq, but insurgents continued to wage guerrilla warfare against the occupying force with devastating results.

John Kerry (left) shakes
hands with George W.
Bush prior to the last
debate before the 2004
election for president.
© Saul Loeb/MCT/Getty
Images

American casualties began to pile up, and support for the war on the
homefront dwindled. The war effort received a major boost when Saddam
Hussein was discovered hiding in a farmhouse near Tikrit in late 2003. He
was arrested, tried, and executed in Baghdad, but his removal did not end
the war. Many Americans hoped that violence in Iraq would de-escalate
with Hussein gone. Bush hailed Hussein's capture as a major step forward
in the war on terror.

The president announced that U.S. forces would remain in Iraq
through his second term in office, which began in 2005. Iraq held its first
general election that year as a major step toward democracy, but the
country itself remained highly unstable and continued to be a source of
conflict and consternation for the U.S. public. By July 19, 2009, the official
death toll for Americans in Iraq neared five thousand, and that number did
not include thousands of nonfatal injuries.

❖ ELECTION 2004: BUSH V. KERRY

When the 2004 election campaign began, war was a central issue
for debate. As the number of American casualties increased and Iraqi

insurgents attacked more coalition forces, Bush's approval ratings fell sharply. Reports of the falsification of the president's so-called evidence for going to war were being publicized, and the 9/11 Commission, a congressional committee developed for investigating the terrorist attacks, found no conspiracy between Iraq and al-Qaeda. It was a low point for Bush.

Bush's opponent, Democratic U.S. senator John Kerry from Massachusetts, focused on the president's foreign policy. Kerry charged that the Bush policy had damaged the U.S. reputation abroad and had used bogus evidence as the justification for war. Bush countered with the argument that Kerry had initially been in favor of the invasion and had long condemned Saddam Hussein.

The Bush campaign took a devastating hit in the spring of 2004 when the media released photos depicting civil rights abuses of Iraqi prisoners of war committed by U.S. soldiers at Abu Ghraib prison. Once an Iraqi prison used to detain and torture civilians, Abu Ghraib had been turned into a U.S. military prison. Detainees were loosely divided into three categories: common criminals, those suspected of committing crimes against coalition forces, and high-value leaders of the insurgency. According to Seymour Hersh of *The New Yorker*, a report of events at the prison, written by Major General Antonio M. Taguba, was leaked to the press. The report, never intended for public reading, described abuses perpetrated by U.S. military personnel. Those abuses included "breaking chemical lights and pouring the phosphoric liquid on detainees … sodomizing a detainee with a chemical light and perhaps a broom stick, and using military working dogs to frighten and intimidate detainees with threats of attack, and in one instance actually biting a detainee."

Photos that accompanied the report were broadcast on CBS's *60 Minutes II* and depicted U.S. soldiers humiliating naked Iraqi prisoners. While the prisoners suffered, the soldiers' facial expressions indicated their enjoyment of what they were doing. While Americans were incensed by these images, Bush insisted that those soldiers were not representative of the majority of forces stationed in Iraq.

Kerry's own military experience and background became a focus of the Bush 2004 campaign. A decorated officer in the U.S. Navy, Kerry had served in the Vietnam War and regularly received support from war veterans at campaign stops. The Bush campaign shed light on Kerry's participation in a Vietnam protest in Washington, D.C., and Kerry fought back with one of the most expensive ad campaigns in history. The presidential hopeful spent $25 million for a three-week television campaign that appeared in nineteen states. In his ads, Kerry promoted his military experience and pointed to negative aspects of Bush's own military record.

As the attacks on Kerry intensified, Bush was forced to address a *60 Minutes II* report in which Bush's National Guard superior officer claimed a young Bush had not fulfilled his duties. The program's host, Dan Rather, eventually admitted that his source's claims could not be verified, and the experienced journalist's reputation was damaged permanently.

Never before had presidential candidates spent such exorbitant sums—in excess of one billion dollars total. Despite all his difficulties, Bush was re-elected on November 3 by the smallest margin (3.3 million votes) of any incumbent president since Woodrow Wilson (286 electoral votes and 277 electoral votes, respectively). Kerry returned to his seat in the U.S. Senate while running mate John Edwards went to work full time at One America Committee, a political action committee he founded in 2001.

There is no denying that the events of September 11, 2001, were still on the minds of voters. Despite two wars and numerous conflicts, Americans had spoken clearly. Turning out in record numbers to cast their votes, the 2004 election had not been about Afghanistan. It was not about Iraq. It was about 9/11. Political blogger John McIntyre wrote in a May 25, 2006, post, "And 2004 was the *first* presidential election after 9/11; the more the Democrats and Kerry talked about Iraq and the war, the more they unwittingly played right into President Bush's strength."

❖ BUSH'S SECOND TERM

Bush's second term was plagued with two wars that refused to end. As of 2004, Osama bin Laden had yet to be found, though the Taliban government that supported him had been dismantled. In 2006, the United States turned over security of Afghanistan to NATO forces. Twelve thousand U.S. troops were left behind to join NATO's twenty thousand. The remainder of U.S. forces continued their search for al-Qaeda extremists. By the end of Bush's term in 2008, bin Laden was still at large, and insurgent conflicts had increased in Afghanistan.

Funding of the Iraq war posed another problem for Bush. In 2005, CNN published a report that Iraq's temporary government—which was led by the United States—had lost $8.8 billion of Iraqi money from the Development Fund for Iraq. An audit uncovered numerous accounting

The Mystery of Pat Tillman

NFL star Pat Tillman left a new wife and a rewarding career that paid him $3.6 million dollars so that he could serve his country in Afghanistan as an Army Ranger. Almost immediately, Tillman became one of the most high-profile soldiers to see action. Praised for his courage and honor, Tillman was a textbook soldier.

The twenty-seven-year-old California native was shot and killed in Afghanistan on April 22, 2004. His wife and mother were informed that he was killed by enemy fire as he was charging up a hill to protect his fellow soldiers.

That story was a lie.

Five weeks later, Tillman's mother was told the truth: Her son was killed by friendly fire (meaning gunfire from his own troops). After speaking with soldiers who were involved in the battle with her son, Mary Tillman believed she understood what happened to him. She explained to Katie Couric, *CBS News* anchor, "In the end, we feel he was hit in the chest ... And it stunned him and he went down. And then they shot him in the head three times."

Mary Tillman believed the Bush administration needed a heroic story to garner public support for the war, and her son's death provided that opportunity. The cover-up was just part of the ploy. Even the coroner refused to sign off on Tillman's body because the report he was asked to sign was false.

errors and questionable bookkeeping strategies. The fund was purportedly to reconstruct Iraq, but poor management and staffing shortages caused problems almost from the beginning.

Bush's challenges were not all overseas. In 2005, the nation witnessed a controversy involving the medical treatment of Terri Schiavo. After suffering brain damage from cardiac arrest in 1990, Schiavo went into a coma that lasted for over two months. After that, doctors diagnosed her as being in a vegetative state, which means she could not survive without life support measures. Her brain was damaged, but her body could live with life support.

In 1998, Terri's husband Michael petitioned the court to remove his wife's feeding tube, an act that would lead to her death. The petition was granted in 2000, and in 2001, the tube was removed. Two days later, another court, appealed to by Terri's parents, reversed the order and demanded reinsertion of the tube. In October 2002, a hearing of the case took place over the course of a week, during which time some doctors said Terri could recover while others insisted she never would. Her feeding tube was again ordered to be removed, and again, the order was reversed.

Terri's story continued with this back-and-forth activity for years until, finally, her feeding tube was permanently removed on March 18, 2005. In an attempt to help her parents prolong their daughter's life, Bush interrupted his vacation on March 21 to fly to Washington, D.C., to sign a bill into law that would give the federal courts authority to decide the case. Under the bill, which became known as the Palm Sunday Compromise, Schiavo's case went before the U.S. Supreme Court. Her parents lost, and Terri died on March 31, 2005.

The right-to-life conflict was covered in-depth by the media, but as emotionally charged as it was, it was soon eclipsed by a natural disaster. On August 24, the tropical storm Katrina became a hurricane, and it hit Florida early on August 25. After a brief period of weakening, the storm regained hurricane status after moving into the Gulf of Mexico. It intensified from a category 3 to a category 5 hurricane in only nine hours. This change means that the winds went from a range of 111 to 130 miles per hour to greater than 155 miles per hour. At the time, it was the strongest hurricane ever recorded in the Gulf of Mexico.

By August 29, Katrina was a category 3 again when it hit land in Louisiana. The hurricane made landfall again near the Louisiana-Mississippi border, still as a category 3. Then it continued into Mississippi before being downgraded to a tropical storm again.

Hurricane Katrina caused widespread severe damage. In New Orleans, Louisiana, alone, 80 percent of the city was flooded. The total damage of Katrina in Mississippi and Alabama was later estimated at $81.2 billion. The death toll neared two thousand. Louisiana mounted a missing persons effort for those not accounted for, but it ran out of money in 2006 and was unable to continue.

President Bush was severely criticized for his delayed response to this predicted national emergency. He eventually signed into law a handful of bills designed to provide aide to those hit hardest by Katrina, but critics and victims saw the effort as inadequate and late. The worst piece of evidence to come to light in the onslaught of criticism was that Bush had been warned several times of the storm's approach and severity; he was told that Katrina could breech New Orleans levees, causing untold death and destruction. The president never asked a question during the briefing.

Another major issue of domestic policy during Bush's second term was immigration. Immigration protests were increasingly frequent and sometimes violent after the proposed legislation known as H.R. 4437. The bill would have raised penalties for illegal immigration and labeled those illegal immigrants and anyone who aided them as felons.

The bill passed the House of Representatives in 2005, but it never made it out of the Senate. Nonetheless, its impact on the immigration reform movement was clear. In response, Bush began enacting legislation to restrict immigration. In October 2006 he signed the Secure Fence Act, which allowed for a 700-mile fence to be built along the U.S.-Mexico border. While other proposals at restriction failed because they included ways for illegal immigrants to gain legal citizenship, the White House began passing immigration initiatives in 2007 that did not require official changes in the law.

❖ 2008 ELECTION: MCCAIN V. OBAMA

Americans were ready for a change as the decade's third presidential election campaign began. Republican candidate John McCain, U.S. senator from Arizona and presidential hopeful in 2000, shocked the nation by choosing Alaska governor Sarah Palin as his running mate. After beating former First Lady and New York senator Hillary Clinton for the Democratic nomination, Hawaiian-born Barack Obama chose U.S. senator Joe Biden of Delaware as his vice presidential candidate.

The two sides made interesting duos. McCain was a seasoned military man and politician, seventy-two years old and conservative in demeanor. Palin was a forty-four-year-old wife and mother with little experience in big-league politics. Yet she was initially a popular choice among Republicans. Obama, by contrast, had already proven himself able to beat Clinton in the primaries, and many Americans started to take the forty-seven-year-old African American U.S. senator seriously. He chose for his running mate a Catholic to whom working-class voters could relate.

Obama based his campaign on hope and change, with the slogan "Yes We Can!" while McCain appealed to the U.S. hunger for conservative family values. In the end, voters revealed that hope and change were what they were looking for after eight years of a Republican president, and Obama became the nation's first African American president.

The Tea Party

In 2009, Tea Party members identified themselves primarily as Republicans, and they supported Republican candidates. The grassroots group derived its name from the Boston Tea Party, seeing its members as willing to protest a big government that was making decisions for them without their consent, just as the original Massachusetts colonists of 1773 protested against the taxation policies of the English monarchy imposed without the colonists' consent.

According to its Web site, the Tea Party asserts the following as its non-negotiable core beliefs:

1. Illegal aliens are here illegally.
2. Pro-domestic employment is indispensable.
3. A strong military is essential.
4. Special interests must be eliminated.
5. Gun ownership is sacred.
6. Government must be downsized.
7. The national budget must be balanced.
8. Deficit spending must end.
9. Bailout and stimulus plans are illegal.
10. Reducing personal income taxes is a must.
11. Reducing business income taxes is mandatory.
12. Political offices must be available to average citizens.
13. Intrusive government must be stopped.
14. English as our core language is required.
15. Traditional family values are encouraged.

Obama's first year in office presented myriad challenges as he worked to fulfill campaign promises. Although he promised to close the Guantánamo Bay detention camp in Cuba, which was established in 2002 by President Bush to detain people during the Afghanistan and Iraq wars, Obama was not able to procure the funds to do so.

Healthcare reform was a cornerstone of Obama's campaign, and yet the reforms he enacted did not satisfy Republicans or Democrats. Obama reversed several Bush-era policies, including one that limited the funding of stem-cell research, but in the area of same-sex marriage, he fell short of his campaign promises and failed to achieve legalization of gay marriage before the end of the decade. Gays, lesbians, and transgendered populations were acutely disappointed in their new president.

Obama selected his former opponent, Hillary Clinton, as his secretary of state, and she worked to repair and build international relationships. As the situation in Afghanistan deteriorated, Obama replaced key military figures and increased troop levels by seventeen thousand in early 2009. In December, he deployed another thirty thousand troops at a cost of $30 billion for the first year, while simultaneously announcing a troop withdrawal date of June 2011.

In 2009, Obama announced to Marines at Camp LeJeune, North Carolina, that U.S. troops would pull out of Iraq within eighteen months: "Let me say this as plainly as I can: By August 31, 2010, our combat mission in Iraq will end." The president held true to his word, and on August 19, 2010, the last U.S. combat troops left Iraq.

❖ GOVERNMENT AS BANK

The United States was already years into an economic recession when Obama took office. Once reputable businesses such as Worldcom and Enron went bankrupt because of the greed of a few men, and the economy continued to worsen as the decade progressed.

The Obama administration's answer to the economic turmoil was the American Recovery and Reinvestment Act (ARRA) of 2009. This stimulus package was designed to save and create jobs first and foremost, but the hope was that it would also provide immediate, temporary relief to those groups hit hardest by the recession. ARRA was worth $787 billion and included spending on education, health, energy, and public infrastructure (for example, roads, bridges, and government buildings). It also was intended to expand programs and provisions already in place.

In March 2009, the federal government stepped in to assist a failing automotive industry; it renewed loans for General Motors (GM) and Chrysler while these companies reorganized after their bankruptcies. Toward that end, the federal government loaned GM and Chrysler about $24.9 billion and got a 60 percent stake in GM. Canada loaned GM $9.5 billion and got a 12 percent stake.

The automakers rebounded from bankruptcy surprisingly fast after receiving the bailout funds. Within two years, much of the money loaned to GM and Chrysler had been repaid to the government, and those companies were reporting strong profits, as was Ford, which had not received any government loans. The automakers began hiring workers once more, although the uncertain economy threatened growth.

❖ POLITICAL SCANDALS

Americans were shocked by one political scandal after another in the 2000s. Some of the more influential ones are listed here.

Valerie Plame

Valerie Plame was a CIA operative whose association with the organization was classified. She worked undercover, relying completely on the secrecy of her identity for her safety. In July 2003, *Washington Post* reporter Robert Novak revealed Plame's identity. This revelation ended Plame's career with the CIA. Plame believed that her identity had been leaked by people close to President George W. Bush. She believed this was done out of revenge because her husband, Ambassador Joe Wilson, had accused Bush of lying about evidence of weapons of mass destruction in Iraq.

Eventually, some powerful men in the White House were implicated in the leak, including presidential advisor Karl Rove and Chief of Staff I. Lewis

New York governor Eliot Spitzer announces his resignation on March 12, 2008, following revelations that he had been a client of a prostitution ring. His wife Silda Wall stands next to him. © *Timothy A. Clary/ AFP/Getty Images*

"Scooter" Libby. For his role in the Plame affair, Libby was indicted on two counts of perjury, two counts of lying to federal investigators, and one count of obstruction of justice. He denied his role in the leak but resigned from his position in 2007. Libby was eventually found guilty on four of the five counts and sentenced to serve thirty months in prison and pay a fine of $250,000, in addition to doing four hundred hours of community service and two years of supervised release. Bush eventually commuted the prison sentence.

Jack Abramoff

In 2006, lobbyist Jack Abramoff stood trial on felony charges of fraud, corruption, and conspiracy. He pled guilty, and in his testimony he implicated several high-profile congressmen, including Republican House Majority Leader Tom DeLay. During Bush's presidential term, Abramoff had secured political favors for his clients by giving generous gifts to congressional and executive branch officials. In addition, he swindled Indian tribes out of millions of dollars. After his conviction, he served forty-three months in prison. DeLay resigned as House Majority Leader in 2006 and was charged with criminal action. His indictment stretched into 2010 when he was found guilty and sentenced to three years in prison.

John Edwards

John Edwards, a former Democratic senator of North Carolina and the running mate of John Kerry in the presidential campaign of 2004, sought the 2008 Democratic presidential nomination. During his bid for the nomination, Edwards was exposed as having fathered a child with Rielle Hunter, a media consultant whom he had met during the campaign. Edwards eventually, though reluctantly, admitted to the affair, and he and his wife, Elizabeth Edwards, separated. She died not long after of cancer. Edwards was later charged for having misused campaign contributions to cover-up his affair with Hunter.

Eliot Spitzer

Eliot Spitzer, Democratic New York governor, announced his resignation in March 2008 after being caught soliciting a prostitute by phone. After the scandal broke, it was discovered that Spitzer had employed the services of prostitutes for many years, and investigators believed he paid almost $80,000 for this illegal activity. Ironically, Spitzer campaigned on ethics reform.

Rod Blagojevich

Illinois governor Rod Blagojevich was impeached and removed from office in January 2009 for abuse of office. In all, he was accused on twenty-four counts of wrongdoing, including wire fraud, conspiracy to solicit bribes, racketeering, and bribery. When his first trial resulted in a hung jury (meaning the jury could not reach a unanimous decision), a mistrial was declared. He was tried again in 2011 and found guilty on seventeen of the charges.

William J. Jefferson

On August 5, 2009, Democrat William J. Jefferson, was convicted of eleven charges of criminal corruption, including bribery, racketeering, and money laundering. He received a thirteen-year prison sentence for his misdeeds. The U.S. congressman from Louisiana had been the subject of a federal investigation and was found hiding more than $100,000 in empty veggie burger boxes in his freezer.

❖ DEATHS OF IMPORTANT INDIVIDUALS

Several influential politicians and the people who kept company with them died in the 2000s:

• Daniel Patrick Moynihan, Democratic U.S. senator from New York and presidential advisor during four administrations from John F. Kennedy to Gerald Ford, died on March 26, 2003, at the age of seventy-six.

• Ronald Reagan, fortieth president of the United States, died on June 5, 2004, at the age of ninety-three.

• Gaylord Nelson, Democratic governor and U.S. senator from Wisconsin, and founder of Earth Day, died on July 3, 2005, at the age of eighty-nine.

• William C. Westmoreland, U.S. Army general and Army chief of staff who served in the Vietnam War, died on July 18, 2005, at the age of ninety-one.

• Rosa Parks, civil rights activist whose refusal to give up her bus seat to a white man sparked the civil rights movement in the 1960s, died on October 24, 2005, at the age of ninety-two.

• Eugene McCarthy, Democratic U.S. congressman and U.S. senator from Minnesota, and presidential hopeful during the Vietnam War, died on December 10, 2005, at the age of eighty-nine.

• Coretta Scott King, widow of Dr. Martin Luther King Jr., died on January 30, 2006, at the age of seventy-eight.

• Caspar Weinberger, secretary of defense and secretary of health, education, and welfare, indicted for perjury and obstruction of justice during the Iran-Contra hearings, died on March 28, 2006, at the age of eighty-eight.

• John Kenneth Galbraith, liberal economist and presidential advisor, died on April 29, 2006, at the age of ninety-seven.

• Strom Thurmund, Democratic governor and U.S. senator as well as Republican U.S. senator from South Carolina, whose party-switching was the catalyst for a postwar political realignment, died on June 26, 2006, at the age of one hundred.

• Gerald R. Ford Jr., thirty-eighth president of the United States, died December 26, 2006, at the age of ninety-three.

• William F. Buckley Jr., political commentator and writer, died on February 27, 2008, at the age of eighty-two.

• Jesse Helms, Republican U.S. senator from North Carolina, whose nickname was "Senator No" for his voting record, died on July 4, 2008, at the age of eighty-six.

• Robert McNamara, U.S. secretary of defense who was credited or blamed for being the architect of the Vietnam War, died on July 6, 2009, at the age of ninety-three.

• Eunice Kennedy Shriver, sister of John F., Robert, and Edward Kennedy, died on August 11, 2009, at the age of eighty-eight.

• Edward "Ted" Kennedy, Democratic U.S. senator from Massachusetts and brother of John F. and Robert Kennedy, who served in politics for nearly four decades, died on August 25, 2009, at the age of seventy-seven.

• William Safire, speechwriter for President Richard Nixon and Pulitzer Prize–winning *New York Times* journalist, died on September 27, 2009, at the age of seventy-nine.

 For More Information
●●

BOOKS

DiMarco, Damon. *Tower Stories: An Oral History of 9/11.* Santa Monica, CA: Santa Monica Press, 2007.

Long, Kim. *The Almanac of Political Corruption, Scandals and Dirty Politics.* New York: Delta, 2008.

Plame Wilson, Valerie. *Fair Game.* New York: Simon & Schuster, 2008.

PERIODICALS

Langer, Gary, and Jon Cohen. "Voters and Values in the 2004 Election." *Public Opinion Quarterly* 69, no. 5 (2004): 744–59. This article can also be found online at http://poq.oxfordjournals.org/content/69/5/744.full (accessed on October 8, 2011).

WEB SITES

"Barack Obama." *The White House.* http://www.whitehouse.gov/about/presidents/barackobama (accessed on October 7, 2011).

"Blagojevich 'stunned,' Guilty on 17 of 20 Counts." *ABC*, June 27, 2011. http://abclocal.go.com/wls/story?section=news/local&id=8217169 (accessed on October 7, 2011).

"Disgraced Lobbyist Jack Abramoff Working in Baltimore Pizza Shop." *Huffington Post*, June 23, 2010. http://www.huffingtonpost.com/2010/06/23/jack-abramoff-pizza-shop_n_622635.html (accessed on October 7, 2011).

Duffy, Michael, et al. "Election 2000: What It Took." *Time Magazine*, November 20, 2000. http://www.time.com/time/magazine/article/0,9171,998530,00.html (accessed on October 7, 2011).

Healy, Melissa. "Post-9/11 Proliferation of PTSD Symptoms Gave Researchers New Insights." *Boston Herald*, September 9, 2011. http://www.bostonherald.com/business/healthcare/view/20110909post-_911_proliferation_of_ptsd_symptoms_gave_researchers_new_insights (accessed on October 5, 2011).

Hersh, Seymour M. "Torture at Abu Ghraib." *The New Yorker*, May 10, 2004. http://www.newyorker.com/archive/2004/05/10/040510fa_fact (accessed on October 7, 2011).

Hughes, John, et al. "GM Begins Bankruptcy Process with Filing for Affiliate." *Bloomberg*, June 1, 2009. http://www.bloomberg.com/apps/news?pid=newsarchive&sid=aw4F_L7E4xYg (accessed on October 7, 2011).

"Timeline: Afghanistan, 10 Years Since War Began." *Reuters*, October 6, 2011. http://www.reuters.com/article/2011/10/06/us-afghanistan-events-idUS-TRE7951PU20111006 (accessed on October 9, 2011).

"U.S. Senator John McCain: Biography." *U.S. Senate.* http://mccain.senate.gov/public/index.cfm?FuseAction=AboutSenatorMcCain.Biography (accessed on October 9, 2011).

Woodward, Bob. "How Mark Felt Became 'Deep Throat.'" *The Washington Post*, June 2, 2005. http://www.washingtonpost.com/wp-dyn/content/article/2005/06/01/AR2005060102124.html (accessed on October 9, 2011).

chapter five *Lifestyles and Social Trends*

2000 February 2 *The Daily Show* on Comedy Central begins its popular satirical election coverage with a series of episodes titled "Indecision 2000," focusing on the primary in New Hampshire.

2000 April 26 Vermont legalizes same-sex civil unions.

2000 May 31 *Survivor* premieres, sparking a national trend in reality television programming.

2001 Toyota begins selling its hybrid model, Prius, in the United States and immediately generates long wait lists, evidence of evolving eco-consciousness and interest in climate change.

2001 January 15 *Wikipedia*, the free, volunteer-driven online encyclopedia site, debuts. Within ten years, it has over 18 million user-generated entries in 279 languages and is hailed by *The New York Times* as one of the ten most popular sites on the Internet.

2001 September The XM Satellite Radio service is launched, providing news, music, and other entertainment.

2001 November 10 Apple debuts its handheld MP3 file-storing device, the iPod, which quickly becomes one of the most sought-after personal electronic devices.

2002 The BlackBerry smart phone is introduced to the U.S. market.

2002 May 19 The science-fiction suspense show, *X-Files*, airs its final episode. With nearly ten years of broadcasts, it is the longest-running science-fiction television series in history.

2002 June 11 *American Idol* debuts. It becomes the only program to be ranked number one in the Nielsen ratings for seven consecutive seasons.

2003 March The social networking site MySpace launches.

2003 March 20 International forces invade Iraq; hundreds of journalists join fighting units in the field, making the Iraq War the most widely covered conflict in history.

2003 April 3 *Washington Post* reporter Michael Kelly is the first journalist killed in Iraq.

2004 February Facebook launches for use by Harvard students only. It is soon made available to the public, and by September 2009 it boasts three hundred million users across the globe.

2004 November 4 Eleven states ban gay marriage in local elections. Voters in exit polls cite "moral values" as the most important issue on the ballot.

2005 February 15 YouTube, a video-sharing Web site, launches.

2005 May The progressive news and blogging Web site *Huffington Post* debuts.

2006 July The online instant-messaging and social site Twitter launches and becomes an almost instant sensation.

2006 September 5 Katie Couric joins *CBS Evening News* as the first solo female evening news anchor. At the same time, the channel begins casting on the World Wide Web.

2006 September 26 Facebook is made available to anyone age thirteen and over with a valid e-mail address.

2007 January 9 Apple unveils the iPhone, which is made available to the public in June and instantly becomes the trendsetter in cell-phone design and technology.

2007 July The 1960s-era *Mad Men* debuts on cable television and prompts a resurgence in the clothing and accessories of the era for both men and women.

2007 November 19 Amazon releases the Kindle, an e-book reader, for $399. It sells out in five-and-a-half hours and remains out of stock for five months.

2008 January The White House begins publishing a blog.

2008 May More than six million copies of the just-released video game *Grand Theft Auto IV* are sold in one week.

2008 September 13 *Saturday Night Live* comedian Tina Fey parodies Republican vice-presidential candidate Sarah Palin. The video becomes an instant sensation on YouTube.

2009 May 19 The musical comedy-drama show *Glee* debuts on Fox, sparking a nationwide phenomenon of "Gleeks" and merchandise related to the show.

2009 June 12 By federal government order, all television shows shift from analog to digital broadcasting.

2009 November 20 Oprah Winfrey announces her retirement from the ever-popular *Oprah Winfrey Show*. The retirement will occur in 2011.

Overview

The media was at the forefront of a series of dramatic events during the first decade of the twenty-first century, including botched elections, natural disasters, the terrorist attacks of September 11, 2001, war, economic recession, and tanking real estate markets, all of which gave worried and weary citizens little rest. It was a decade that saw the rise of online newsgathering as traditional television stations took to the Internet with blogs and news magazines capable of real-time updates while many print newspapers ceased paper publication in favor of online editions. While the Internet was largely considered a progressive tool in the field of news reporting, its flipside was that news could now be reported by anyone at any time. Anyone could write a blog or post online articles; accuracy could not always be assumed. In the more traditional news media, Americans said their final goodbyes to television news anchormen such as Peter Jennings (1938–2005) and Walter Cronkite (1916–2009), while tuning in to radical radio shock jocks such as Howard Stern and Rush Limbaugh and outspoken conservative television talk show hosts such as Bill O'Reilly and Glenn Beck. The progressive online news site *The Huffington Post* provided continual coverage of all things newsworthy but with a decided emphasis on politics and the people who work in government. For those in search of a more lighthearted presentation of U.S. politics, viewers turned to the dry humor of cable news talk shows such as *The Daily Show* with Jon Stewart and the news parody *The Colbert Report* with Stephen Colbert. Whatever their preferences for newsgathering, Americans no longer had to read a printed newspaper or magazine, and the five o'clock and ten o'clock news hours no longer cornered the market.

Technology shaped many people's leisure habits and set new trends as well. Millions of people embraced online social networking sites such as Facebook, Twitter, Friendster, and MySpace. Even professionals recognized the value in online networking as they joined sites such as LinkedIn. E-commerce reached new heights as millions of shoppers took advantage of the convenience of the online stores Amazon.com and eBay, while artisans reveled in making their crafts and wares available to a global community through sites such as Etsy.com. Twenty-first century technology gave Americans their two most popular new tools and toys: the mp3 player and the cell phone. E-readers like Kindle and the Nook made reading more accessible and affordable as people paid a fraction of the price of print books and found the classics online through sites such as the Gutenberg Project. Video gaming was increasingly popular in the 1990s and hit all-time highs in the 2000s as people searched for ways to entertain themselves or socialize with friends without spending money during the economic downturn.

If there is one part of a society that never seems to change despite economic challenges, it's fashion. During this decade fashion and lifestyle often seemed to overlap. Emo was a music genre as well as a fashion statement, as was Hipster. Scene youth, a subculture of pop punk, sported choppy haircuts, skinny jeans, heavy makeup, and fashion styles that worked for both sexes. Low-slung, baggy pants were all the rage among teen and young adult men in urban areas where gangsta or hip-hop fashion ruled. Skater kids wore Vans skate shoes and t-shirts featuring logos popular in the skating and surfing world such as Billabong, Volcom, and Quicksilver. Girls and women sported clunky suede boots by Ugg while Converse All-Star sneakers and Chuck Taylors made a comeback from the 1970s. Crocs took the fashion world by storm in the first half of the 2000s. The Boulder, Colorado-based company premiered its foam-resin sandals to much acclaim for their comfort and criticism for their appearance.

Americans paid untold amounts of money on their looks in the 2000s. Plastic surgery, liposuction, and Botox injections became common procedures from coast to coast, while tanning salons enjoyed increased memberships. Pilates was a popular form of exercise, and diets such as South Beach and Atkins made their developers rich and famous. Americans became enamored of energy drinks and could not get enough of their Starbucks coffee. Yet as many individuals sought to become less natural with their appearance, there was a marked shift across the country as the concept of "green" living became more popular.

Families in the first decade of the century did not resemble those found at the beginning of the previous century. As the number of single-parent families increased, so did the number of stay-at-home dads. Same-sex couples fought for (and sometimes won) the right to marry, and divorce rates were down, possibly because cohabiting was more widely accepted.

Glenn Beck (1964–)   Glenn Beck is a self-proclaimed conservative radio host, author, political commentator, and entrepreneur whose outspokenness has earned him a loyal fan base as well as vocal enemies. His company, Mercury Radio Arts, includes a number of broadcasting, publishing, and Internet entities. After holding a series of radio broadcasting jobs, Beck aired the *Glenn Beck Program* in Florida in 2000. Two years later, the local show became national when it was launched on forty-seven stations across the country. By 2008, the show was ranked fourth in the nation and boasted more than 6.5 million listeners. He joined Fox News Channel as host of the television show *Glenn Beck* in 2009 and also had a regular stint on Fox's *The O'Reilly Factor.* *(© AP Photo/Mike Mergen)*

Stephen Colbert (1964–)   Stephen Colbert is the host of Comedy Central's popular satirical news program, *The Colbert Report.* Colbert accepted a job in 1997 on *The Daily Show* with fellow comedian Craig Kilborn. Two years later, Jon Stewart replaced Kilborn as host. Although Colbert served as both actor and writer, it was his writing skill that earned him Emmys in 2004, 2005, and 2006. In 2005, Colbert began hosting *The Colbert Report.* His character is a news reporter who mocks modern television news broadcasting conventions, with particularly sharp jabs at conservative talk show hosts such as Bill O'Reilly and Glenn Beck. His 2007 book, *I am America (And So Can You!)*, includes political satire similar to the format used on his show. Colbert has won numerous awards for his performances as well as for his influential personality. *(© AP Photo/Charles Sykes)*

Al Gore (1948–)   Al Gore was the forty-fifth vice president of the United States, having served under Democratic president Bill Clinton from 1993 to 2001. Although his political activities brought his name to the forefront of American culture and society, Gore's efforts as an environmental activist have been equally influential. Gore publicized facts and concerns about climate change throughout the first decade of the twenty-first century, and his documentary on the subject—*An Inconvenient Truth*—won an Oscar in 2007. That same year, Gore was honored with the Nobel Peace Prize for his work to raise awareness of man-made climate change. Although Gore has won numerous awards for his work, he is not without his critics, some of whom accuse him of making inaccurate scientific claims. Other critics claim there is a conflict of interest in his environmental activities because he has invested financially in green technology. *(© Daniele Mascolo/Getty Images)*

Rachael Ray (1968–) Rachael Ray's cooking show *30 Minute Meals* launched on the Food Network in November 2001, and before the decade was over, the energetic queen of the kitchen had built herself a media empire that included four Food Network programs, a line of cookware, an olive oil, the popular magazine *Every Day with Rachael Ray*, and more than a dozen bestselling cookbooks. Her magazine was named Magazine of the Decade by *AdWeek* in 2009, and her syndicated talk show, *Rachael Ray*, led *Newsweek* to describe her as "the most down-to-earth TV star on the planet." The show debuted in 2006. In 2007 she founded Yum-O!, a nonprofit organization dedicated to empowering children to develop healthy relationships with food and cooking. *(© Jean Baptiste Lacroix/WireImage)*

Rick Warren (1954–) Evangelical Christian minister Rick Warren founded the Saddleback Church in 1980. By 2009 the church stood in Lake Forest, California, and boasted a weekly attendance of approximately twenty thousand, making it the eighth-largest church in the country. Warren is probably best known for his 2002 bestselling devotional book, *The Purpose Driven Life*. Within five years of publication, the book had sold more than thirty million copies. In 2008, Warren was invited by President-elect Barack Obama to give the invocation at his inauguration ceremony. Warren is criticized by people who see his views as extreme. However, the minister's impact on the decade was undeniable, as *Time* magazine called him one of the "Fifteen World Leaders Who Mattered Most in 2004" as well as one of the "One Hundred Most Influential People in the World" in 2005. In 2008, Warren was featured on the magazine's cover as the most powerful religious leader in the United States. *(© AP Photo/Charles Sykes)*

Oprah Winfrey (1954–) In 1985, Oprah Winfrey turned a local Chicago television talk show into *The Oprah Winfrey Show*. Within a year, the show was broadcasting nationally and took the number-one slot in national syndication. The show won three Emmys, and Winfrey received the Broadcaster of the Year Award from the International Radio and Television Society. Her acting talent was evident in the 1985 film adaptation of Alice Walker's bestselling novel, *The Color Purple*, and in 1986, she formed Harpo Productions Inc., her own production company. Winfrey became the first woman in history to own and produce her own talk show when Harpo bought *The Oprah Winfrey Show* from Capitol Cities/ABC. Throughout the 2000s, Winfrey's show continued to dominate the daytime talk show field, and Winfrey herself branched out with her business interests. She partnered with Oxygen Media, a cable channel aimed at women's programming, and in 2000 she began publishing *O; The Oprah Magazine*. By 2003, Winfrey was a billionaire,

the first African American woman to achieve such financial status. Winfrey chose to retire her talk show after twenty-four seasons and shortly thereafter, she launched another cable television channel, the Oprah Winfrey Network. *(© AP Photo/Chris Pizzello)*

Mark Zuckerberg (1984–) In 2004, Mark Zuckerberg and Harvard classmates Dustin Moskovitz, Eduardo Saverin, and Chris Hughes cofounded Facebook, a social networking site. Zuckerberg had already earned a reputation as something of a genius even before he got to Harvard. Once there, he wrote two software programs prior to releasing Facebook. CourseMatch allowed students to form study groups, and Facemash published photos of students and encouraged users to vote on the best-looking among them. At the same time, students were clamoring for Harvard to produce a school-only site that would list students with their contact information. Zuckerberg answered that call with Facebook. Soon, the team made Facebook available to the world. After a little more than six years in operation, Facebook reached the five-hundred-million-member mark. In 2009, Zuckerberg was number 158 on *Forbes* list of the "Four Hundred Richest Americans." He was also the youngest. Within two years, he would jump to number 14 on the list, still the youngest. *(© AP Photo/Paul Sakuma)*

DIVIDED AMERICA, CHANGING FAMILIES

The United States was a nation divided throughout the first decade of the twenty-first century. One reason for the split was related to political differences as the 2000 presidential election was decided by recount a full month after voters had cast their ballots. Controversy engulfed the process, and when Republican George W. Bush was declared the winner, those who had voted for Democrat Al Gore doubted the accuracy of the recount. Gore had won the popular vote, but Bush allegedly won the electoral vote. The controversy left many Americans with a "them" and "us" attitude.

As the decade progressed, Americans had to deal with some intensely difficult events. The terrorist attacks on the World Trade Center in New York City and the Pentagon in Washington, D.C., shocked the country and its citizens. An atmosphere of fear and uncertainty blanketed the nation even as the beliefs that divided people faded into the background as strangers helped each other, friends and families consoled one another, and grief held Americans captive. The resulting wars in Iraq and Afghanistan lasted far longer than most people initially believed they would.

By the middle of the decade, the wartime economy was worsening and the housing bubble that many had taken advantage of suddenly burst. Property values plummeted as the nation entered an economic recession, and the outlook had not improved even by decade's end. Unemployment in January 2009 was at 7.2 percent, the highest it had been in fifteen years, according to the Bureau of Labor and Statistics. Even more troubling was the fact that, had the unemployment rate been figured using the same calculations as were used right before the Great Depression of the 1930s, that rate would have been 17.5 percent.

Americans were losing their jobs at an alarming rate, and men were the hardest hit because they generally earned more money and worked in professions where layoffs were highest. As a result, there were more stay-at-home dads in the 2000s than in previous decades. As this necessity became more common, the idea of working mothers and stay-at-home fathers became more accepted. By 2007, the Census Bureau reported that the number of stay-at-home dads had tripled over the decade and now numbered around 159,000. Web sites and blogs were developed to tap into and support this new demographic, and even the media joined in on the trend with movies such as *Daddy Day Care* (2003). So pervasive was this paradigm shift that public restrooms began to be outfitted with changing tables in the men's room.

A woman works from home. There was a sharp increase in the number of telecommuters during the first decade of the twenty-first century. © AP Photo/ Amanda Smith/The Register-Guard

Ironically enough, although it became more socially acceptable for dads to stay at home with the children, working mothers still faced scrutiny from those who feel that mothers should stay at home with their children. Moms continued to struggle with the financial need to work and the critics who claimed that children in homes with working mothers are more at risk.

As jobs became scarcer and companies looked for ways to downsize without losing their best employees, telecommuting (working from home and traveling to the office fewer than five days of the traditional work week) became a viable option. According to the research organization Gartner Group, thirteen million workers telecommuted at least one day a week in 2007, a 16 percent increase from 2004. In 2008, Forrester Research reported that twenty-two million Americans ran a business from home. This trend allowed for increased flexibility for families, a benefit for parents and children alike.

Mothers and fathers had more to worry about than losing their jobs in the 2000s. The trend up to that point had, for about ten years, been to overparent children by protecting them from health or well-being threats

Why Civil Unions Are Not Enough

R egarding gay rights, heterosexuals often wondered why civil unions do not satisfy gay couples who want to formalize and legalize their relationship. By 2009, same-sex partners could legally form domestic partnerships or legal unions in twelve states. These arrangements were not equal to each other in terms of rights, nor were any of them equal to the rights granted to married couples.

Marriage gives a couple more than one thousand federal- and state-level legal benefits; civil unions provide more than three hundred state-level benefits. In addition, married partners enjoy greater and more far-reaching benefits in terms of taxes, medical decisions, death benefits, child support and alimony, and immigration rights.

Rights and benefits aside, gays and lesbians make the argument that if they are considered equal to heterosexual individuals, then they should have the same rights and privileges. In the United States, marriage is an important institution that carries with it a certain amount of socially recognized respect. It is a tradition that many believe should be extended to all people, regardless of sexual orientation.

(real or imagined), micromanaging their children's lives, or overscheduling them. Professionals who worked with these children labeled the phenomenon "helicopter parenting." Now that the economy was in a downward spiral and families were having to make do with less money, children who had grown accustomed to participating in numerous, often expensive activities had to face the fact that their parents could no longer afford to pay for them. Psychologists were, at the same time, warning parents that trying to shield children from making mistakes or failing or making their own decisions would, in the long run, be detrimental to their independence and overall balance. Published studies supported this claim, and the trend lost some steam as parents began giving their children breathing room.

Divorce rates were lower in the 2000s than in the previous decade. According to the U.S. Census Bureau, the divorce rate per one thousand people in 2005 was 3.6, the lowest it had been since 1970. The marriage rate was down as well from 7.8 in 2004 to 7.5 in 2005. Single-parent families, which peaked in the 1980s, declined into the 2000s. In 2002,

28 percent of all children lived in single-parent homes. By 2009, that number had decreased to 26.2 percent. Another trend was that of cohabitation as a stepping stone to or replacement of marriage. The surge over the decades was remarkable: In 1960, 439,000 American couples lived together without being married. In 2007, more than 6.4 million couples did.

Same-sex couples noted a shifting attitude toward them and their rights as the decade progressed. In 2000, the Bush administration ordered the Census Bureau to re-code same-sex couples who identified themselves as married so that they would be counted as unmarried partners. The Obama administration reversed that policy in 2009, thereby recognizing same-sex couples as legitimately married. According to the 2010 census, the number of gay Americans revealing that they are living with same-sex partners almost doubled between 2000 and 2009. By 2009, gay marriage had been legalized in Massachusetts, Connecticut, Iowa, and Vermont. New York and California recognized out-of-state gay marriages.

❖ LEISURE TIME IN A TOUGH ECONOMY

Although the economic downturn left people with less disposable income, they did not let that stop them from finding ways to entertain themselves and socialize. Technology played a large part in this endeavor as more people turned to networking sites Friendster (2002), MySpace (2003), Facebook (2004), and Twitter (2006). Personal relationships took on a whole new meaning as millions of social networking members created profile pages and posted comments and events online for everyone to see. Of these sites, Facebook was the most popular, and by September 2009 it claimed more than 300 million active users. This new method of developing and managing relationships blurred the line between the private and the public, and younger users especially struggled to understand what type of information is appropriate to post. As a result, cyberbullying took on a life of its own among teens. A 2009 Cyberbullying Research Center study reported that one in five middle-school students were victims of online harassment. Although harassment was not as much an issue for them, adults had their own unfamiliar territory to traverse with a trend known as "cyberdating." Adults would meet online—and never in person—and develop cyber relationships, some of which went beyond casual flirting and included what was called cybersex.

In addition to social networking, technology produced the tiny but powerful mp3 player, a device that made a monumental impact on the

Foreign Language for the Twenty-First Century

With millions of cell phone users, it was only a matter of time before texting—also known as SMS messaging—developed its own language. Indeed, when using those little keyboards, people immediately appreciated the usefulness of a shortcut or abbreviation. Here is a list of some of the more commonly used abbreviations:

BRB: be right back
CU: see you
G2G: got to go
IDK: I don't know
KK: OK
LOL: laugh out loud
MYOB: mind your own business
OMG: oh my god
PAW: parents are watching
ROFL: rolling on the floor laughing
SRY: sorry
TTYL: talk to you later

music industry and transformed how people listen to music. Although other mp3 devices were available, Apple debuted the iPod in 2001, and the music recording and sales industries were forever changed. Also introduced in 2001 was iTunes, a media player computer program that can manage the contents on the iPod. Capable of storing thousands of songs, music videos, television shows, podcasts, movies, and more, iPods can be connected to iTunes, where all of these various forms of entertainment can be purchased. Various versions of the iPod have won numerous awards for engineering as well as innovation. Many consumers found the iPod irresistible; in fact, a September 2009 presentation at the Apple "It's Only Rock and Roll" Event, revealed that cumulative sales of the mp3s had exceeded 220 million.

Cellular phones, also known as cell or mobile phones, were not brand new in the 2000s, but they became a staple to the American lifestyle during that decade. In particular, the BlackBerry took the cell phone world by storm when it was first introduced in the United States in 2003. Considered a smart phone, the BlackBerry supports e-mail, text messaging, mobile talking, Web browsing, Internet faxing, and other wireless features. In June 2000, 97 million Americans subscribed to a cell phone service. By June 2010, that number had reached 293 million. Likewise, computers—particularly laptops—became more popular as they became more affordable and convenient. By the end of the decade, one thing was absolutely clear: Americans relied on technology for human connection.

Beyond connection, technology made having fun even more fun. Video games became one of the country's favorite pastimes, and gamers spent millions of dollars on music, role playing, arcade sports, and other genres of video games. As the decade progressed, graphics improved greatly, as did the level of play. Gamers had a variety of consoles to choose from, including the best-selling console in history, the Sony PlayStation 2. Microsoft's Xbox was a close second, followed by Nintendo's GameCube. Nintendo released the Wii in 2006, which in 2009 broke the record for best-selling console in a single month in the United States. Nintendo's handheld DS system came in a close second. Video gaming was a multi-billion-dollar industry. In 2007 alone, video game hardware sales totaled $6.6 billion, and software another $15.8 billion.

Three young men show off many of the fashion trends of the first decade of the twenty-first century, including Converse shoes, skinny jeans, and gelled or side-swept hair. © Ilan Rosen/PhotoStock-Israel/ Alamy

❖ FASHIONS AND FADS

The 2000s did not have one particular fashion or fad all its own but was rather a blend of fashions from past decades mixed with newer styles. Without a doubt, some of the fashions from the 1990s lingered, but as the decade progressed, they became more refined.

Even in a decade of fashion fusion, there are certain fads or trends that remain dominant throughout. In the 2000s, those trends included Converse high-top sneakers—also known as Chuck Taylors or Chucks—in colors ranging from black to lime green to patterned; Ugg boots; skinny jeans; and hoodies. This is not to say that everyone wore these fashions, but at any given time across the decade, one could easily find them being worn by someone, somewhere.

As has often been the case, the country's youth determined fashion direction in the 2000s. It was a time when music heavily influenced

Bag the Sagging

"Sagging" is the term given to a trend in wearing jeans or other pants well below the waist so that much of a person's underwear is visible. Primarily a male fashion statement of the 2000s, some social scientists believe the trend was borrowed from the prison system, where inmates are forbidden to wear belts because they can be used as weapons. Hip-hop artists in the 1990s made the look popular, and in the 2000s sagging was a symbol of rejecting mainstream social values.

Public reaction to sagging was so strong that local governments, schools, public transportation agencies, and some airlines enacted bans against the trend. Eventually, a number of metropolitan areas—including Brooklyn, New York, and Dallas, Texas—implemented billboard campaigns designed to fight sagging.

fashion, and there was a strong counterculture flare as American teens expressed their individuality through styles such as emo, hipster, skater, goth, hip-hop, and scene. The latter trend in particular was a blend of various styles, including emo, indie, pop, and even Japanese glam rock. Scene kids sported choppy hairstyles, Vans shoes or Chuck Taylors, and sometimes trucker hats. As the decade progressed, this style incorporated hoodies, skinny jeans, and bright colors.

The hairstyles worn by American teens were almost as varied as the clothing. Shorter hair was "in" for boys in the early part of the decade, but that soon gave way to longer, more free-flowing hair. By the end of the decade, boys and girls alike found it acceptable to wear heavily gelled hairstyles with hair often dyed bright colors. Eyeliner was a fashion staple for both sexes, and the androgynous look was all the rage. For those youth not wanting to join the Scene scene, hair was kept longer, with side-swept bangs and styles made possible only through the regular use of a hair straightener.

Fashion for adult Americans began with a decidedly feminine flare that included ponchos, denim, and tank tops. The mid-2000s brought leggings and tunics as well as flirty dresses inspired by the hippie/bohemian era of the 1960s. Crocs were all the rage, and soon after their 2006 debut, the company designed new styles. By the end of the decade, women were wearing headbands, message bracelets, and denim.

Men began the decade with a new trend called metrosexuality. The metrosexual was a heterosexual male who cared about his image and spent money on things traditionally thought of as women's habits: skin care, pedicures and manicures, massage, colorful clothes, and expensive designer jeans. Salons began targeting men as they offered facials and waxing treatments designed specifically for them, and marketing data supported the idea that men would spend money on grooming products developed just for them.

❖ LOOKING YOUNG AND FIT

Americans were suffering from a severe obesity crisis by the dawn of the twenty-first century. Health and medical experts warned that the consequences of obesity were much more far-reaching than simply not feeling good about oneself. Serious health risks such as heart disease, cancer, diabetes, and stroke were real threats. Something needed to be done.

Many Americans turned to dieting as a response to being overweight. The most popular diet was originally introduced in the 1970s by Dr. Robert Atkins. The diet enjoyed renewed popularity in the early years of the decade; followers avoided carbohydrate-heavy foods such as breads and desserts. Instead, they doubled up on proteins and fats. Using this strategy, dieters could eat bacon and butter but not white bread and pie. As interest in the diet surged, food manufacturers began introducing "low-carb" versions of products such as beer and soda. Followers of Atkins experienced quick weight loss, but the diet was difficult to follow in the long term because of its limitations. By the end of the 2000s, the diet's popularity had fizzled out.

Another diet closely related to Atkins was the South Beach diet, which became popular around the same time. Although it, too, is a low carbohydrate diet that prohibits foods rich in simple carbs, it does not ask dieters to give up carbohydrates completely or to even measure their intake. Instead, it emphasizes the glycemic index, which measures the effect of different carbs on blood sugar level. A 2006 report published in the *Journal of General Internal Medicine* found that a mere 33 percent of the claims made in the South Beach diet book could be confirmed by results of scientific research. Other trendy diets were the blood type diet, the best life diet, and the paleo diet.

When dieting did not give Americans the body or lifestyles they yearned for, people turned to medical procedures. One of the most popular cosmetic treatments of the decade was Botox, a toxin that is directly injected into the face to smooth away wrinkles. By 2002, Botox topped the charts as the most common cosmetic procedure in the country. In 2008 alone, more than two million people tried the drug, and the number of injections administered throughout the decade multiplied by five times. In addition to Botox, Americans turned to gastric-bypass surgery for quick and intense weight loss. One of the most high-profile people to have this surgery was TV weatherman Al Roker, whose physical image changed drastically after having surgery performed. Liposuction, in which fat is suctioned out of the body, was another commonly performed cosmetic procedure, and in 2006 alone, it was performed on nearly 404,000 patients. It was during this year that the Food and Drug Administration approved laser liposuction as an alternative and less invasive procedure than standard liposuction, which uses a syringe to remove body fat.

Americans found other ways to improve their body image even if they could not afford surgery or liposuction. Millions turned to indoor tanning facilities. In 2005, the Indoor Tanning Association reported that about thirty million Americans used tanning beds each year. While users cited the benefits of being able to control the amount of ultraviolet rays and vitamin D they are exposed to, skin care and medical experts lamented the use of tanning beds because of the increase in the rate of skin cancer (an estimated one million new cases yearly). The U.S. Department of Health and Human Services took an official stand in 2006 when it announced that the UV radiation from the sun as well as sun lamps and tanning beds is carcinogenic. In 2007, Utah and Virginia joined twenty-five other states that legally limited the use of tanning beds by teens. The limitations infuriated the industry, which was earning five million dollars annually from tanning salon use, much of it spent by teenage girls.

Some treatments that gained in popularity in the 2000s were more than cosmetic, among them the corrective laser eye surgery known as LASIK. In the early part of the decade, market research indicated that between 1.1 and 1.4 million patients had the LASIK procedure performed. This represented more than two billion dollars in doctor fees every year. By early 2009, procedures were down 50 percent in some clinics, compared to early 2008. Experts cited the failing economy as the primary reason for the decrease. Later in the decade, the expensive procedure became more affordable as competition forced down prices and clinics developed innovative payment plans.

Exercise continued to be the mainstay of healthy lifestyles, and the beginning of the decade saw a renewed interest in the stationary bike. Spin classes, which are group classes that use stationary bikes, were offered at health clubs and gyms across the country. Yoga was the major trend in the exercise industry in the 2000s. A 2005 study reported that 16.5 million Americans practice yoga to the tune of $2.95 million dollars a year.

Green Living

As Americans struggled to keep themselves healthy and balanced, collective awareness of the health and balance of the environment slowly increased throughout the decade. Recycling was not enough of an effort any longer, and environmentally conscious citizens began preferring to buy locally at farmers' markets or at least to shop the organic produce section of the supermarket. Reusable shopping bags were a wise alternative to the traditional plastic bags, and those who could afford them bought hybrid cars such as the Toyota Prius. Home energy bills were reduced by replacing incandescent lights with compact fluorescent bulbs, which were four times more efficient.

Former vice president Al Gore played a key role in the green movement as he focused his efforts on increasing public awareness of the issue of global warming. Due in large part to his award-winning 2006 documentary *An Inconvenient Truth*, climate change and its imminent dangers became a topic of concern for individuals and corporations alike.

According to an Associated Content article, participation in yoga and tai chi more than doubled between 2002 and 2009. Strength and core training workouts also drew attention as exercise programs such as Pilates were added to basic local recreation center offerings as well as health and fitness clubs. For this decade, the key was balance and stress reduction.

A controversial trend in health and fitness was the consumption of energy drinks. Though not new to the market in the 2000s, energy-drink sales saw unprecedented growth during the decade. Between 2000 and 2005, the industry multiplied by seven times. By 2007, the energy-drink industry was a $5.4 billion market. A report published by the International Food Information Council Federation correctly forecasted that the United States was "the largest energy drink consuming country in the world by 2009." Health and medical experts denounced energy drinks as dangerous, especially to their targeted teen audience. The primary concern with the drinks was their caffeine content, which, unlike soft drinks, is not limited by the Food and Drug Administration. In addition to caffeine, the drinks often contained high amounts of sugar and also unregulated herbal stimulants. *Pediatrics* cited heart palpitations, seizures, strokes, and sudden death as possible side effects of consumption. Popular drinks included Red Bull, Monster, Rockstar, and Full Throttle.

Discussion about health and fitness trends in the 2000s would be incomplete without mention of Starbucks coffee. Whereas Dunkin' Donuts once cornered the market on coffee shops, Starbucks had used its upscale coffeehouse ambience, music, and food menu to eclipse Dunkin' Donuts. The first Starbucks opened in 1971 in Seattle, Washington, and by the end of the 2000s it boasted around fifteen thousand stores in fifty countries. Growth was explosive beginning in the 1990s and continued through the first half of the 2000s. By 2008, however, the economic recession had taken its toll on Starbucks' profits, but Americans still managed to find a way to pay four dollars for a cappuccino.

❖ MEDIA MAYHEM: AN ERA OF CHANGE

Never before in the history of the nation had media been in the spotlight as it was in the 2000s. Traditional television and radio news programs needed to find new ways to reach audiences as more people turned to the Internet for their news and entertainment. One particularly popular avenue for gathering news was the Web log, commonly known as the blog. Anyone could write blogs, and by 2006, 140,000 new bloggers were appearing each month. Reading blogs was equally appealing, and by 2009 the World Wide Web boasted 126 million active blogs. Once accepted as a legitimate news source, blogs literally changed the landscape of media by challenging print newspapers and newsmagazines. In short, blogs brought about the democratization of media, for ordinary individuals now had a way to publicize their opinions and expertise along with the professionals in the news industry. News could now be published in real time, and as more Americans purchased devices that could access the Internet, newspaper circulation declined rapidly. While print newspaper circulation declined steadily throughout the decade, online audience readership grew. According to the *New York Times* newspaper, Web sites drew 73 million unique visitors every month in the first quarter of 2009, a 10.5 percent increase over the first quarter of 2008.

As it became clear that Americans were ready to receive their news at any time of day or night, cable television began hosting news shows with a twist. One such show was *The Daily Show* with Jon Stewart that took a satiric look at the news. Stephen Colbert hosted a similar program known as *The Colbert Report*, in which Colbert satirized conservative political talk shows and their hosts by portraying them as poorly informed caricatures of themselves. Comedy Central broadcasted both shows.

The set of the television talk show *The View* in 2003 with hosts (from left to right) Meredith Vieira, Star Jones, Joy Behar, and Barbara Walters. © AP Photo/ Ed Bailey

While *The Daily Show* won Emmys, it was Colbert and his show that became something of a cultural phenomenon. In the pilot episode that aired on October 17, 2005, Colbert introduced the word "truthiness," which refers to the truth a person believes based on his gut instinct and absolutely no evidence, logic, or fact. The American Dialect Society named it the Word of the Year in 2005, and Merriam-Webster did the same the following year. Ironically, the word that had such an impact on society was not even in the script. Colbert chose to use it when he decided the word "truth" was not absurd enough.

Satirical news reporting became something of a trend as Americans learned to take its political pundits with a chuckle. The entertainment newspaper *The Onion* did in print what comedians such as Stewart and Colbert did on the air, and the paper's circulation in 2009 was four hundred thousand. In 2007, *The Onion* began publishing satirical news via audios and videos on its Web site. According to the company, the site got around 7.5 million unique viewers per month after debuting the material, which is broadcast under the name "Onion News Network." The company was rewarded for its efforts with the Peabody, a medal usually given annually to radio and television shows that nurture the human spirit. This degree of success for a newspaper that began as a free, low-budget project run by college juniors in Madison, Wisconsin, is remarkable, but it is a perfect example of how journalism and newsgathering need to be flexible in order to survive in a technologically changing society.

Conservative talk shows on both television and radio gained wider audiences as Americans chose political sides. Glenn Beck and Bill O'Reilly hosted television talk shows, but it was *The O'Reilly Factor* that became the most-watched cable news show in 2007 and 2008. It had been the number-one U.S. cable news show for 106 consecutive months by the end of the third quarter of 2009. In radio, Rush Limbaugh hosted *The Rush Limbaugh Show,* the highest-rated talk-radio program in the country. Although Limbaugh was plagued with personal challenges in the 2000s—he admitted to being addicted to painkillers and to being nearly completely deaf—he still managed to be chosen in a 2008 Zogby International poll as the most trusted news personality in the nation.

Radio shock jock Howard Stern spent the first half of the decade hosting *The Howard Stern Radio Show* on CBS affiliates across the nation. Stern's choice of controversial material caused 24 stations to drop his show in less than a year. In October 2004, Stern signed a five-year contract with Sirius Satellite Radio, and he began fulfilling that contract in January 2006. He left his ABC position with his show syndicated in sixty North American markets and a reported peak audience of twenty million listeners. Before the end of the decade, Stern made *Time* magazine's list of the 100 most influential people and Forbes' Celebrity 100 list.

Daytime talk shows aimed at women enjoyed success in the 2000s. Oprah Winfrey's long-running show (25 seasons) *The Oprah Winfrey Show* was the highest-rated talk show in U.S. television history. In addition to featuring celebrities and exploring ways to empower average Americans through self-improvement, the show was popular for its book club. Any book featured in Oprah's club was guaranteed to be an instant bestseller. Another popular talk show was the all-female hosted *The View,* which debuted in the late 1990s but gained momentum in the 2000s. With seasoned journalist Barbara Walters at the helm, the show was hosted by five female moderators who discussed issues as much among themselves as with their guests. The platform is nothing out of the ordinary: Celebrities are interviewed, and social issues are discussed. What set *The View* apart from other shows was that viewers got an intimate glimpse into the lives of famous women, and they appreciated the humanity they saw. These moderators were not perfect, and they did not pretend to be. Watching the Emmy-winning show, millions of viewers felt a connection with these intelligent women of varying backgrounds and beliefs.

Saying Goodbye to these Late Greats

As the 2000s ushered in great change in nearly every facet of media, Americans said goodbye to some of the most beloved pioneers of television and radio broadcasting:

- Fred Rogers (2003) was better known to the public as the host of the PBS children's show, *Mr. Rogers' Neighborhood*.
- Johnny Carson (2005), known as the King of Late Night, hosted *The Tonight Show* for thirty years. Many future stars made their television debut on Carson's talk show.
- Peter Jennings (2005) was the only anchor of the CBS news program, *World News Tonight* for the last twenty-two years of his life. Together with Tom Brokaw and Dan Rather, Jennings dominated the evening network news for three decades.
- Merv Griffin (2007) hosted *The Merv Griffin Show* for twenty-one years beginning in 1965. The show earned eleven Emmys and was known for covering more controversial topics than other talk shows of the day were willing to risk. Griffin was also a game show host and producer.
- Ed McMahon (2009) was Johnny Carson's sidekick for thirty years and best known for his nightly introduction, "Here's Johnny!"
- Walter Cronkite (2009) was an exceptional broadcast journalist who is remembered for his nineteen-year stint (1962–81) as anchorman of the *CBS Evening News*. Throughout the 1960s and 1970s, Cronkite was often called "the most trusted man in America" for the compassionate yet professional way in which he covered the news.

For More Information

BOOKS

Garner, Abigail. *Families Like Mine: Children of Gay Parents Tell It Like It Is*. New York: Harper, 2005.

Jones, Jen. *Fashion Trends: How Popular Style Is Shaped*. Mankato, MN: Capstone Press, 2007.

Zengotita, Thomas de. *Mediated: How the Media Shapes Your World and the Way You Live in It*. New York: Bloomsbury, 2006.

PERIODICALS

Bridges, Andrew. "Survey: 24% Between 18–50 Tattooed." *USA Today*, June 11, 2006. This article can also be found online at http://www.usatoday.com/news/health/2006-06-11-tattoo-survey_x.htm (accessed on November 14, 2011).

Cohen, Noam. "Wikipedia." *The New York Times*. Updated May 29, 2011. This article can also be found online at http://topics.nytimes.com/top/news/business/companies/wikipedia/index.html (accessed on October 4, 2011).

Shaver, Katherine. "Stay-at-Home Dads Forge New Identities, Roles." *The Washington Post*, June 17, 2007. This article can also be found online at http://www.washingtonpost.com/wp-dyn/content/article/2007/06/16/AR2007061601289.html (accessed on October 4, 2011).

WEB SITES

Arango, Tim. "Fall in Newspaper Sales Accelerates to Pass 7%." *The New York Times*, April 27, 2009. http://www.nytimes.com/2009/04/28/business/media/28paper.html (accessed on October 4, 2011).

Crouch, Andy. "Ten Trends of the 2000s." *Culture Making*, January 1, 2011. http://www.culture-making.com/articles/trends_of_the_2000s (accessed on October 4, 2011).

"Gay Marriage Facts and Statistics." *The Gay Marriage Research Center*. http://www.gaymarriageresearch.com/gay-marriage-facts-statistics/ (accessed on, October 4 2011).

Kotkin, Joel. "Skipping the Drive: Fueling the Telecommuting Trend." *New Geography*, August 18, 2008. http://www.newgeography.com/content/00180-skipping-drive-fueling-telecommuting-trend (accessed on October 4, 2011).

"Living Arrangement of Children Under 18 Years Old, 1970–2010." *Child Trends Data Bank*. http://www.childtrendsdatabank.org/sites/default/files/59_Tab01.pdf (accessed on October 4, 2011).

"Mark Zuckerberg." *Forbes*, September 2011. http://www.forbes.com/profile/mark-zuckerberg (accessed on October 4, 2011).

Nussbaum, Paul. "The Purpose Driven Pastor." *Philadelphia Inquirer*, January 8, 2006. http://www.time.com/time/covers/0,16641,20080818,00.html (accessed on October 4, 2011).

"Oprah Winfrey." *Academy of Achievement*, October 21, 2010. http://www.achievement.org/autodoc/page/win0bio-1 (accessed on October 4, 2011).

"Rachael's Bio." *Rachael Ray Show*. http://www.rachaelrayshow.com/show-info/rachaels-bio/ (accessed on October 4, 2011).

"Unemployment Rate: A Visual Guide to the Financial Crisis." *Mintlife*, January 22, 2009. http://www.mint.com/blog/trends/a-visual-guide-to-the-financial-crisis-unemployment-rates (accessed on October 4, 2011).

"U.S. Divorce Statistics." *Divorcemagazine.com*. http://www.divorcemag.com/statistics/statsUS.shtml (accessed on October 4, 2011).

Medicine and Health

2000 January 17 The Clinton administration calls for Food and Drug Administration (FDA) regulation of online pharmaceutical sales.

2000 January 31 Michael J. Fox retires as an actor from the hit show *Spin City* due to the effects of Parkinson's disease, a condition that he had disclosed to the press in 1998. He will continue to appear in guest roles and launches the Michael J. Fox Foundation for Parkinson's Research.

2000 June 5 Ten-year-old North Carolinian Candace Newmaker, diagnosed with mental health and learning problems, dies while undergoing a so-called rebirthing program of intense breathing exercises (meant to be therapeutic and establish a bond with her adoptive mother) in Colorado. Charges are brought against her mother and the therapists; the therapists are found guilty and receive prison terms.

2001 February 2 Former Wisconsin governor Thomas George "Tommy" Thompson takes over as secretary of the Department of Health and Human Services (HHS), replacing Donna Shalala.

2001 May 14 The Supreme Court rules unanimously in *United States v. Oakland Cannabis Buyers' Cooperative* that marijuana cannot be legally used for medical purposes.

2001 July 2 Fifty-nine-year-old Robert Tools receives the first fully implantable, battery-powered artificial heart at Jewish Hospital in Louisville, Kentucky. The surgery is performed by Laman A. Gray Jr. and Robert D. Dowling. Tools survives 151 days.

2001 August President George W. Bush restricts federal support of stem-cell research on surplus embryos obtained from fertility clinics.

2002 Nearly 4,200 cases of West Nile virus infection are reported during the year; 284 people die from the disease.

2002 October 29 The San Francisco federal court of appeals rules that doctors cannot have their licenses revoked for prescribing marijuana as a pain reliever.

2003 February 17 Federal judge Robert Sweet dismisses a suit brought by Samuel Hirsch against McDonald's fast food restaurant on behalf of obese teenagers.

2003 October 21 The U.S. Senate passes legislation banning partial-birth abortions; President Bush signs the legislation on November 5.

2004 The bodies of U.S. soldiers killed in Afghanistan or Iraq are autopsied and given full CAT scans in order to build databases used in developing new techniques, procedures, and equipment to save lives in the future. One immediate change is lengthening the tube used to reinflate collapsed lungs.

2004 June 5   Former president Ronald Reagan dies after deteriorating health due to Alzheimer's disease. His family publicly supports stem-cell research as an avenue for potential cures.

2004 October 8   Congress passes the Anabolic Steroid Control Act, which reclassifies some performance-enhancing drugs as controlled substances and stiffens penalties for companies trying to work around steroid laws.

2005 March 18   In Florida, the feeding tube of patient Terri Schiavo is removed following approval from the Supreme Court. Schiavo, who suffered from severe brain damage and was in a coma for fifteen years, dies on March 31.

2005 August 31   Emergency-power generators fail at Memorial Medical Center in New Orleans, as floodwaters caused by damage inflicted by Hurricane Katrina (which hit the city 48 hours earlier) inundate the lower floors, trapping patients and staff in the stifling-hot building. Critically ill patients with the least chance of survival are placed last on the

evacuation list. Some patients on ventilators begin to die. On September 1, hospital staff members administer drugs to patients deemed beyond saving and leave the facility. Ten days later, 45 bodies are removed from the shuttered hospital.

2006 June 8   The FDA approves Gardasil, touted as the first-ever cervical cancer vaccine, for blocking infections associated with the human papillomavirus.

2006 August   Seventeen patients under the care of the National Cancer Institute show regression of advanced melanoma due to the use of genetically engineered white blood cells.

2006 December 19   President Bush signs a bill promoting awareness and funding of autism research.

2007 June 1   Right-to-die advocate Dr. Jack Kevorkian, who was serving a 10-to-25-year sentence for a second-degree murder conviction in 1999 for assisting in a suicide, is released from prison on parole.

2008 December   Cleveland (Ohio) Clinic doctors perform the world's first near-total facial transplant surgery.

2009 January 26   Unemployed, single mom Nadya Suleman (known derisively in the media as "Octomom") gives birth to eight babies after fertility treatments. Already a mother of six other children, she is accused of wishing to become famous, misusing fertility treatments, and wanting to "cash in" on the birth of her children.

2009 March New York City establishes a Bedbug Advisory Board to deal with an infestation of the pests. Within two years, the United States will suffer from an epidemic of these bloodsucking insects.

2009 March 7 President Barack Obama overturns his predecessor's stem-cell policy and allows the National Institutes of Health to fund research on embryonic stem cells beyond previous restrictions.

2009 October 24 President Obama declares the swine-flu pandemic (H1N1) a national emergency.

2009 December Federal health officials estimate that more than ten thousand Americans have died from the recent swine-flu outbreak.

Health care was a major focus of attention on all fronts throughout the first decade of the twenty-first century. While politicians debated the costs of various health plans and options, doctors and their staff dealt with epidemic levels of obesity and autism. Teen health was in the news as young adults continued to experiment with drugs and alcohol as well as sex and other risky behaviors. A wartime culture brought post-traumatic stress disorder (PTSD) to the attention of everyone as soldiers returned home and struggled to adjust to civilian life, while threats such as anthrax and various strains of the flu fueled a fear-based, post-terrorism mentality.

Obesity (having too much body fat) reached all-time record levels in the early 2000s as more Americans consumed high-calorie fast food more often and ate larger portions at each meal. The trend in the increase of obesity diagnoses was not limited to adults; across the nation, childhood obesity was on the rise. According to the Centers for Disease Control and Prevention (CDC), the incidence of childhood obesity had tripled since the 1980s. Obesity puts individuals at greater risk for stroke, type 2 diabetes, coronary heart disease, sleep and respiratory disorders, and a host of other health problems. Because it is a negative influence on various other physical conditions and had increased across all age groups, obesity became a public-health issue that garnered public funding in an effort to educate American consumers.

Childhood health disorders were continually in the spotlight throughout the early 2000s. Diagnoses of autism (a brain disorder that affects and hinders social interaction, communication, and behavior) and its related disorders increased sharply between 2000 and 2009, a rise that actually began in the 1990s. According to the U.S. Department of Education data, a comparison of rates from 1992 to 1993 and those from 2000 and 2001 shows that the incidence of autism among American children increased six and a half times. In May 2010, the CDC announced that an estimated one in 110 children was affected by some form of autism.

In addition to obesity and autism, American children in the first decade of the new millennium were being diagnosed with attention deficit disorder (ADD) and attention deficit hyperactivity disorder (ADHD) at an alarming rate. Both disorders indicate a problem with inattentiveness; the second one combines inattentiveness with over-activity. A 2009 CDC report indicated that five million children (9 percent) between the ages of three and 17 suffered from ADHD.

Teen health garnered equal concern. A Guttmacher Institute report published in 2010 but featuring statistics only through 2006 indicated that while the 2005 U.S. teen pregnancy rate had reached its lowest point in 30 years with a 41 percent decrease since its peak in 1990, it rose for the first time in more than a decade the next year, by 3 percent. According to the CDC, the upward trend continued for another year but by 2008 had reversed again and continued to decline in 2009. Underage drinking continued to be a concern, as alcohol was the most commonly used drug among young people, exceeding tobacco and illicit drugs. Marijuana, a drug popular among the youth population, was consistently in the news as one state after another voted on legalizing its medical use to control various symptoms such as nausea and loss of appetite.

People in the United States were concerned about several viruses in the early 2000s. The September 2001 anthrax attacks that killed five people and infected 17 more caused one of the largest FBI investigations in U.S. history. At the end of the decade, the world experienced a flu pandemic (epidemic that spreads on a global scale) involving the H1N1 flu strain—commonly known as swine flu. What began officially as an outbreak in April 2009 had killed 18,000 people by July 2010, according to the World Health Organization.

Veterans of the war in Afghanistan (begun in 2001) and the Iraq War (begun in 2003) suffered from post-traumatic stress disorder (PTSD), a type of anxiety disorder that can occur after an experience involving threat of injury or death. Experts in 2009 estimated that 35 percent of military forces from these wars would eventually be diagnosed with PTSD. Survivors of the terrorist attacks on the World Trade Center in 2001 as well as those who helped clean up the damage also suffered from PTSD. *Science Daily* reported that researchers found incidence of PTSD associated with an increased risk for suicidal thoughts.

It was not all bad news in health and medicine in the early 2000s. Despite its controversial nature, stem cell research progressed throughout the decade. Also, the first human face transplant to be performed in the United States took place in Cleveland, Ohio, in December 2008. Research continued on bionic technology to develop prosthetic limbs that perform like natural limbs.

Richard Carmona (1949–) Appointed by the George W. Bush adminis-
tration, Richard Carmona was the seventeenth surgeon general of the
United States (2002–06). This was quite an accomplishment for the high-
school dropout who had grown up in poverty. Carmona joined the U.S.
Army in 1967 and served with distinction in the Special Forces during the
Vietnam War (1954–75). After active service, he earned his medical degree
at the University of California Medical School, graduating as the top
student of his class. During his varied professional life, Carmona worked as
a police officer, SWAT team leader, nurse, trauma surgeon, and university
professor. After his stint as surgeon general, Carmona publicly denounced
the Bush administration for suppressing medical information. He claimed
he was silenced on many issues, including information related to stem-cell
research and sex education. In his later career, Carmona shifted his focus
from treatment to prevention. *(© Chris Maddaloni/Roll Call/Getty Images)*

Deepak Chopra (1964–) Deepak Chopra is a medical doctor, writer, and
public speaker who began his career as an endocrinologist. Chopra and his
family immigrated to the United States in 1968, and the young doctor
completed his clinical internship and residency in the States. In 1985, he
began studying Ayurveda (an alternative medicine system that originated
in India). Throughout the 1990s, Chopra made a name for himself as an
Ayurveda guru, and in 1996, he and fellow doctor David Simon founded
the Chopra Center for Wellbeing in California. Having authored several
health and wellness books, Chopra became a celebrity in the 2000s as his
public speaking career flourished. He reaches millions of listeners weekly
through his Sirius XM radio show. Readers turn to his weekly column in
the *San Francisco Chronicle*, and he is a regular contributor to the
Washington Post as well as the popular online news outlet, *Huffington Post*.
Chopra has won numerous awards for his work and influence on public
health. *(© Bill Olive/Getty Images)*

Connie Culp (1963–) Connie Culp suffered severe facial trauma when her
husband, Thomas G. Culp, shot her in a failed 2004 murder-suicide
attempt. The blast destroyed most of her face. Her face was embedded with
hundreds of shotgun pellets and bone splinters, and she required
intubation to breathe. Culp went to the Cleveland Clinic in Ohio, where
she met with Dr. Risal Djohan. An uncertain Djohan began reconstructing
Culp's face a little at a time. Thirty operations later, she was still unable
to eat solid food, smell, or breathe on her own. On December 22, 2009,
Dr. Maria Siemionow and her team of surgeons replaced 80 percent of

Culp's face in a 22-hour operation. Using the bone, muscles, nerves, skin, and blood vessels from an organ donor who had just died, Siemionow conducted the fourth face transplant in the world, but the first one performed in the United States and the most extensive one to date. Within a month, Culp was eating solid foods, drinking, and living a relatively normal life. *(© AP Photo/Jason Miller)*

Sanjay Gupta (1969–)   Born October 23, 1969, in Detroit, Michigan, Sanjay Gupta earned his medical degree from the University of Michigan in 1993, with a specialization in treating brain and spinal injury. In 1997 Gupta was named a White House fellow. He became well known in the early 2000s when he began reporting on health and medical issues on Cable News Network (CNN). Although still practicing medicine, Gupta reported on the anthrax scare that followed the September 11, 2001, terrorist attacks on the United States. This visibility, combined with his reporting from Kuwait during the Iraq War, made Gupta a widely recognized medical expert throughout the United States. His reporting efforts after 2005's Hurricane Katrina garnered him an Emmy award. In 2009, president-elect Barack Obama expressed his desire to see Gupta serve as the U.S. surgeon general, but the medical media star turned down the offer, citing a desire to maintain a healthy balance between his professional and personal life. *(© Michael Loccisano/FilmMagic)*

❖ THE POLITICS OF HEALTH

Health care was an issue of primary concern to many Americans in the early 2000s. As medical costs rose, politicians debated many facets of health care, including types of healthcare coverage, how to fund it, and distinctions between state and federal government roles. As the economy fell into recession and unemployment rose, the number of individuals without health insurance coverage increased, and the idea of mandatory, affordable health care for everyone became a topic of debate. Many conservatives argued that every person should be held responsible for his own coverage, whereas many liberals argued that a universal healthcare insurance program ought to be established.

As medical technology advanced and life expectancy increased, medical costs skyrocketed. Twenty-eight percent of spending through Medicare, a federally funded program designed to help pay the medical expenditures of Americans age 65 and over as well as younger people with certain disabilities, was devoted to just 5 percent of patients who were in the final year of life. Public insistence on Medicare reform increased, but because much of the voting population was made up of people over age 65, politicians were reluctant to support efforts that would limit funding, impose expenditure ceilings, and restrict access. They wanted to avoid alienating a large number of voters. In 2003, President George W. Bush signed the Medicare Prescription Drug Improvement and Modernization Act, which gave Medicare patients a choice in prescription plans and placed deductibles on a sliding scale (the higher the income of the patient, the higher the deductible).

Certain health issues, such as obesity, autism, and health-related lifestyle choices, became targets of federal funding as the White House became involved in promoting a healthier citizenry. Individual communities across the country enacted smoking bans in public places, while schools sought to ban student access to fast food and carbonated soft drinks on campuses. One controversial public health issue facing Americans in the early 2000s was medical marijuana. By the end of 2009, 13 states had legalized the use of marijuana for medical purposes.

❖ OBESITY BECOMES EPIDEMIC

Obesity became a public-health issue in the 2000s as more than half of all adults were estimated to be overweight or obese. By the end of the decade, nine states could claim adult populations in which at least 30 percent

Where East Meets West

The 2000s saw a gradual acceptance of Eastern alternative medicine, not as a replacement for Western practices but as a complement to them. Also known as integrative medicine, this healing program takes into consideration an individual's unique needs and physiology and incorporates those healing practices that hold the most promise for effective treatment.

Alternative therapies include homeopathy (treatment using small doses of natural substances that in much larger doses would produce symptoms of disease in a healthy person); aromatherapy (use of plant extracts and essential oils, usually by inhalation and/or massage); body massage; chiropractic; and acupuncture.

Thanks largely to the popular doctor Deepak Chopra, Ayurvedic medicine also gained momentum in the United States in the early 2000s. Originating in India, Ayurvedic medicine is a comprehensive system that emphasizes body, mind, and spirit equally. It relies on diet, exercise, yoga, meditation, massage, herbs, and medication. Each of these programs is tailored to the individual's needs.

of individuals were obese; by contrast, not one state could claim that in 2000. Sadly, the problem was not limited to adults. According to the Centers for Disease Control and Prevention (CDC), childhood obesity more than tripled between 1980 and 2010. In 1980, 6.5 percent of children ages 6 to 11 years old were obese; that percentage jumped to 19.6 in 2008. Among children ages 12 to 19, the percentage increased from 5.0 to 18.1.

The obesity epidemic took its toll on the health of millions of Americans young and old alike, leading to increased risk of heart disease, sleep disorders, type 2 diabetes, stroke, cancer, bone and joint problems, and a host of other health issues. The increase in health problems resulted in major medical expenses. According to the CDC, obese individuals spent $1,429, or 42 percent more for medical care in 2006 than did persons of normal weight. The annual health cost of obesity in the United States ran as high as $147 billion.

As Americans struggled with their weight, many solutions to the crisis were proposed. In response to the public outcry for fast-food industry

2005

1992

Food Guide Pyramid
A Guide to Daily Food Choices

MyPyramid.gov
STEPS TO A HEALTHIER YOU

regulation as well as the obvious need to rethink nutrition requirements and guidelines, the Department of Agriculture released a revised food pyramid in 2005, one that included the need for regular exercise. The White House closed the decade with a commitment to address childhood obesity; early in 2010 it established a task force, which eventually unveiled Let's Move! a program designed to educate adults and children on nutrition and healthy lifestyle choices.

The U.S. Department of Agriculture released revised food pyramid guidelines (left) in 2005, replacing the 1992 food pyramid (right). The new pyramid emphasized the importance of daily activity in addition to healthy eating. © Joe Raedle/Getty Images

❖ OTHER PHYSICAL HEALTH CONCERNS

The first decade of the twenty-first century saw the same health concerns as the 1990s where adults were concerned. Cancer continued to receive research funding, and the most significant advance was in targeted therapy. Whereas chemotherapy destroys all rapidly dividing cells, targeted therapy focuses on destroying proteins found only in cancer cells. Still in its early stages, targeted cancer therapy provided new hope for people with cancer.

Breast cancer remained one of the most pervasive types, with 200,000 new cases being diagnosed annually. Ovarian cancer was one of the most dangerous types of the disease, as there existed no reliable screening test, so many cases were not diagnosed until it was too late to save the patient. Melanoma, the most serious form of skin cancer, was diagnosed at a rate of more than one million cases each year. Approximately 75 percent of all

Portion Control

Food portions have grown significantly over the years in the last twenty years. The National Heart, Lung, and Blood Institute of the National Institutes of Health chronicled the phenomenon it termed "portion distortion" on a web site at http://hp2010.nhlbihin.net/portion/index.htm. The site provides some startling examples of how the increase in portion sizes has resulted in a large increase in calorie intake between 1990 and 2010.

COMPARISON OF PORTIONS AND CALORIES FROM 1980 TO 2010

	Portion (1980)	Calories	Portion (2010)	Calories
Bagel	3 diameter	140	6 diameter	350
Cheeseburger	1	333	1	590
Spaghetti w/ meatballs	1 cup sauce, 3 small meatballs	500	2 cups sauce, 3 large meatballs	1,020
Soda	6.5 ounces	82	20 ounces	250
Blueberry muffin	1.5 ounces	210	5 ounces	500

skin cancer deaths each year were attributed to melanoma, according to the American Cancer Society. Incidence of melanoma was on the rise throughout the decade, and experts cited high-risk tanning behaviors for the increase. Awareness of colorectal cancer increased as emphasis on early detection was supported by TV news anchorwoman Katie Couric, whose own colonoscopy was televised live in 1998. In the immediate years following that broadcast, the number of colonoscopies performed spiked by 20 percent.

Human immunodeficiency virus/acquired immune deficiency syndrome (HIV/AIDS) had infected more than 40 million people across the globe by 2006. Drugs were available to those who could afford them, and they were effective. Beginning in the 1990s, physicians prescribed a combination of antiretroviral drugs that inhibited the growth and spread of HIV in the body. Known as highly active antiretroviral therapy (HAART), this combination of drugs was introduced in 1996 and decreased the annual rate of infection by 52 percent in 2009. New cases of HIV infection between 2001 and 2008 decreased by 17 percent, partly because the cost of treatment fell from $10,000 each year to $100 or less by 2010.

Heart disease remained the leading cause of death in both men and women. According to the CDC, 26 percent of all deaths in the United States—more than one in every four—was caused by heart disease in 2006. By 2010, it was estimated that in the United States heart disease would cost $316.4 billion in medications, health care, and lost productivity.

In the early 2000s several viruses spread throughout the United States, infecting young and old, weak and strong alike. West Nile Virus, which is carried by infected mosquitoes and passed to humans by the insect's sting, became a national health threat in 2005 when 3,000 cases were reported. Of those people infected, 119 died. Toward the end of the decade, the H1N1 flu strain, also known as the swine flu, spread so rapidly that it became a pandemic (global epidemic). Initially designated an outbreak in April 2009, the flu claimed the lives of 18,000 people worldwide by mid-2010, according to the World Health Organization. Humans were responsible for another virus attack when someone mailed letters containing deadly anthrax spores to a number of news media offices in 2001. Five people were killed and another 17 infected. Although the FBI accused government bio defense lab employee Bruce Ivins for the terrorist act, many experts questioned whether he acted alone. Total damages to the dozens of buildings contaminated as a result of the anthrax mailings exceeded $1 billion, according to the FBI.

❖ **THE RISE OF PSYCHOLOGICAL AND NEUROLOGICAL DISORDERS**
In the early 2000s, an increase in the incidence of mental health disorders, primarily among children, was noted. Autism (a brain disorder that affects and hinders social interaction, communication, and behavior) and its spectrum (related) disorders (ASDs) were repeatedly in the headlines due to the significant increase in the number of diagnoses. The increase itself was not new: A comparison of data for the years 1992–93 and 2000–01, as reported by the U.S. Department of Education, showed nearly 5.5 times as many cases of autism. By decade's end, the CDC announced that one in 110 children was affected by some form of autism, and some experts believed that statistic to be closer to 1 in 67. Approximately 75 to 80 percent of those affected also suffered some form of mental retardation. Autism was more common among children than multiple sclerosis, cystic fibrosis, and cancer. Boys were three to four times more likely to be affected by autism or one of its disorders. Although the exact number of Americans afflicted with an autism spectrum disorder was not known, experts at the

An autistic student is escorted by a teaching assistant in the hallway of a school in Ohio that specializes in the treatment of autistic children in 2006. The student is wearing a full-body sack to minimize stimuli and increase his sense of security. © *AP Photo/Thomas Ondrey*

CDC, the National Institutes of Health (NIH), and other reputable institutions estimated that number to be as high as 1.5 million.

Each disorder has its own set of symptoms, though all autism spectrum disorders inhibit social interaction and both verbal and nonverbal communication to one degree or another. In many children, the warning signs do not become obvious until the child is more than one year of age. Some autistic babies appear to develop normally and then suddenly lose their acquired language or social skills. Autism was first diagnosed in 1943, and it was considered a rare disorder for the next several decades. The rate of diagnoses accelerated rapidly beginning in the early 1990s, and by the end of the first decade of the twenty-first century, the incidence of autism and its spectrum of disorders caused some to see the disorder as an epidemic.

The causes of autism remained a mystery by the end of the first decade of the twenty-first century. Although many medical experts agree that autism and its spectrum disorders have a strong genetic basis, those genetics are complex, and some people believe outside factors such as diet, environmental features, and even routine vaccinations influence the

The Aftermath of 9/11 and Middle East Wars

The terrorist attacks on New York City's World Trade Center on September 11, 2001, were devastating solely for the number of lives lost. But the aftermath of the event in terms of health reached beyond that. As more than 1.2 million tons of rubble were removed from Ground Zero, exposure to the debris and dust affected survivors and workers alike. More than seven hundred specialists were dispatched to clean up asbestos, radiation from medical equipment, Freon from air conditioners, and other toxic waste. Workers were at risk for development of respiratory disease, and those who suffered from symptoms linked specifically to the cleanup site were diagnosed with World Trade Center syndrome. About 40 percent of firefighters developed coughs so severe they had to be treated with steroids.

Some of those citizens exposed to the terrorist attacks were diagnosed with post-traumatic stress disorder (PTSD), a type of anxiety disorder that can occur after an experience involving the threat of injury or death. In 2009, experts estimated that 35 percent of military personnel who had served in the wars in Iraq and Afghanistan would eventually be diagnosed with PTSD. A study in the journal *Military Medicine* revealed that 62 percent of service personnel reported receiving some form of mental health care after returning home.

development of the disorder. One particularly controversial theory that gained momentum in the early 2000s suggested that childhood vaccines directly caused autism. The measles-mumps-rubella (MMR) vaccine in particular was suspect because of a scientific study conducted by British researcher Andrew Wakefield and published in the medical journal *The Lancet* in 1998, which directly linked the vaccine to the diagnosis of autism in 12 children. The study's finding was not supported by other research, but the fear incited by the suspicion was enough to cause millions of children to go unvaccinated throughout the decade. Wakefield was later charged with falsifying his findings and lost his license to practice medicine; however, the debate over his study continued. British journalist Brian Deer began investigating Wakefield and the validity of the study in 2004, but the decade was over before Deer was able to publicly declare the study a fraud.

Attention deficit disorder (ADD) and attention deficit hyperactivity disorder (ADHD), two more related disorders, were being diagnosed with greater frequency in the 2000s. Both disorders are characterized by a combination of inattentiveness, over-activity, an inability to assert self-control, and other symptoms. According to the CDC, rates of ADHD diagnosis increased an average of 3 percent each year between 1997 and 2006 and an average of 5.5 percent each year from 2003 to 2007. Scientists did not identify the reasons for the significant increase, which amounted to a diagnosis of ADHD for one in every ten American children. Some believed an increase in awareness and improved screening methods accounted for the increase, whereas others surmised that since there was no absolute test for conclusive diagnosis, doctors may have misdiagnosed symptoms as ADHD.

❖ TEEN HEALTH

Teen health in the first decade of the new millennium was in the spotlight for many reasons. A Guttmacher Institute report published in 2010 featured statistics through the year 2006 and indicated that although the 2005 U.S. teen pregnancy rate had reached its lowest point in 30 years with a 41 percent decrease since its peak in 1990, it rose for the first time in more than a decade the following year, by 3 percent. Teen pregnancy increased again in 2007 but resumed its downward trend in 2008 and 2009.

Experts did not have explanations for the two-year increase in teen pregnancy. Some people cited the increase in popularity of abstinence-only sex education programs that did not provide information on contraception. Others placed blame on movies that seemed to glorify teen pregnancy, such as the 2007 Academy Award-winning film *Juno*. Juno is a fiercely independent teenage girl confronted with an unplanned pregnancy. Starring Ellen Page and Michael Cera, the movie made many top-ten lists. It had its share of critics, however, and when 17 students under the age of 16 became pregnant at a Massachusetts high school in 2008, *Time* magazine dubbed it the Juno effect.

Underage drinking—long a concern of public health officials, educators, and parents alike—continued to receive attention, although there was virtually no change in the use of alcohol by underage populations between 2002 and 2006. Rates were remarkably similar in small metropolitan areas (28.9 percent), large metropolitan areas (27.8 percent), and rural areas (29.1 percent), according to the U.S. Department of Health and Human Services. The 2009 National Survey on Drug Use and Health reported that 10.4 million American youth (nearly 27 percent) between the ages of 12 and 20 consumed alcohol. In an effort to combat underage drinking, various states funded initiatives designed to educate young people. The Office of the Surgeon General developed the Interagency Coordinating Committee on the Prevention of Underage Drinking, and dozens of federally-funded drug education programs were developed in response to underage drinking.

Although the drug of choice for youth was alcohol, teens continued to use illicit drugs such as marijuana and various narcotics. As music raves became more popular among teens, drugs common to nightclub populations also became more attractive to youth. According to the National Institute on Drug Abuse, 2.8 million Americans age 12 and older had used 3,4-methylenedi-oxymethamphetamine (MDMA, or Ecstasy) in 2009, including 4.7 percent of tenth graders and 4.5 percent of twelfth graders. Club drugs such as gamma-hydroxybutyric acid (GHB) and Flunitrazepam (Rohypnol) are sedatives and were referred to as date rape drugs because they incapacitate their victims, leaving them vulnerable to assault.

Pharmaceuticals gained in popularity among teens and young adults in the 2000s. "Pharm parties" became common weekend occurrences across the nation as party hosts would hand out baggies containing a so-called trail mix, a dangerous mix of pain killers, psychotropic drugs such as Zoloft and Prozac, and the tranquilizer Xanax as well as any other pharmaceuticals found in household medicine cabinets. A 2006 *USA Today* article on prescription drug use in teen culture indicated that overdoses of pharmaceuticals and over-the-counter drugs accounted for approximately one-fourth of the 1.3 million drug-related emergency room admissions in 2004. The following year, a survey by the Partnership for a Drug-Free America revealed that 19 percent of American teens (4.5 million) had admitted taking painkillers or stimulants recreationally. By 2005, OxyContin and Vicodin were more popular than cocaine or Ecstasy.

❖ PROGRESS AND PROMISE

Stem-Cell Research

Stem cells are generic cells that can replicate themselves indefinitely. Found in all multicellular organisms, stem cells can produce specialized cells for a variety of tissues throughout the body, including heart muscle and brain tissue. Because scientists can maintain stem cells indefinitely, they are an attractive research material. Stem cell research has the potential to contribute to the scientific understanding of genetics, which could lead to disease prevention. Treatment of diseases that occur in people with a genetic predisposition for them, such as Alzheimer's, Parkinson's, diabetes, arthritis, and some cancers, could be revolutionized by advances in stem cell research.

Scientists use embryonic stem cells and adult stem cells in their research. Embryonic stem cells come from embryos created as part of fertility treatments; fertility clinics donate unused embryos with the donor's consent for scientific research. Embryonic stem cells are valuable to scientists because they can be grown relatively easily in a lab environment and are highly versatile. Adult stem cells, on the other hand, are individual cells taken from an organ or tissue that can renew itself; they are not nearly as plentiful as stem cells from embryos and are harder to extract; they are also specialized to the tissue from which they were taken, so they are not as versatile.

The use of embryonic stem cells caused considerable controversy throughout the first decade of the twenty-first century because their use requires the destruction of a fetus. In 2001, President George W. Bush passed a law prohibiting federal funding of research on stem cell lines created after August 1, 2001. Then, in 2006, he vetoed the Stem Cell Research Enhancement Act of 2005 passed by Congress, which would have authorized federal funding for research using stem cells derived from unused human embryos that had been donated from fertilization clinics. In March 2009, President Obama repealed the Bush-era ban and signed a memorandum granting federal science policies and programs increased independence and federal funding.

In 2007, scientists began using a more ethically neutral method, focusing on induced pluripotent stem cells (iPSCs). These are adult cells that have been reprogrammed so that they function like embryonic stem cells. The reprogramming is introduced to a cell using a virus, which can sometimes cause cancer. For this reason, iPSCs must be studied more before they can be used in any treatment for humans.

Advances in Transplants and Prosthetics

Even as researchers continued to conduct stem-cell research to cure disease, doctors and scientists made major breakthroughs in other areas of medicine. The first successful human face transplant to be performed in the United States took place in December 2008 at the Cleveland Clinic in Ohio. The patient was forty-six-year-old Connie Culp, who was left without a nose, lower eyelids, upper jaw, palate, and other facial features when she suffered a shotgun blast to the face in 2004. Doctors used the bone, muscles, nerves, skin, and blood vessels from the face of a woman who recently died in order to create a new face for Culp. Eighty percent of Culp's face was replaced in the 22-hour-long surgery. Within a month of the surgery, Culp was able to lead a relatively normal life.

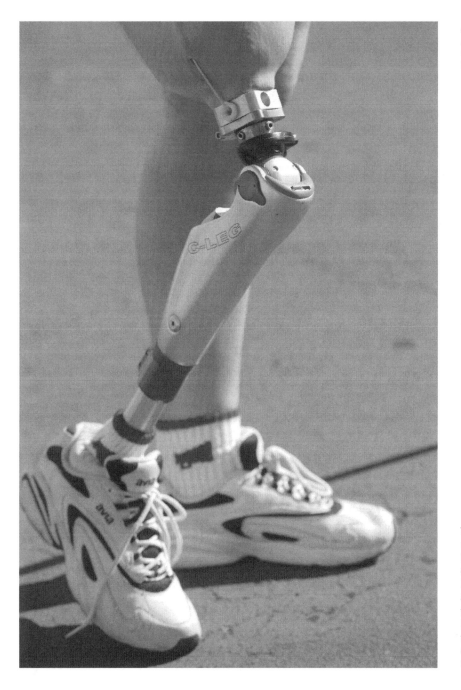

The C-Leg prosthetic limb revolutionized artificial limb technology in that it could sense the weight loading of the foot and ankle while also detecting the exact angle of the knee joint so that its wearer could move correctly. © *AP Photo/Las Vegas Sun, Steve Marcus*

Scientists also made an important breakthrough in the development of prosthetics. In 2008, scientists succeeded in implanting sensors into a monkey's brain, which allowed the monkey to move a mechanical arm with his thoughts. Researchers hoped this breakthrough in the field of neuroprosthetics would lead to a re-evaluation of physically disabled people and an improvement in their quality of life as they performed daily tasks with mind-controlled gadgets. Whereas bionic people were once mere fictional characters, as for example Steve Austin in "The Six Million Dollar Man," they now became examples of what might actually be achieved in the 2000s. The C-Leg, for example, is computerized to sense the weight loading of the foot and ankle, and it detects the exact angle of the knee joint so that its wearer can move correctly. The Utah Arm contains microchips that sense the reaction time of muscles, thereby leading to precise movement. The i-Limb is a mechanical prosthesis powered by myoelectric signals. The five individual digits move just like normal fingers.

 For More Information
....

BOOKS

Insel, Paul, Don Ross, Kimberly McMahon, and Melissa Bernstein. *Nutrition*. Mississauga, ON: Jones & Bartlett, 2010.

Sears, Robert. *The Vaccine Book: Making the Right Decision for Your Child*. New York: Little, Brown, 2007.

Siri, Ken, and Tony Lyons. *Cutting-Edge Therapies for Autism, 2010–2011*. New York: Skyhorse, 2010.

PERIODICALS

Guttmacher Institute. *U.S. Teenage Pregnancies, Births and Abortions: National and State Trends and Trends by Race and Ethnicity* (January 2010): 2.

Luscombe, Belinda. "The Truth about Teen Girls." *Time Magazine U.S.*, September 11, 2008. This article can also be found online at http://www.time.com/time/magazine/article/0,9171,1840556-2,00.html (accessed on August 19, 2011).

U.S. Department of Health and Human Services. *Summary Health Statistics for U.S. Children: National Health Interview Survey, 2009* Series 10, no. 247 (December 2010): 5.

WEB SITES

"Attention-Deficit/Hyperactivity Disorder (ADHD)." *Centers for Disease Control and Prevention*. Last updated December 10, 2010. http://www.cdc.gov/ncbddd/adhd/data.html (accessed on August 16, 2011).

"Autism Spectrum Disorders: Data & Statistics." *Centers for Disease Control and Prevention*. Last modified May 13, 2010. http://www.cdc.gov/ncbddd/autism/data.html (accessed on August 16, 2011).

Chuphal, Pramod. "Dr. Deepak Chopra." *The Boston 10.* http://boston10.cityspur. com/2009/10/19/dr-deepak-chopra (accessed on August 16, 2011).

"Connie Culp, Nation's First Face Transplant, Emerges." *The Huffington Post,* May 5, 2009. http://www.huffingtonpost.com/2009/05/05/connie-culp-nations-first_n_197187.html (accessed on August 16, 2011).

Fermoso, Jose. "Prosthetic Limb Research Could Lead to Bionic Athletes, Gadgets Controlled by the Brain." *Gadget Lab,* July 29, 2008. http://www. wired.com/gadgetlab/2008/07/prosthetic-limb (accessed on August 16, 2011).

"H1N1 Pandemic Officially Over: WHO." *CBCNews,* August 10, 2010. http:// www.cbc.ca/news/health/story/2010/08/10/who-h1n1-swine-flu-pandemic. html (accessed on August 16, 2011).

"Heart Disease Facts." *Centers for Disease Control and Prevention.* Last modified December 21, 2010. http://www.cdc.gov/heartdisease/facts.htm (accessed on August 16, 2011).

Leinwand, Donna. "Prescription Drugs Find Place in Teen Culture." *USA Today,* (June 13, 2006). http://www.usatoday.com/news/health/2006-06-12-teens-pharm-drugs_x.htm (accessed on August 16, 2011).

"Study Estimates Medical Cost of Obesity May Be as High as $147 Billion Annually." *Centers for Disease Prevention and Control,* July 27, 2009. http:// www.cdc.gov/media/pressrel/2009/r090727.htm (accessed on August 16, 2001).

"Underage Drinking Research." *The Century Council.* http://www.centurycouncil. org/learn-the-facts/underage-drinking-research#889 (accessed on August 16, 2011).

Science and Technology

2000 May 1 Under the executive order of President Bill Clinton, the selective availability restriction for the civilian use of the global positioning system (GPS) is lifted.

2000 July 25 Air France Flight 4590, a Concorde flight, crashes in Gonesse, France. All 109 people onboard are killed, along with four others on the ground.

2000 December 15 IBM releases its first Universal Serial Bus (USB) flash drive, whose 8 MB storage capacity is more than four times that of most publicly available floppy disks.

2001 The Toyota Prius, the first mass-produced hybrid (powered by both gasoline and electricity) automobile, is made commercially available worldwide.

2001 August President George W. Bush restricts federally supported stem-cell research to studies conducted using a limited number of stem-cell lines, significantly slowing progress in the field.

2003 February 1 The space shuttle *Columbia* disintegrates upon reentering the atmosphere above Texas at approximately 9:00 AM. The entire crew, comprising six Americans and Ilan Ramon, Israel's first astronaut, is killed in the accident.

2003 April The Human Genome Project announces that it has successfully completed its goal of sequencing the human genome, although small portions remain unsequenced due to technological and practical limitations.

2003 August The social networking Web site MySpace is launched and quickly becomes one of the most popular and profitable Web-based companies in history—so much so the company's name itself becomes almost synonymous with the suddenly inescapable social media phenomenon.

2004 June 21 *SpaceShipOne*, an air-launched spacecraft conceived of and developed by Mojave Aerospace Ventures, completes the first private (not affiliated with government) manned spaceflight. Its pilot and sole passenger, Mike Melvill, becomes the first licensed commercial astronaut in the United States.

2004 December 26 An earthquake with a magnitude of 9.1 on the moment magnitude scale (the third most powerful earthquake ever measured with a seismograph) occurs in the Indian Ocean. The resulting force produces a tsunami as powerful as it is unexpected, which causes destruction in fourteen countries and kills more than 230,000 people.

2005 January 5 While examining images of space taken in 2003, a team of astronomers discovers Eris, a planet (by the accepted, albeit broad, definition used in determining planethood prior to 2006) more massive than Pluto, which is later determined to be one of the most distant objects in the solar system.

2005 February A research team at the University of Michigan is able to cure deafness in guinea pigs by delivering genes that promote growth of hair cells in the cochlea, the part of the inner ear that registers sound.

2005 August Hurricane Katrina ravages the U.S. Gulf Coast, causing more than 1,800 deaths and billions of dollars in damage to Louisiana alone.

2006 August 21 Physicist Marusa Bradac and her team at the Kavli Institute for Particle Astrophysics and Cosmology at Stanford University make the first observation of dark matter.

2006 September 14 Members of the International Astronomical Union (IAU) meet to determine how best to classify the recently discovered Eris and longtime ninth planet Pluto. They decide to assign Pluto, Eris, and the former asteroid Ceres the newly created title of dwarf planet, thereby lowering the number of planets in the solar system from nine to eight.

2007 November Developmental biologist James Thompson and his team report a method for deriving cells with properties similar to those of stem cells from human skin, thus ending the need for the destruction of a human embryo to collect stem cells.

2008 July Google completes indexing of one trillion Web pages for its search engine.

2008 July 31 NASA's *Phoenix* Mars Lander detects water in a Martian soil sample using its onboard thermal and evolved gas analyzer (TEGA).

2008 September 10 The Large Hadron Collider successfully fires and circulates proton beams through its entire main ring.

2009 The online microblogging service Twitter has more than 75 million user accounts by the end of the year.

2009 March President Barack Obama overturns President Bush's policy on stem-cell research, allowing the National Institutes of Health to fund research on embryonic stem cells beyond the previously allotted sixty cell lines.

2009 October 1 Scientists announce the discovery of Ardi, a 4.4-million-year-old fossilized skeleton that is thought to be the closest genetic link between humans and chimpanzees.

2009 November 13 NASA announces the discovery of water on the Moon.

Overview
....

The twenty-first century began on a note of uncertainty, as fear of the "Y2K bug," an anticipated data-storage problem associated with digital record-keeping practices, swept the United States. Computing experts warned that digital records used in banking and other automated technology that relies on digital data-storage systems could be totally wiped out with the transition from 1999 to 2000, prompting many citizens to envision ripple effects throughout the heavily computer-reliant U.S. society. Fortunately, the Y2K problem did not materialize, and the speed of technological and scientific progress moved ahead without a glitch into the first decade.

The unusually fast pace of innovation in the first decade of the twenty-first century resulted from a high level of collaboration and cooperation among scientists and researchers worldwide. Revolutionary breakthroughs were made in many areas of study as scientists and researchers worked together via the Internet on pursuits such as the Human Genome Project, an international study of DNA, and the Large Hadron Collider, a high-energy particle accelerator designed to explore certain questions pertaining to high-speed physics.

While such highly complicated scientific experimentations were underway, the lives of ordinary people in developed countries around the world were being transformed by technology designed for everyday use, such as cell phones, satellite radio systems, digital television, wireless Internet, and social networking Web sites. Suddenly people were in touch around the globe on a scale and scope that would have been unimaginable in 1990.

Scientists gained a better understanding of the human organism from such developments as the discovery of the fossilized remains of a previously unknown human ancestor and the development of gene therapy techniques, while discoveries such as water on the Moon, new planets, and the confirmed existence of dark matter enlarged astronomers' and planetary geologists' views of the solar system and the universe beyond it. Among consumers in general, concerns about climate change prompted growing interest in green—meaning environmentally friendly—technologies such as solar and wind power, electric and hybrid automobiles, and carbon-neutral production methods.

The perpetual state of technological change that characterized the years from 2000 through 2009 prompted people to ask different questions about the human existence, about the environment on Earth and its fate, and to consider the history of the solar system in new ways. All of this activity caused people to consider lifestyle changes and prompted them to envision changes in the decades to come.

Paul Allen (1953–) By 2004, Paul Allen had co-founded Microsoft (one of the most successful corporations in history), donated hundreds of millions of dollars to charity, purchased two American professional sports teams, survived cancer, and become one of the wealthiest people in the world. He added to these accomplishments by single-handedly financing the development and construction of *SpaceShipOne,* a spacecraft that became the first nongovernment craft to carry a man into space. By doing so, Allen proved that private spaceflight is possible and may soon develop into a large industry, providing untrained citizens the once-unthinkable opportunity to travel into space. *(© Slaven Vlasic/Everett Collection/Alamy)*

Ardi (Ardipithecus ramidus) In 1994 anthropologist Tim D. White and his team uncovered the fossilized skeleton of a female *Ardipithecus ramidus* in Ethiopia. They estimated that the skeleton is 4.4 million years old, which would make it the oldest known human ancestor. Over the next fifteen years the team painstakingly excavated and studied the bones, finally announcing their discovery on October 1, 2009. Nicknamed "Ardi," the skeleton provides evolutionary biologists with important clues regarding human ancestry. Ardi's unique physical characteristics, which represent an intermediate evolutionary stage during which hominids (human-like animals) alternated freely between living in trees and walking upright on the ground, dispel common beliefs regarding a so-called missing link between chimpanzees and humans, leading scientists to claim that the two began divergent evolutionary patterns much earlier than was predicted previously. Although there is still much to be learned about Ardi, her discovery has led to a significant reappraisal of mankind's evolutionary ancestry. *(© HO/Reuters/Corbis)*

Mike Brown (1965–) After earning a PhD in astronomy from the University of California, Berkeley, in 1994, Mike Brown joined the faculty of his alma mater, where he conducted research in and taught astronomy. He specialized in the systematic survey of remote parts of the solar system. Brown discovered and studied fourteen trans-Neptunian objects (TNOs; minor planets that orbit the Sun from a distance beyond the orbit of Neptune) ever since his first discovery, of Quaoar, in June 2002. He is most widely known for discovering Eris, the largest object to be discovered in the solar system since the discovery of Neptune 150 years earlier. By announcing his discovery, Brown became inadvertently responsible for the creation of the dwarf planet category of celestial body and the resultant removal of Pluto from the official list of planets. *(© AP Photo/Damian Dovarganes)*

Steven Chu (1948–) Steven Chu worked in many fields, including atomic physics, energy science, public administration, laser technology, molecular biology, and polymer physics. His contributions to such areas of study were recognized with innumerable awards, notably the Nobel Prize for Physics, which he was awarded in 1997 for his research in cooling and trapping atoms with laser light, and the numerous honorary degrees he holds. His interest in and advocacy for renewable energy technologies earned him appointment as United States secretary of energy on January 21, 2009, a position he used to assist anti-climate change efforts in the United States.

(© Larry Downing/Reuters/Landov)

Leroy Hood (1938–) A pioneer in the fields of biology and medicine, Leroy Hood made his reputation through his involvement in the development of the technology that made the Human Genome Project (HGP) a reality. The HGP—a massive, cooperative effort to form a complete map of all the genes in the human body—saw success largely due to Hood's early participation in it and his advocacy for the medical opportunities it represented. His knowledge of the biotechnology field, along with his contributions to the medical and scientific communities, earned him many prestigious awards. He also had considerable success in the commercial biotechnology industry, founding more than 14 companies. He was elected to the National Academy of Sciences, the National Academy of Engineering, and the Institute of Medicine, making him one of only ten people to be elected to all three as of 2009. *(© AP Photo/Dale Degabriele/ PRNewswire)*

James Thomson (1958–) After earning a PhD in molecular biology from the University of Pennsylvania in 1988, James Thomson joined the faculty at the University of Wisconsin, Madison, where he and his research team became the first to report the derivation of stem cells (cells that can divide infinitely and can turn into any other type of cell and can thus potentially be used to treat degenerative disorders) from human embryos. Despite the medical potential of Thomson's work, stem-cell research was met with ethical outrage by many because it required the destruction of a human embryo. Then, in 2007, Thomson's team announced that they had established a method for turning skin cells into cells with properties highly similar to those of stem cells, effectively eliminating the necessity of destroying human embryos and paving the way for future medical applications. *(© Reuters/Landov)*

Elias A. Zerhouni (1951–) After earning his medical degree from the University of Algiers School of Medicine in 1975, Elias A. Zerhouni moved from his home country of Algeria to the United States, where he completed a residence at Johns Hopkins University of Medicine in 1978. For the next thirty years he held a variety of research and instruction positions at several U.S. universities, in addition to founding five start-up businesses and acting as a consultant to numerous scientific organizations. Zerhouni's ground-breaking research in the field of radiology led to many technological and procedural advances in magnetic resonance imaging (MRI) and computerized axial tomography (CAT) scanning. In 2002 he became one of the most high-profile Arab Americans to work for the Bush administration when he was appointed director of the National Institutes of Health, a position he left in October 2008. *(© Chris Kleponis/Bloomberg/Getty Images)*

Topics in the News
....

❖ BIOLOGY: EXPLORING THE HUMAN ORGANISM

The Human Genome Project

In a decade characterized by revolutionary discoveries and amazing inventions, the successful completion of the Human Genome Project (HGP) stands alone as perhaps the most remarkable scientific achievement of its time. The HGP was an ambitious, incredibly expensive undertaking initiated and coordinated by the U.S. Department of Energy and the National Institutes of Health with the stated goal of determining the sequence of the three billion chemical base pairs that make up human deoxyribonucleic acid (DNA) and of identifying all of the genes in human DNA. Thanks to an unprecedented level of international and interdisciplinary cooperation and support, the project was completed two years ahead of schedule in 2003.

The $3 billion HGP was officially founded by the U.S. government in 1990, when it began providing funding to universities, research centers, and private laboratories for purposes of gene sequencing research. Joined by researchers in China, Japan, France, Germany, and Great Britain, American scientists quickly set about using technologies pioneered by Leroy E. Hood (1938–) to identify and map the twenty-five thousand human genes (the pieces of genetic information that code for specific proteins) and thus determine how the human body is constructed. The project required millions of man-hours of painstaking research and systematic study of the human genetic code before successfully producing a reference sequence of the entire human genome (all the hereditary information stored in human DNA).

Those involved in the research combed through billions of pieces of so-called junk DNA, much of which does not serve any known biological function, to find the genes and determine their corresponding effects on the cellular construction of the human organism. Rather than slow progress by competing against one another, research teams and lab staffs shared their findings freely, compiling an open Internet database for easy access to the information. This methodology ensured that the human genetic sequence will remain public property so it will not be subject to intellectual property restrictions or exploitation for financial gain. This network model of research also served to hasten analysis of the information gathered, as everyone in the world had and continues to have access to all information and research involving any specific gene.

The information gathered for the HGP is of immeasurable value to the practice of medicine because it allows researchers to determine and perhaps successfully treat many genetically-caused diseases and disorders. By forming a complete map of the human genome and its variations, the genes responsible for these diseases and disorders can be isolated and studied, with the hope that doing so will lead to more effective and less-intrusive treatment programs for patients. These treatments would be designed to interact specifically with the problem-causing genes. Medical applications of this information include often simple, affordable genetic testing, which may provide clues regarding individuals' predisposition to specific physical problems and possible preventative measures.

The Human Genome Project is anticipated to form the basis of future developments in medicine, biology, and genetics, and it is viewed as a monument to the benefits of global scientific collaboration.

Stem-Cell Research

Apart from the successful sequencing of the human genome, biologists had many reasons to celebrate accomplishments during the first decade of the twenty-first century. One accomplishment was advances in stem-cell research. This research, which focuses on cells that can be turned into any type of specialized bodily cell (such as skin or muscle), progressed when researchers figured out how to collect cells from sources that do not require the destruction of a human embryo (fertilized egg), which was the case after James Thomson (1958–) derived the first stem-cell line in 1998. In 2001 President George W. Bush stated his objection to the use of human embryos in this research, and he mandated restricting tests to a limited number of cell lines. Stem-cell research was revitalized in 2007 when Thomson discovered a method by which almost any human cell could be turned into a stem cell. Stem-cell research is anticipated to provide an important part of treatment programs for conditions such as cancer, multiple sclerosis, and Parkinson's disease. It may also greatly enhance medical treatment of spinal cord injuries.

Gene Therapy

Another important research field is gene therapy. This approach involves correcting defective genes that cause diseases and genetic orders by using modified viruses to deliver therapeutic genes into a patient's genome. This approach, however, faces certain complications. Conditions that arise from mutations in multiple genes (such as Alzheimer's disease, arthritis, and diabetes) are not easily treated using a viral delivery mechanism. Furthermore, introducing foreign genes into a patient's body can provoke a dangerous, even fatal, immune-system response. Despite a number of such deaths, scientists continue their research in this field. Using gene-therapy techniques, doctors have successfully treated deafness in laboratory animals (February 2005), a bone-marrow failure syndrome (March 2006), advanced melanoma (August 2006), and a type of inherited childhood blindness (2009), among other conditions.

Cloning

In the first decade of the twenty-first century, cloning proved to be one of the more surprising and morally murky areas of biological research. Cloning is the process of creating a genetic copy of a living organism's nuclear DNA, which scientists accomplish by transferring genetic material from an adult cell of the organism being cloned to a host egg that has had its primary genetic material removed. The egg is then implanted in the uterus of a female host, where it develops until the cloned fetus is born. Since the first animal cloning, which took place in 1997 in Scotland and produced a cloned sheep, researchers have successfully cloned goats, cats, mice, rabbits, monkeys, and many other species. In 2008 the U.S. Food and Drug Administration approved human consumption of meat from cloned livestock, although cloned meat was not expected to be sold in stores due to the impracticality of large-scale cloning operations.

Despite its appeal for scientists, many people object to cloning research. One objection focuses on what cloned animals suffer. These animals tend to have immune-system deficiencies and genetic abnormalities that cause tumor growth, and they often die prematurely. As cloning research continues, scientists anticipate more of its medical and scientific benefits will be understood, and others continue to pose their objections to this line of investigation.

❖ ASTRONOMY: A NEW LOOK AT THE SOLAR SYSTEM

During the 1990s, powerful telescopes were built with the capacity of looking far out into the Milky Way and beyond it. The first decade of the twenty-first century, however, uncovered major astronomical developments nearer to Earth on the solar system (the Sun and the objects bound to it by gravity). Some discoveries in this research radically changed the way scientists define and interpret this small part of the universe.

One such discovery came on January 5, 2005, when astronomers Mike Brown, Chad Trujillo, and David Rabinowitz located a new planet larger than Pluto and orbiting the Sun. They had captured photographs of it using a high-powered telescope in October 2003 but failed to recognize it as a planet until reviewing the photographs two years later. On September 13, 2006, the planet and its moon were officially named Eris and Dysnomia, respectively. Eris was calculated to be the largest object found in the solar system since Neptune was discovered in 1846, as well as one of the most distant. It orbits the Sun at a maximum distance of almost ten billion miles.

The discovery of Eris prompted debate about how to classify planets. The term *planet* has long been defined as any major natural body orbiting the Sun, which since Clyde Tombaugh's discovery of Pluto in 1930 included Mercury, Venus, Earth, Mars, Jupiter, Saturn, Uranus, Neptune, and Pluto. However, this definition was clearly inadequate because astronomers recognize various other objects that orbit the Sun, including the icy Ceres, lopsided Haumea, gaseous Makemake, and now Eris. In order to refine the term *planet*, the International Astronomical Union (IAU) convened to establish, by popular vote, a more comprehensive and useful definition of planethood. On August 24, 2006, IAU members established an official set of criteria that an object must meet in order to be classified as a planet. It must (a) orbit the Sun, (b) have enough mass that its gravity gives it an almost-round shape, and (c) have become gravitationally dominant in its own orbital zone (meaning no objects exist near it that are not controlled by its gravitational force).

By these criteria, neither Eris nor Pluto could be considered planets because they fail to satisfy the third criterion: They coexist with several other bodies of similar size, mass, and composition that are independent of their gravitational influence. As a result, they were placed in the new dwarf planet category along with Ceres, Haumea, and Makemake. The demotion of Pluto, although ultimately beneficial to the scientific community, led some in the general public to lament the loss of the beloved ninth planet.

Another important discovery had to do with water. Although abundant on Earth, water is scarce elsewhere in the solar system, a fact that constitutes an impediment to human colonization of other planets and the feasibility of extraterrestrial (alien) life ever having existed within the solar system. Long speculated but never before proven, the existence of water on both the Moon and Mars came as a welcome surprise to astronomers around the world.

Evidence of water on Mars was detected on July 31, 2008, by analysis of soil samples taken by the National Aeronautics and Space Administration (NASA) *Phoenix* Mars lander. The *Phoenix* first touched down near the Martian north pole in May 2008, revealing geometric patterns in the terrain similar to those that occur in arctic regions of Earth, believed to be caused by the seasonal expansion and shrinking of subsurface ice. Scientists were able to test Martian soil samples remotely using *Phoenix* to prove that water molecules were indeed released when the samples were heated to 32 degrees Fahrenheit (0 degrees Celsius), the temperature at which ice

A NASA illustration shows an artist's conception of the Phoenix Mars Lander on the surface of Mars. Phoenix landed on Mars in 2008. © *NASA/JPL/Getty Images*

melts. In addition to this important discovery, the *Phoenix* project provided detailed photographs of the Martian surface and information regarding the chemical composition and weather patterns of the planet's atmosphere. On November 10, 2008, the *Phoenix* project was concluded and the craft was left on the Martian surface.

Little more than a year later, on November 13, 2009, NASA announced that Anthony Colaprete and his research team had discovered water on the Moon. Using the Lunar Crater Observation and Sensing Satellite (LCROSS) and Lunar Reconnaissance Orbiter (LRO), the scientists were able to verify the existence of frozen water in one of the Moon's permanently shadowed craters. By examining data collected from the project, astronomers have identified several other spots on the lunar surface that are likely to contain water, increasing the viability of constructing a permanent space station on the Moon (theoretically, the ice could be melted and filtered to provide drinking water and broken down into breathable oxygen).

Not every space-related occurrence during the first decade was cause for celebration, however. On February 1, 2003, the U.S. space shuttle *Columbia* was destroyed as it re-entered Earth's atmosphere, killing the seven-person crew. The shuttle, having completed sixteen days of orbiting Earth, disintegrated as hot atmospheric gases entered a hole that had formed in the wing during takeoff. The interior support structure was destroyed, and fragments of the shuttle were scattered across several southern states. The tragedy prompted a massive overhaul of the NASA space shuttle program, which was essentially halted for two years.

While many criticized the government-operated space program, the aerospace technology company Mojave Aerospace Ventures was working toward the privatization of the spaceflight industry. The company was founded by billionaire Paul Allen and engineer Burt Rutan with the express purpose of developing and successfully launching a craft capable of carrying passengers into space. An air-launched spaceplane called *Space-ShipOne* successfully completed the first-ever privately manned spaceflight on June 21, 2004, when it carried pilot Mike Melvill into space during a 24-minute flight. The historic craft was retired soon after and, on December 7, 2009, was replaced by *SpaceShipTwo*, which was designed specifically to establish a for-profit spaceflight service for curious (and wealthy) space enthusiasts.

❖ PHYSICS

Astronomers were not the only scientists to benefit from the study of space. Physicists working at the Kavli Institute for Particle Astrophysics and Cosmology, an independent laboratory located at Stanford University, made the first observations of dark matter in isolation in August 2006. Physicists had long speculated about the existence and properties of dark matter, a substance that comprises approximately one-fourth of the mass in the universe. Dark matter does not emit light or heat but may explain discrepancies between the predicted gravitational forces of galaxies and their actual, observed gravitational forces. Unequivocal proof of its existence came when physicist Marusa Bradac and her team compared X-ray images of the Bullet Cluster, a unique area in space where two galaxy clusters are passing through each other at ten million miles per hour. The researchers created a map of all the mass in each galaxy cluster and determined that the dark matter was traveling faster than the other matter, leaving small clumps of regular matter trailing behind the gravitational force of the dark matter. Able to observe dark matter directly, physicists learned about how this material functions and thus more about the universe it affects.

Instead of focusing on massive bodies in outer space, other physicists study tiny particles of matter. Research scientists with the European Organization for Nuclear Research (CERN), the world's largest particle physics laboratory, constructed the Large Hadron Collider (LHC). This structure was built with international collaboration among thousands of scientists and engineers. The LHC is a ring 16.5 miles (27 kilometers) in circumference that lies in a tunnel beneath the border between Switzerland and France. Its purpose is to accelerate individual particle beams at a speed just slightly slower than the speed of light, causing them to collide. Scientists want to observe the results of particle collisions to learn more about fundamental laws of matter. For example, they would like to discover if there is a particle that gives mass to matter.

The LHC experiment involves propelling particle beams around the ring with super-powered electromagnets until they have reached a certain speed, at which point they are made to collide with one another. The LHC successfully circulated its first particle beam on September 10, 2008, and was officially inaugurated on October 21 of that year. Although not scheduled to operate at full power until 2014, the LHC has already given physicists valuable clues as to the nature and function of the most basic particles of matter.

❖ CLIMATE CHANGE

At the beginning of the twenty-first century, climate change was a politically divisive and socially controversial topic. Skeptics remained unconvinced that climate change is occurring, despite much scientific evidence and scholarly analysis. The documentary *An Inconvenient Truth,* increased people's awareness of the problem, and the consensus reached by most scientists and many ordinary people was that certain human activities, such as burning fossil fuels, were responsible for a rise in the average temperature of Earth's atmosphere and oceans. In the United States and elsewhere in developed countries, people studied the environmental effects of urban, consumerist lifestyles. Governmental agencies began to revise regulations concerning fuels and other harmful chemicals, but in many cases, doing so was met by partisan controversy and industry resistance.

The United Nations Intergovernmental Panel on Climate Change (UNIPCC) named the most important contributing factor of climate change to be greenhouse gas emissions. Greenhouse gases in Earth's atmosphere absorb and emit longwave (infrared) radiation. These gases occur naturally and are important in regulating climate. However, an imbalance in these gasses is caused by the combined effect of fossil fuel emissions, deforestation, leaking chlorofluorocarbons, and fumes from nitrous-based fertilizers. Diverse and pervasive human activities contaminate the environment, which in turn affects global temperatures; these

Vehicles travel across the Sierra Nevada on Interstate 80 in January near Emigrant Gap, California, a stretch normally covered with snow. Warmer temperatures caused by global warming threaten to melt the Sierra snow pack, a main watershed for the state. © *AP Photo/Rich Pedroncelli*

changes alter weather patterns and cause polar icecaps to melt. The melting causes oceans to warm and sea levels to rise. By analyzing ice core samples and fossils, scientists find evidence that in the decades since the beginning of industrialization in the early nineteenth century, atmospheric carbon dioxide levels increased by at least one-third and methane levels more than doubled. As a result, more heat is being trapped inside Earth's atmosphere, causing abnormally high temperatures, glacial melt, and rising sea levels.

Alterations in environmental conditions caused several large-scale events that dramatically announced a warming planet. In 2002, the Larson B ice shelf, a large span of floating ice that has been attached to the Antarctic Peninsula for thousands of years, collapsed and broke apart. In 2003, an estimated thirty-five thousand Europeans died as a result of an extreme heat wave, a phenomenon scientists agreed would become more common as the century progresses. In August 2005, Hurricane Katrina caused an estimated 1,800 deaths and billions of dollars in property damages along the U.S. Gulf Coast. In New Orleans, alone, an estimated ten billion dollars in damage occurred to infrastructure such as roads, bridges, and utilities. Studies conducted that year found that the number of category 4 and 5 hurricanes (having winds exceeding 130 and 155 mph, respectively) had more than doubled worldwide between 1975 and 2005, while the speed and duration of all hurricanes had increased by 50 percent.

In 2007, the melting arctic ice cap was so significant that the Northwest Passage, a group of shipping channels from Europe to Asia across the top of North America, was fully navigable for the first time in recorded history. During the summer of the same year, the surface area of all the sea ice in the Arctic Ocean was almost 23 percent below the previous record low in 2005. Studies conducted around this time also confirmed that the rapid melting of snow and ice in the Northern Hemisphere is causing a drastic reduction in the Arctic polar bear population. The U.S. Geological Survey projected that, due to the destruction of their habitat, two-thirds of the polar bears would disappear by 2050. This statistic, along with pressure from environmentalist and wildlife preservation groups, led to the classification of polar bears as a protected species under the Endangered Species Act in 2007.

The U.S. Forest Service provided additional compelling evidence of the urgent state of the global climate when it found that over the previous one hundred years the Sierra Nevada tree line has receded by as much as 100 feet as a result of heat and drought. It also found that warmer winters enabled many more mountain pine beetles in Canada and the United States to survive into the following year; the enlarged population has destroyed tens of millions of acres of pine forest, which has been measured via satellite.

As Americans became more aware of the realities of climate change, they made efforts to reverse the negative effects of human activity or at least prevent further harm to their ecosystems. Policies were adopted that aimed to reduce greenhouse gas emissions, increase energy efficiency, and move away from fossil fuel dependency and towards renewable energy sources such as solar, wind, and hydroelectric power. Carbon capture and storage, a process by which carbon dioxide is captured and stored rather than being released into the atmosphere, began seeing large-scale implementation. Public transportation programs received increased funding, as did recycling programs and energy-efficient urban development.

Many in the international community viewed the U.S. government's environmental policies as inadequate. This criticism became especially strong after the failure of the United States to adopt the Kyoto Protocol. The Kyoto Protocol is an international agreement to reduce global greenhouse gas emissions—specifically carbon dioxide, methane, nitrous oxide, hydrofluorocarbons, perfluorocarbons, and sulfur hexafluoride—by up to 10 percent of their 1990 levels over the period from 2008 to 2012. U.S. president Bill Clinton (1946–, served 1993–2001) committed the United States to a program of pollution containment with the goal of a 7 percent emissions reduction by signing the Protocol in 1998, but President George W. Bush (1946–, served 2001–09) refused to ratify it, withdrawing the United States from obligatory participation in 2001. The Protocol took effect on February 16, 2005, with a total of 141 nations agreeing to its terms and emissions-reduction requirements at that time. However, without the participation of the United States, which was responsible for about 25 percent of global greenhouse gas emissions throughout the decade, the decade ended without much hope for the Protocol's success.

Between December 7 and 18, 2009, representatives from 193 countries met in Copenhagen, Denmark, for the United Nations Climate Change Conference. Their goal was to establish and commit to firm, verifiable greenhouse gas emissions targets. Discordant and hostile, the negotiations resulted in an accord frustratingly limited in scope and ambition. An agreement was reached between the United States, China, India, South Africa, and Brazil, which provided a system for monitoring progress towards pollution reduction. The agreed-upon goal was to limit the global temperature rise to 2 degrees Celsius above pre-industrial levels by the year 2050, although the accord did not commit any of its members to legally binding measures. Many scientists viewed this goal as too little, too late.

❖ AUTOMOBILE TRAVEL

One of the publicly vaunted methods of combating climate change came in the form of hybrid automobiles. Hybrids are vehicles that combine small internal combustion engines, which burn gasoline, with a more fuel-efficient power system, such as an electric energy storage system. By combining multiple power sources, automobile manufacturers are able to make vehicles that use the acceleration benefits of traditional combustion

Segway Personal Transport

American inventor Dean Kamen (1951–), the same man who gave the world the first insulin pump, was not interested solely in medical technology. He was also responsible for the invention of the Segway PT (short for "personal transport"), a two-wheeled, self-balancing electric vehicle which was heavily advertised as the future of personal transportation. Unveiled in December 2001 and mass-produced in 2002, the Segway allows a rider, standing upright, to travel at up to 12.5 miles per hour (20.12 km/hr) simply by shifting his or her weight forward and backwards, and to steer from left to right with handlebars. The device maintains its balance by utilizing gyroscope technology and uses an electric propulsion system.

Despite its high visibility with the public when it debuted, the Segway PT did not sell particularly well, with only about thirty thousand units being sold from 2001 to 2007. This rate was attributed in part to the high cost of the vehicle and in part to the fact that the device is not even legal for street use in many parts of the United States. Particular sectors, however, such as police and private security forces and tour guide services, adopted the technology to generally favorable effect. Product lines competing with the Segway in the personal transportation sector include the two-wheeled Toyota Winglet scooter and the one-wheeled Honda U3-X. Although promoted as a replacement for larger automobiles, the Segway was expected to be relegated to the dusty corners of transportation obscurity.

engines with the lower level of greenhouse gas emissions associated with so-called clean energy sources. Although created during the 1990s, hybrid technology saw extensive development and growing sales figures during the 2000s, with the release of popular sedan models such as the Toyota Prius, Chevrolet Volt, Honda Insight, and Ford Fusion, as well as hybrid SUVs, motorcycles, trucks, and vans. The United States and Japan are large markets for hybrid vehicles, largely due to the environmental awareness of the nations' populations and partly because consumers were thrilled at the prospect of getting about 30 more miles of transport for each gallon of gas burned than traditional gasoline-only vehicles.

Along with more environmentally friendly transportation technology, the 2000s introduced automobile drivers to the global positioning system (GPS), a technology that changed the way people find their way to their destination. GPS uses satellites to provide location information to a receiver unit anywhere on Earth, allowing individuals to easily navigate unfamiliar roads and arrive at their destination. The number of satellites varies because new ones are regularly introduced as old ones are decommissioned, but at any time there are at least 24 of them orbiting Earth at a speed of 12,000 miles per hour (19,312.19 km/hr). GPS was fully operational in 1994, but civilian use was restricted by the U.S. Department of Defense, which conceived and constructed the system. In May 2000 an executive order by President Bill Clinton took effect, lifting the restrictions. After that, public use became widespread, as GPS receiver-equipped vehicles and cell phones enabled Americans to have quick access to a global street map.

❖ COMMUNICATION

As the first decade progressed, a fundamental shift occurred in the way people interact with technology and with each other. The increased availability and versatility of the Internet, paired with an astounding increase in the speed, computing power, and affordability of electronic technology, had the effect of connecting people from around the world on an unprecedented scale.

An iPhone displays the tweets of celebrity Twitter fan Stephen Fry in 2009. Twitter was a popular way to send out short messages electronically at the end of the twenty-first century. © *ICP/incamerastock/Alamy*

Throughout the 2000s a radical changed occurred in the way information was created and consumed on the Internet. Its potential was more thoroughly explored each day as millions of Americans (and millions of others internationally) accessed the World Wide Web (WWW or just Web) with such devices as mobile phones, handheld game consoles, portable music devices, and traditional laptop and desktop personal computers. The decade saw the advent of blogs, short for *web logs,* which serve as easily updated online information diaries and allow diverse writers—including published authors, scientists, politicians, and artists, along with ordinary private individuals—a way to reach a large audience. Blogging was used by so many that it practically replaced traditional news media like newspapers and television as the primary source of news.

File sharing is another method by which Internet users are able to share with each other. File sharing is the process of providing access to digitally stored data, such as music, video, and text files, through the Internet. Millions of Web users share files, sometimes containing copyrighted material, in this manner, and these uses forced many industries to reinvent their business strategies in order to avoid missing out on revenue lost due to sharing. People across the world are also able to share ideas and media files in a different way with incredible speed by using electronic mail (e-mail) services. E-mail allows users to send electronic text messages with the Internet the same way that the Postal Service allows them to send physical letters, drastically reducing the wait time between correspondences.

The idea of user-generated content found its most versatile outlet with the development of social networking sites, which provide services that let users manage an online profile, through which they can interact with other users by sharing conversations, posting photographs and videos, and linking to other sites. Social networking sites were astoundingly popular during the 2000s, with sites such as Friendster, MySpace, Facebook, LinkedIn, and Twitter being used by members of every demographic to keep in touch with friends, organize social events, share information about special interests, make professional connections, and promote personal businesses or social causes. By 2009, the number of Facebook users worldwide exceeded the population of Indonesia, the fourth largest country in the world. Social networking became one of the world's favorite uses of the Internet, changing the context in which the majority of people, Americans included, interacted with each other on a daily basis.

Another manifestation of the power of user-generated content came in the form of WikiPages, a collaborative software that utilized *crowdsourcing,* the process of letting users contribute their own content to create a webpage or online service. The largest and most popular WikiPages-based service on the Web is Wikipedia, a digital encyclopedia. Wikipedia contains user-written and -edited articles, numbering more than 13 million in 2009, generating a scope and volume of information unmatched by print publications.

Much of the expansion of the Internet's capabilities can be attributed to the concurrent growth of electronic technology. The principal contributing factor was continuing advances in the processing power and memory capacity of computers, which stemmed from the ability of manufacturers to fit more transistors into hardware than had been possible in the 1990s. As the affordability, availability, and capability of personal computers

The Digital Switch

....

As television broadcasting technology was developed and standard-ized during the 1940s and 1950s, the only method of encoding picture and sound relied on the use of an analog signal. Analog signals are those in which the content of the broadcast is encoded in variations in the amplitude and frequency of the signal. All television programming thus had to comply with rigid standards of analog broadcasting while still undergoing modification in order to implement new technologies and formats, including color imaging, stereo sound, and closed captioning. Limitations in the number of modifications that could be made to a given analog signal also contributed to its inefficiency. With the development of digital television broadcasting technology in the 1990s and 2000s came increased efficiency and performance versatility, but digital television services were costly to operate and not free to the public in the United States.

Fortunately for broadcast engineers, an international agreement was made in 2006 by which all countries are required to make the transition from analog television broadcasting to digital by June 17, 2015. Several European nations made the switch easily and early, but the United States had a slightly more difficult time. Full-power analog broadcasting in the country was scheduled to end after February 17, 2009, with the aid of federally sponsored digital converter box coupons, which would alleviate much of the cost to consumers of purchasing the device used to receive digital television signals. An unexpected number of Americans were interested in receiving the benefits of the coupon program, however, and the government was forced to delay the transition to digital television until June 12, 2009. By the day of the original deadline, 36 percent of all full-power broadcasters in the United States had already made the transition and were broadcasting entirely in digital.

Although not every American was fully prepared for the digital switch, as it was commonly known, the nation's television stations were successful in changing to all-digital, although low-power broadcasters were allowed to maintain analog signals without any dates being set on when they would be required to make the switch.

increased, so did public interest in using them. Many, however, would never have gained regular Internet access if not for the invention of wireless local area networks (WLAN) and its complementary operational standard, known as Wi-Fi. The two, operating together, provide any device with a wireless Internet antenna the ability to connect to a network remotely, without having to physically connect the device to the source of the network. The practical implication of wireless Internet and Wi-Fi is that Americans are able to access the Web from anywhere there is a wireless signal.

Also instrumental in the increased use of the Internet that accompanied the 2000s was the implementation of broadband technology. Broadband refers to digital subscriber line (DSL) and cable modem Internet access, which uses highly efficient coaxial and fiber optic cables to transmit electronic data from the Internet. By widely adopting broadband technology, usage of which grew by 24 percent in the United States between 2000 and 2003, the typical Internet connection doubled in information transfer speed. This allowed for real-time audio, video, and image streaming, as well as video chat services such as Skype.

In addition to these advances in Internet technology, innovation in other sectors contributed significantly to the changing nature of communication in the United States and elsewhere in the world. The rise of cellular phone technology impacted just about everyone in the United States, as the relatively simple send/receive call models were replaced by mobile phones with built-in MP3 music players, digital cameras, GPS units, hands-free headsets, and touch screens, offering a seemingly endless choice of services such as Web access, text messaging, e-mail, video conferencing, and applications (apps), specialized software designed to perform specific tasks. Cell phone networks themselves underwent a period of rapid evolution, with the first third-generation (3G) network capable of transferring information at speeds of up to 3 megabits per second (Mbps). Cell phone use generated 200 million customers from 2003 to 2007.

Radio technology also saw improvement in the form of satellite radio, a technology that uses satellites orbiting Earth to relay radio signals to an extraordinarily broad geographical area. FM radio stations have a limited broadcast range and often only provide local programming, whereas satellite radio services allow users to listen to a wide range of program choices, with some channels entirely free of commercials, advertisements, and even disc-jockey (DJ) interruptions. The first satellite broadcast began on January 5, 2001, and by July 2009, satellite radio had over 18.5 million subscribers.

✦ ARCHAEOLOGY

On October 1, 2009, a team of paleontologists co-directed by Tim White of the University of California, Berkeley, announced the discovery of the oldest fossilized skeleton of a human ancestor, which belonged to a female member of a species known as *Ardipithecus ramidus*. The skeleton, affectionately nicknamed Ardi, was uncovered and excavated in 1994 in the Ethiopian desert and carefully studied for the next fifteen years. Researchers determined that the skeleton was approximately 4.4 million years old, making it more than a million years older than the skeleton of Lucy, the *Australopithecus afarensis,* which had been the oldest known human ancestor species for the previous twenty years.

Ardi's discovery rocked the anthropological community by dispelling the popular notion that a missing evolutionary link tied the ancestry of chimpanzees and humans. Instead of branching from the primate family tree after chimpanzees, Ardi's skeleton indicates that humans began a separate evolutionary path much earlier than had previously been known. Scientists based this conclusion on Ardi's peculiar mix of primitive and advanced physical traits, which suggest that she walked on two legs on the ground but used all four limbs to move through trees. Scientists have also used the fossils as a basis for the theory that human characteristics not found in all other primates, such as monogamous sexual pairing and cooperation between males, actually occurred in human evolutionary history before tool use rather than after (as had traditionally been assumed by archaeologists). By continuing to study Ardi and the bones from 36 of her relatives that were discovered at the same site, researchers will be able to gain a better understanding of human ancestral history.

 For More Information
• •

BOOKS

Agar, Jon. *Constant Touch: A Global History of the Mobile Phone.* London: Totem, 2004.

Brown, Mike. *How I Killed Pluto and Why It Had It Coming.* New York: Spiegel Reilly, 2009.

Kiessling, Ann A., and Scott Anderson. *Human Embryonic Stem Cells: An Introduction to the Science and Therapeutic Potential.* Sudbury, MA: Jones and Bartlett, 2003.

Lincoln, Don. *The Quantum Frontier: The Large Hadron Collider.* Baltimore: Johns Hopkins University Press, 2009.

Palladino, Michael A. *Understanding the Human Genome Project.* San Francisco: Benjamin Cummings, 2001.

Scientific American. *Understanding Cloning.* New York: Grand Central, 2002.

Time Magazine. *Time: Hurricane Katrina: The Storm That Changed America.* New York: Time, 2005.

WEB SITES

"The Digital TV Transition: What You Need to Know About DTV." *DTV.gov.* http://www.dtv.gov/ (accessed on June 17, 2011).

GPS.gov. http://www.gps.gov/ (accessed on June 17, 2011).

"NASA—Columbia." *NASA* http://www.nasa.gov/columbia/home/index.html (accessed on June 17, 2011).

"NASA finds 'significant' water on moon." *CNN Tech.* November 13, 2009. http://articles.cnn.com/2009-11-13/tech/water.moon.nasa_1_lunar-crater-observation-anthony-colaprete-solar-system?_s=PM:TECH (accessed on June 17, 2011).

Paul Allen: Idea Man. www.paulallen.com (accessed on June 15, 2011).

"Profile: Dr. Leroy Hood." *Institute for Systems Biology.* http://www.systemsbiology.org/scientists_and_research/faculty_groups/Hood_Group/Profile (accessed on June 15, 2011).

Segway http://www.segway.com/ (accessed on June 17, 2011).

Shreeve, Jamie. "Oldest Skeleton of Human Ancestor Found." *National Geographic News.* October 1, 2009. http://news.nationalgeographic.com/news/2009/10/091001-oldest-human-skeleton-ardi-missing-link-chimps-ardipithecus-ramidus.html (accessed on June 15, 2011).

"Solar System Exploration: Planets: Dwarf Planets." *NASA.* http://solarsystem.nasa.gov/planets/profile.cfm?Object=Dwarf (accessed on June 17, 2011).

"Stem Cell Basics [Stem Cell Information]." *National Institutes of Health.* Last modified April 28, 2009. http://stemcells.nih.gov/info/basics/ (accessed on June 16, 2011).

chapter eight *Sports*

2000 June 19 The Los Angeles Lakers win their first title in twelve years after beating the Indiana Pacers in the National Basketball Association (NBA) finals, winning the series four games to two.

2000 July 8 Venus Williams wins her first Grand Slam title at Wimbledon by defeating Lindsay Davenport in women's singles. Pete Sampras wins men's singles, his thirteenth Grand Slam title.

2000 August 12 Evander Holyfield becomes the first boxer in the sport's history to hold four heavyweight championship titles when he beats John Ruiz in twelve rounds by unanimous decision.

2000 September 15 The 2000 Summer Olympic Games commence in Sydney, Australia. American track-and-field athlete Marion Jones becomes the only female ever to win five medals in that sport by earning three gold and two bronze medals. The U.S. Olympic squad takes home a total of ninety-two medals, thirty-seven of which are gold.

2000 October 1 The U.S. Anti-Doping Agency, an organization that monitors performance-enhancing substance use in American athletes, begins operation.

2001 February 18 Dale Earnhardt, beloved NASCAR driver, dies in an accident during the final lap of the Daytona 500.

2001 April 8 Tiger Woods becomes the first golfer to hold all four of the sport's major titles at the same time when he wins his second Masters Golf Tournament.

2002 February 8 The U.S. Olympic team wins thirty-four medals, ten of which are gold, at the XIX Winter Olympic Games in Salt Lake City, Utah.

2002 August 30 Following lengthy deliberation, a last-minute agreement is reached between Major League Baseball (MLB) officials and the players' union to avoid a labor strike for the remainder of the 2002 season. The bargain negotiated includes player consent to mandatory testing for performance-enhancing drugs.

2003 June 3 Chicago Cubs power-hitter Sammy Sosa shatters his bat while playing against the Tampa Bay Rays at Wrigley Field, revealing that it has cork inserted into the barrel. This violation of MLB regulations casts doubt on the legitimacy of Sosa's recent five-hundredth home run.

2003 September 3 A federal raid of a Bay Area Laboratory Co-operative (BALCO) office reveals widespread steroid abuse in professional sports. The subsequent investigation uncovers connections between the company and high-caliber athletes such as Barry Bonds, Bill Romanowski, and Marion Jones.

2004 January 10 Hawaiian surfer and windboarder Pete Cabrinha rides the largest wave ever, a seventy-footer arising near the coast of Maui.

2004 August 13 The opening ceremony of the 2004 Summer Olympics takes place in Athens, Greece, marking the beginning of a highly successful run for the United States; the U.S. team goes on to earn 103 medals, 35 being gold.

2005 January 17 *The Ultimate Fighter*, a reality competition television show that chronicles the training, fights, and personal lives of aspiring mixed martial arts (MMA) fighters, makes its first appearance. The Ultimate Fighting Championship (UFC)-sponsored series goes on to inspire public interest in MMA.

2005 April 4 The Washington Nationals make their debut appearance in the MLB. Two days later they record their first win.

2005 July 24 Cyclist Lance Armstrong wins his seventh consecutive Tour de France and announces his retirement.

2006 February 10 The first day of the XX Winter Games takes place in Turin,

Italy. U.S. athletes go on to claim nine gold, nine silver, and seven bronze medals at the Games.

2006 July 27 Floyd Landis, who had been announced as the winner of the Tour de France four days earlier, fails his obligatory drug test. He is forced to forfeit his win to Oscar Pereiro, only the second time in the race's history that the winner has been disqualified.

2007 May 25 NHL Phoenix Coyotes assistant coach Rick Tocchet pleads guilty to running a gambling ring, allegedly with Mafia connections.

2007 July 9 Veteran NBA referee Tim Donaghy resigns amid allegations that he bet on games in which he was working as a game official.

2007 August 7 Barry Bonds hits his 756th home run, surpassing Hank Aaron to claim the major league career home run record.

2007 October 5 Track star Marion Jones pleads guilty to lying to federal agents about her steroid use and forfeits all titles and race results dating back to September 2000, among them her five medals from the 2000 Summer Olympics.

2008 April 20 Danica Patrick's first-place finish at the Indy Japan 300 makes her the first woman to win an IndyCar race.

2008 August 8   The Summer Olympics in Beijing, China, commence.

2008 August 16   U.S. swimmer Michael Phelps wins his eighth gold medal of the 2008 Summer Olympics, setting a new record for gold medals won by an individual at a single Olympics.

2009 June 14   The Los Angeles Lakers, in their record-setting thirtieth appearance in the NBA finals, earn their fourth championship of the decade by outperforming the Orlando Magic.

2009 June 24   A stunning upset against the heavily favored Spanish team at the Fédération Internationale de Football Association (FIFA) Confederations Cup leads to the U.S. men's soccer team placing second overall in the championship.

2009 November 4   The New York Yankees defeat the Philadelphia Phillies four games to two in the World Series. The win earns the team its twenty-seventh championship title, making the Yankees the most successful professional sports franchise in U.S. history.

2009 December 21   Jimmie Johnson, winner of four consecutive NASCAR championships, becomes the first racecar driver to be named Associated Press Male Athlete of the Year.

The twenty-first century's first decade saw unprecedented sporting achievement by athletes in both the United States and elsewhere. Various records were shattered as the insatiable human drive for physical triumph, coupled with advances in training techniques, materials, and sports medicine, compelled a new generation to push the boundaries of athleticism to extremes. Sports fans were treated to spectacular and highly entertaining performances, while the competitors themselves were rewarded with incredibly high salaries and lucrative sponsorship deals. The ever-increasing profitability of professional sports was illustrated by the size and cost of the stadiums, fields, and other structures built to house athletic competitions.

College sports commanded larger audiences than ever before, and tournaments sanctioned by the National Collegiate Athletic Association were broadcast to audiences of record size. As a result, many college athletes gained international prominence and celebrity and were prompted to join the ranks of pro sports rather than finish earning their degrees. The American palette for sports changed, too, as extreme sports and mixed martial arts gained mainstream attention, even as public interest dwindled in traditional sports such as boxing. Although it failed to garner the level of attention in the United States as it did abroad, professional soccer made solid progress in the United States, establishing itself as a legitimate competitive sport and earning television broadcasting contracts and high-end endorsements.

Not every development in U.S. sports during the 2000s was cause for celebration, however. Sex scandals, cheating, recruiting violations, and rampant steroid abuse ensured that no sport managed to evade entirely the specter of controversy. Such transgressions disillusioned fans and the sports media regarding the integrity of athletes, officials, and others involved in U.S. sports. For both positive and negative reasons, then, the decade was expected to go down in sports history as remarkable.

Lance Armstrong (1971–) Lance Armstrong was instrumental in renewing U.S. interest in the sport of competitive bicycling. As a child, it became apparent that he was a particularly skilled cyclist. He won the U.S. National Amateur Championship in 1991. Armstrong joined the U.S. Olympic cycling team and took fourteenth place in the road race at the 1992 Olympic Games. The exceptional performance by such a young cyclist drew the attention of sponsors and clubs, allowing Armstrong to become a professional, full-time racer. He was remarkably successful during his early career, participating in some of the most prestigious competitions in the professional cycling circuit. His rapid rise to cycling dominance was halted, however, when in 1996 he was diagnosed with cancer. Fortunately the cancer was successfully treated, allowing Armstrong to return to competition. The following decade saw one of the most notable achievements in sporting history, as the recovered Armstrong won the Tour de France, the most highly esteemed bicycle race in the world, seven years consecutively, a feat never before accomplished. After his seventh Tour win, Armstrong retired from cycling and devoted himself to the Lance Armstrong Foundation, a nonprofit that raises money for cancer research and cancer survivors. *(© Robert Laberge/Getty Images)*

Barry Bonds (1964–) Barry Bonds became one of the most accomplished players in contemporary baseball, collecting an impressive number of awards and records. He was also a flashpoint for controversy, as he came to embody an era of steroid abuse in the sport despite never failing a drug test. As a child, Bonds was good at many sports, but he was particularly good at baseball. In 1985, he was drafted by the Pittsburgh Pirates, and he made his debut in 1986. Bonds performed well both as a left-fielder and as a powerful batter, consistently topping the MLB statistics charts. Bonds earned multiple Gold Glove awards, Silver Slugger awards, MVP titles, and All-Star honors. Bonds broke MLB records for home runs in a single season (73) and walks drawn in a season (198) as a San Francisco Giant. In 2003 the slugger became the first MLB player to steal five hundred bases and hit five hundred home runs in his career, and four years later he broke the all-time career home run record by hitting his 756th. That 2007 season was to be his last during the decade. Over the course of his baseball career Bonds set the record for single-season home runs and career home runs, walks, and intentional walks, and number of MLB awards. These achievements did not earn him unconditional exaltation, however, as he was implicated in a steroid-use scandal that permanently cast doubt on the legitimacy of his career. *(© Robert Laberge/Getty Images)*

LeBron James (1984–) LeBron James was one of the most well-known athletes of the 2000s. Aided by a massive 6-foot 8-inch frame and a competitive disposition, James first demonstrated his extraordinary talent at basketball while in high school in Akron, Ohio, earning three successive spots on the All-USA First Team and as many Ohio "Mr. Basketball" titles. The national sports media proclaimed him the most promising new talent in U.S. sports and heralded his rise to basketball dominance. He was chosen as the first pick in the 2003 National Basketball Association (NBA) Draft by the Cleveland Cavaliers and graduated straight from high school to professional basketball. James performed spectacularly during his rookie season, earning the NBA Rookie of the Year award and a spot on the 2004 U.S. Olympic basketball team. James was also chosen to play in seven consecutive All-Star games and he helped the 2008 U.S. Olympic basketball team take home the gold medal. James played seven seasons with the Cavaliers, during which he broke many long-standing NBA career records. James ended his time in Cleveland in 2010 when he announced that he was leaving to play for the Miami Heat, where he thought he would have a better chance at winning an NBA championship. The move generated intense criticism from the fervent Cleveland sports culture. James led the Heat to the NBA finals his first year with the team, but ultimately lost to the Dallas Mavericks. *(© AP Photo)*

Michael Phelps (1985–) Michael Phelps was single-handedly responsible for getting Americans to pay more attention to the traditionally less popular sport of swimming with his incredible performance at the 2008 Summer Olympics, earning an unprecedented eight gold medals. As a child, Phelps shined as a competitive swimmer. He qualified for the 2000 Summer Olympics when he was only fifteen years old. Less than a year later Phelps broke the 200-meter butterfly-stroke world record, making him the youngest male to set a world swimming record. He claimed gold medals in the 2002 Pan Pacific Championships, the 2003 World Aquatics Championships, the 2004 Summer Olympics, the 2005 World Aquatics Championships, the 2006 Pan Pacific Championships, and the 2007 World Aquatic Championships, breaking world records with each successive performance. By the time Phelps entered the pool at the 2008 Olympic Games, it seemed that he was unstoppable. Phelp's reputation of total superiority over his challengers was established as fact when he broke Mark Spitz's thirty-six-year-old record of seven as the most gold medals won by a single athlete at any Olympic Games. Early the next year Phelps found himself in a scandal with the publication of a photo showing him using a water pipe, presumably to smoke marijuana. After observing his ban from competition, Phelps returned to win five gold medals and one silver at the 2009 World

Aquatics Championships. By the end of the decade Phelps had cemented his place in the record books by setting a total of 39 world records, the most records set by any swimmer in history. *(© Robert Laberge/Getty Images)*

Dana White (1969–)   Dana White single-handedly maneuvered the sport of mixed martial arts (MMA) fighting from general obscurity to a position of prominence and profitability. White developed an interest in combat sports during his teens, eventually moving to Las Vegas, where he opened gyms and managed local fighters. Building off his success at operating sparring rings and managing boxers, White became involved with the Ultimate Fighting Championship (UFC). The UFC was on the verge of collapse and financial ruin at the time White purchased it with the assistance of investors. White became president of the UFC under the conditions of the buyout agreement. He immediately set about changing the image of MMA, which had traditionally been considered barbaric and tasteless. He was able to make the sport more acceptable to public sensibilities by restructuring the rules and instituting mandatory medical exams for fighters. White's business acumen benefited the UFC immensely. Moreover, the television program *The Ultimate Fighter,* which chronicled the lives and training of aspiring MMA fighters, generated new interest in the UFC and helped to confirm the UFC's legitimacy as an athletic organization. *(© Claire Greenway/Getty Images)*

Shaun White (1986–)   The popularity and success of action sports such as skateboarding and snowboarding grew throughout the first decade of the 2000s, with the formerly unstructured and convention-averse nature of the sports giving way to formatted competitions with rules and scoring systems. Shaun White was one of the first athletes to embrace this legitimization of action sports, and his enormous influence and inventiveness have directed the development of snow- and skateboarding. White spent his youth in a frenzy of activity despite having a congenital heart defect, making a name for himself by receiving his first snowboarding sponsorship at age seven and by being adopted as the protégé of skateboarding legend Tony Hawk. White entered the professional skateboarding scene at age seventeen, cultivating a mythical reputation as the only skater to have landed a frontside heelflip 540 body variable. The board-sport acrobat justified the praise of his fans by consistently outperforming his competition, capturing gold medals at high-level championships such as the X Games and the 2006 and 2010 Winter Olympics. In 2003 he became the first athlete to medal in both the Summer and Winter X games in two different events. White's highly publicized success and fame had the effect of ensuring the future popularity of competitive action sports. *(© AP Photo/Richard Drew)*

Venus (1980–) and Serena (1981–) Williams   Sisters Venus and Serena Williams rose together to dominate women's tennis for over a decade. As children, the siblings attended the training academy of esteemed tennis coach Rick Macci, although they participated in only a few competitions at the behest of their father, Richard Williams, who wanted them to focus on their schoolwork. In 1995 Richard Williams removed the girls from Macci's academy and assumed the role of their trainer and coach. This unorthodox preparation for competitive tennis proved to be beneficial when they made their professional debuts, with both sisters quickly accumulating wins and establishing themselves as accomplished players. By 2000 the Williams sisters had qualified for the prestigious Wimbledon Cup championship, the penultimate tournament in the world of professional tennis. There the pair won the women's doubles title, and Venus took the women's singles title after defeating Serena in the semifinals. For the next ten years the sisters alternated holding the coveted position of tennis world champion, frequently facing off against one another in title matches. Serena attained the World number one ranking on July 8, 2002, usurping Venus at the top of the world leaderboards. This represented the beginning of a good-natured sibling rivalry that forced increasingly impressive performances from the sisters, culminating in Serena winning thirteen Grand Slam singles titles and Venus winning seven, as well as a unified Williams team taking the gold medal in women's doubles at the 2000 and 2008 Summer Olympics. *(© AP Photo/Kirsty Wigglesworth)*

Tiger Woods (1975–)   Eldrick "Tiger" Woods distinguished himself as an exceptional golfer in a decade defined by unsurpassed sporting achievement. As a young boy, Woods displayed incredible talent as a golfer, receiving coverage in *Golf Digest* at the age of five and winning his first junior tournament at age seven. From 1988 to 1991 Woods won every Junior World Championship, and in 1991, he became the youngest player ever to win the U.S. Junior Amateur Golf Tournament. The following year Woods became the first person to win the U.S. Junior Amateur Golf Tournament twice, and he participated in his first Professional Golf Association (PGA) Tour event. He received a golf scholarship to attend Stanford University in 1994, became a professional golfer in 1996, and by 1997 had won the prestigious Masters Tournament, making him the event's youngest winner. Having established himself as golf's top athlete, Woods spent the next decade dominating the professional rankings. He won three more Masters, four PGA Championships, and three U.S. Open Championships. Woods was also named PGA Player of the Year ten times, Associated

Press Male Athlete of the Year, and in 2009 he became the first athlete to make $1 billion in career earnings. Although idolized by many, Woods garnered negative publicity in 2009 when several women admitted to having affairs with the married golfer, tarnishing his otherwise immaculate image. *(AP Photo/Lenny Ignelzi)*

◆◆◆ *Topics in the News* ·

Sports

TOPICS IN THE NEWS

❖ BASEBALL

Professional baseball saw a resurgence in popularity during the 2000s, as droves of fans flocked to games (or their television sets) to watch a new generation of athletes compete for coveted Major League Baseball (MLB) titles. The predictability that had characterized the sport during the preceding decade was replaced with a persistent sense that no game had a guaranteed outcome; team rosters were so saturated with star power that upsets occurred frequently, as a single athlete's performance could easily determine the final score of a game. Although traditionally confined in popularity to the United States and its immediate neighbors, heightened international enthusiasm for baseball resulted in an influx of high-caliber talent from across the Pacific Ocean, such as Japanese stars Hideki Matsui, Ichiro Suzuki, and Hideo Nomo; Korean pitcher Chan Ho Park; Taiwanese left-fielder Chin-Feng Chen; and Chinese pitcher Wang Chao. From this dynamic new atmosphere emerged a host of memorable sporting achievements and exciting matchups.

Baseball's most storied and celebrated occurrence during the decade was the triumph of the Boston Red Sox at the 2004 MLB World Series. Long haunted by the "curse of the Bambino"—purportedly incurred upon trading famed hitter Babe Ruth to the New York Yankees in 1919—the Red Sox had not won a World Series championship in eighty-six years before emerging victorious over the St. Louis Cardinals, whom they tidily swept four games to none to claim the 2004 title. Compounding the jubilation of the substantial Red Sox fan population was the additional satisfaction of having defeated their long-time rivals, the Yankees, in the American League Championship Series (ALCS), recovering from a three-game deficit to qualify for competition in the World Series. This reversal of fortune for the Red Sox persisted throughout the decade, culminating in another perfect World Series win, this time against the Colorado Rockies in 2007.

Aside from being beaten by the Red Sox, the New York Yankees were highly successful during the 2000s. Propelled by the remarkable skill of stars such as third baseman and power-hitter Alex Rodriguez, shortstop Derek Jeter, second baseman Alfonso Soriano, and pitcher Roger Clemens, the franchise established itself as a dominant force in professional baseball, making the World Series playoffs every year of the decade until 2008. The Yankees also bookended the decade with World Series wins, claiming their third consecutive title by defeating the New York Mets in 2000 and conquering the defending champions the Philadelphia Phillies in 2009, thus making the Yankees and Red Sox the only two clubs to win more than one World Series during the decade. Although the franchise had the highest win-loss ratio of the decade, team manager Joe Torre grew so disheartened by a losing stint and perceived decline in competitive ability that he left the Yankees in 2007, to be replaced by former catcher Joe Girardi.

The change that permeated the world of professional baseball throughout the 2000s was exemplified by the establishment of the Washington Nationals. The MLB resolved to contract the league in 2001, making plans to collectively purchase and dissolve the Minnesota Twins and the Montreal Expos. The next year, complications forced a delay in the plan, which was rescheduled to be effected four years later. In the meantime, the MLB elected to transfer the Expos from Canada to Washington, D.C., where they were renamed the Nationals ("Nats," for short). The move was not universally supported, however, as the owner of the Expos appealed, ineffectually, to cancel the plan, and the Baltimore Orioles management expressed concern that the new team might detract from their fan base. In spite of such resistance, the Expos were transformed into the Nationals, losing their first game to the Philadelphia Phillies on April 4, 2005. Two days later the team won their inaugural home game at the new RFK Stadium; however, the fledgling organization went on to struggle through its infancy, recording a humiliatingly low fifty-nine wins in their 2009 season.

In addition to the Nationals' RFK Stadium, several baseball teams established new home fields, including the Detroit Tigers (2000), San Francisco Giants (2000), Houston Astros (2000), Milwaukee Brewers (2001), Pittsburgh Pirates (2001), Cincinnati Reds (2003), San Diego Padres (2004), Philadelphia Phillies (2004), St. Louis Cardinals (2006), New York Mets (2009), and New York Yankees (2009).

Noteworthy sporting achievements abounded during the decade. The most remarkable took place on August 7, 2007, when Giants left-fielder Barry Bonds hit his 756th career home run to best Hank Aaron's 31-year-old career home run record. Bonds would go on to end the season with a total of 762 home runs. Also of note were the two perfect (in which no member of the opposing team reaches base) games that took place during the 2000s, the first pitched by Arizona Diamondbacks legend Randy Johnson on May 18, 2004, and the second by Chicago White Sox ace Mark Buehrle on July 23, 2009.

❖ BASKETBALL: PROFESSIONAL

In comparison to other sports, the course of professional basketball during the 2000s was relatively unremarkable. Despite solid, star-laden rosters and consistently entertaining play, National Basketball Association (NBA) teams failed to generate the same level of excitement for fans as they had during the previous decade, resulting in a low-key period for the sport.

Steroids

S candal rocked American professional sports when in 2003 it was revealed that the Bay Area Laboratory Co-operative (BALCO), a company operating under the guise of offering blood and urine analysis for athletic competitions, had been supplying a new and previously undetectable steroid called tetrahydrogestrinone (referred to in the media as "the clear") to several high-profile athletes. Subsequent investigation conducted by the federal authorities linked BALCO to big-name stars, including MLB players, most notably Barry Bonds; Olympic athletes such as track star Marion Jones and Dwain Chambers; a number of NFL Oakland Raiders team members; and several cyclists. The results of the scandal were devastating, forcing Marion Jones to forfeit her three gold and two bronze medals from the 2000 Summer Olympics and casting a permanent shadow of doubt on the legitimacy of the record-breaking performances that took place during the decade.

That is not to say, however, that there were no notable developments in the NBA. The league was primarily dominated by two organizations—the perennially successful San Antonio Spurs and the storied Los Angeles Lakers. The Lakers, under the guidance of new head coach Phil Jackson, were such a powerhouse that they made appearances at six NBA championship games (2000–02, 2004, 2008–09), winning four of them (2000–02, 2009). Much of the Lakers' success can be attributed to guard Kobe Bryant, whose talent garnered him NBA All-Star honors every year of the decade, as well as the league Most Valuable Player (MVP) award in 2008 and an NBA Finals MVP title in 2009. Bryant was also the league's scoring leader for both the 2006 and 2007 seasons. He was supported by an extremely capable roster that included stars such as centers Shaquille "Shaq" O'Neal and Karl Malone; guards Gary Payton, Ron Harper, and Derek Fischer; and forwards Lamar Odom, Pau Gasol, and A.C. Green.

While the Lakers were enormously successful, the San Antonio Spurs competed with them to be the league's premier team. In 2003, upon the departure of the team's top players David Robinson, Steve Kerr, and Danny Ferry, the team looked to center Tim Duncan to carry on its winning tradition. Duncan's virtuosity on the basketball court (he was named league MVP in 2002 and 2003 and played on the NBA All-Star team every year of the

Women in Sports

The first decade of the twenty-first century was a period in which women's sports gained significant media coverage and drew more public interest than ever before. Nowhere was this trend more apparent than in the success of the Women's National Basketball Association (WNBA), which gained an eight-year contract with sports broadcaster ESPN to have its games televised. Women also found unprecedented success in sports that had previously been the exclusive domain of men. In 2008, female racecar driver Danica Patrick became the first woman to win an IndyCar race by triumphing at the Indy Japan 300, just one of her many achievements on the racetrack. In 2000, in a similar overturn of sporting conservatism, Michelle Wie (pronounced "wee") became the youngest player to qualify for a U.S. Golf Association amateur championship at ten years of age. In 2006 Wie became the first female medalist in a Men's U.S. Open golf event, and by the next year she was one of professional golf's highest-earning competitors.

decade), combined with the strong leadership of head coach Gregg Popovich and the reliability of teammates Tony Parker, Robert Horry, and Manu Ginobili, allowed the Spurs to claim NBA championship titles in 2003, 2005, and 2007, and to end the decade with the league's highest win-loss ratio.

❖ BASKETBALL: COLLEGE

The tame state of professional basketball during the 2000s stood in stark contrast to the dynamic, high-intensity play exhibited by collegiate players during the decade. The National Collegiate Athletic Association (NCAA) Men's Division I Championship, more commonly referred to as "March Madness" or the "Big Dance," continued to attract enormous public attention by enticing fans with the possibility of obscure, low-ranked teams upsetting big-name favorites to claim the national title. In 2001 an additional team slot was added to the tournament in order to allow non-ranked schools the opportunity to earn a chance to participate, raising the number of teams in the contest to sixty-five. The highly anticipated Final Four showdowns invariably rewarded audiences with entertaining action, both on and off the court; wagers placed by gamblers on the outcome of such games totaled an estimated $50 billion annually.

The two most successful college basketball teams during the decade were the University of North Carolina Tar Heels and the University of Florida Gators. The Tar Heels, already established as a major contender in the Atlantic Coast Conference, won the Division I Championship in 2005 by defeating the University of Illinois Fighting Illini, and again in 2009 with a victory over the Michigan State Spartans. They also held five regular season conference titles and made it to the Final Four in 2000 and 2008. The Gators were the only other team to claim two March Madness wins during the decade, with back-to-back titles in 2006 and 2007. They were also one of the most consistent collegiate teams, qualifying for the championship every year from 2000 to 2007.

The North Carolina Tar Heels play against the Michigan State Spartans in the NCAA men's basketball championship game in 2009. The Tar Heels victory in the game cemented their place as a dominant team in college basketball. © *Gregory Shamus/Getty Images*

❖ OLYMPICS

Throughout the 2000s, the United States Olympic team continued the cherished American tradition of annihilating its competition at the Summer Games, but it failed to win the overall medal count at any of the Winter Games. Host city Sydney, Australia, set the stage for the first

Summer Olympics of the new millennium, where more than ten thousand athletes from 199 different countries competed in three hundred events with hopes of taking home gold medals. Two events—tae kwon do and triathlon—were added to the Olympic itinerary, and women participated in weightlifting and pentathlon events for the first time in the history of the Games. The American women's softball team achieved a stunning comeback when, having lost three consecutive games, they rebounded to defeat each of the teams that they had lost to and claim the gold medal. Other noteworthy performances were the U.S. women's 4 × 100-meter medley relay swim squad, which broke the world record in the event to earn the gold medal, and the U.S. men's basketball team's narrow triumph over France and Lithuania for the highest spot on the award podium. Tennis players Venus and Serena Williams won a gold medal in women's doubles. The United States ultimately won the overall medal count with 92 (37 gold).

The 2002 Winter Olympics, held in Salt Lake City, Utah, were attended by almost 2,400 athletes representing 77 nations. Women's bobsled was introduced, bringing the total number of events to 78. Global broadcast records were shattered as more than two billion viewers tuned in to watch the competition, witnessing China and Australia's first-ever gold medals at the Winter Olympics. Highlights included American figure skaters Sarah Hughes and Michelle Kwan earning gold and bronze medals, respectively, in women's singles; and skier Bode Miller managing two silvers, in giant slalom and Alpine combined. The Games were ultimately disappointing for the American team, however, as their 34 medals (10 gold) came just short of overcoming the Germans, who won a record-setting 36 medals.

"Welcome Home" was the motto of the 2004 Summer Olympics, which marked the first time since 1896 that the Games were held in Athens, Greece, where they originated. The American team performed exceptionally by all standards, earning the most overall medals (103) and the most gold medals (35) of all competing nations. The American women's 4 × 200-meter swim relay team captured the gold with a world record performance, and swimmer Michael Phelps claimed an astounding eight medals (six gold and two bronze). Americans Misty May-Treanor and Kerri Walsh became the most successful beach volleyball duo in Olympic history by taking the gold medal without recording a single loss, and funambulist Carly Patterson became only the second American to win the all-around gold in gymnastics. Paul Hamm, an American gymnast, was erroneously awarded a gold medal over South Korean Yang Tae Young due to scoring confusion, but he was allowed to retain it despite appeals from Korean officials because the Olympic committee feared the consequences of setting such a precedent. The only major disappointment suffered by the U.S. Olympic team was the third-place finish of the men's basketball team, which was the first time since professionals were permitted to compete in the event that the United States did not take the gold.

The 2006 Winter Olympics, held in Turin, Italy, involved more than 2,500 athletes. The addition of team pursuit speed-skating, team sprint cross-country skiing, and snowboard cross raised the total number of events to 83. The 2006 Games were relatively uneventful for the United States team, which once again placed second to Germany in overall medal count, 25 to 29. American speed-skater Apolo Ohno provoked an unprecedented level of interest in short track skating by earning one gold and two bronze medals, and he went on to become the most decorated American in Winter Olympic history.

The final Olympiad of the decade was also the largest, the most viewed, and by far the most extravagant. The Games, for which host city Beijing, China, had constructed twelve new competition venues, were attended by almost 11,000 athletes representing 204 teams. The new Olympic structures served as a theater for 40 world records and 130 Olympic records, although much of the resultant pageantry and festiveness were diffused by allegations of human rights violations cast against the Chinese government. Nonetheless, the U.S. team had much cause for celebration, as athletes had outstanding performances in several events. Swimmer Michael Phelps returned to win an Olympic record of eight gold medals, and in the course of doing so broke seven speed records. Swimmer Natalie Coughlin became the first American female athlete to win six medals in a single Olympics and the first woman in history to win two consecutive gold medals in the 100-meter backstroke race. Sisters Venus and Serena Williams managed to take home a gold medal in women's doubles tennis, and the American doubles women's beach volleyball team once again went undefeated to claim the gold. Despite such exemplary success, the U.S. team did not win the overall gold medal count (which went to China for the first time), but it did maintain its customary highest total medal count, with 110 (36 gold).

❖ FOOTBALL: PROFESSIONAL

Although National Football League (NFL) quarterbacks have always been among the most high-profile athletes in professional football, their public stature during the 2000s grew to levels typically reserved for religious leaders and elected officials. Nearly all discussion of football during the decade centered on quarterbacks, and a team's success (or lack thereof) was frequently attributed to the skill of the man making the passes.

This trend was exemplified by quarterback Tom Brady, who led the New England Patriots to establish a total dominance over the rest of the NFL that lasted for much of the decade. Under the guidance of head coach Bill Belichick, Brady and the Patriots won the Super Bowl (the league championship game) in 2001, 2003, and 2004, with Brady named MVP of the first two appearances. They also boasted the league's first undefeated regular season in 2007, although they lost the Super Bowl that year to the New York Giants. As a result of his brilliance on the field and the success of his team, Brady was named *Sports Illustrated* Sportsman of the Year (2005) and awarded a bevy of honors, including AP Male Athlete of the Year (2007), AP NFL MVP (2007), and AP NFL Offensive Player of the Year (2007). He was hailed by the sports media as one of the greatest quarterbacks of all time and was a six-time Pro Bowl selection, and he set the record for the most passing touchdown completions in a regular season in 2007, with fifty.

Certainly the most polarizing figure in professional football was quarterback Brett Favre (pronounced "Farve"). Favre had cultivated an enormous fan base as starting quarterback for the Green Bay Packers, with whom he spent most of his professional career (1992–2007), by leading the team to win seven division championships, four conference championships, and one Super Bowl. However, Favre drew the scorn of the notoriously passionate Packers fan population when, having announced his retirement from the NFL in 2008, he promptly returned to play for the New York Jets for that year's football season. This betrayal, as it was interpreted by many, did not pay off for Favre, as he spent the season wracked by injury and failed to perform as well as he had with the Packers. The famed quarterback supposedly retired permanently after completing the 2008 season, but much to the surprise of football fans everywhere, he returned once again to professional football, this time to play for the Minnesota Vikings. Given the long-standing rivalry between the Vikings and the Packers, this transition was seen as even more egregious than the move to New York. Regardless of public opinion regarding his loyalty, Favre was expected to be remembered for his outstanding career, during which he broke several NFL records, including total career touchdown passes, career passing yards, career pass completions, career victories, and number of consecutive games as a starter.

Favre's records, however, were threatened by several other outstanding quarterbacks who ended the decade poised to overtake them. Peyton

Manning, quarterback for the Indianapolis Colts, had a standout decade, over the course of which he led his team to win one Super Bowl and had the most NFL wins as a starting quarterback, the most touchdown passes, the most passing yards, and the most pass completions. He also set the all-time NFL records for highest single-season passer rating, most career seasons with more than four thousand passing yards, most consecutive seasons with more than four thousand passing yards, most single-season pass completions, and the most games with a perfect passer rating. Peyton's brother Eli Manning, quarterback for the New York Giants, also made a name for himself by leading his team in 2007 to win the Super Bowl over the heavily favored Patriots. Ben Roethlisberger, who played for the Pittsburgh Steelers, was famous for his excellence as a "double threat" who was equally adept with passing and rushing plays and for winning the 2005 and 2008 Super Bowls. Drew Brees of the New Orleans Saints gained a reputation near the end of the decade, receiving the 2008 NFL Offensive Player of the Year Award and directing the Saints to win the 2009 season Super Bowl.

There were, of course, some standout NFL players who were not quarterbacks. Wide receiver Randy Moss, who played for the Vikings, Patriots, and Oakland Raiders during the 2000s, was popular for his high-intensity play and, in 2007, set the league record for most receptions in a season, with 23. Marvin Harrison, a wide receiver for the Indianapolis Colts, had the distinction of being the only player in NFL history to catch at least one pass in every single game he played, averaging more than 84 receptions per season and earning more than 1,400 receiving yards each season from 2000 to 2002. LaDainian Tomlinson, running back for the San Diego Chargers, set the all-time NFL record for single-season touchdowns, with 31 in 2006. During the same season he also broke the 45-year-old league record for the most points scored in a single season, with 186. By far the decade's best defensive player was Baltimore Ravens linebacker Ray Lewis, who was twice named NFL Defensive Player of the Year (2000 and 2003), and following his team's victory at the 2001 Super Bowl, he became the first defensive player from the winning team to earn Super Bowl MVP honors. He was a Pro Bowl selection eight times during the decade, as well as being named to the NFL 2000s All-Decade Team.

❖ FOOTBALL: COLLEGE

The most prominent force in college football during the 2000s was the University of Southern California (USC) Trojans, coached by Pete Carroll. With seven consecutive Pacific-10 conference titles (2002–08),

USC football coach Pete Carroll (second from left) embraces star football player Reggie Bush (third from left) during a game against rival UCLA on December 3, 2005. USC was a potent force in college football during the 2000s. © *Jay Drowns/ Sporting News/Getty Images*

seven straight Bowl Championship Series appearances (2002–08), and three consecutive national championship titles (2003–05), the Trojans were a genuine powerhouse. Much of this success was due to star running back Reggie Bush, who in 2005 was awarded the coveted Heisman Trophy, the Walter Camp award, the Doak Walker award, and the AP Player of the Year award. Scandal dimmed public appreciation for these achievements, however, when in 2006 it was revealed that the USC staff had made several NCAA recruiting violations, including giving gifts such as cars, houses, and cash to Bush and his family members as incentives for him to remain on the team. Consequentially, Bush was stripped of all of his major collegiate football awards, and the USC was forced to forfeit their 2005 Orange Bowl victory.

Although the USC Trojans were not a part of it, the Southeastern Conference (SEC) retained its position as one of the marquee conferences in college football. Teams from the conference won half of the total national championship titles of the decade, with Bowl Championship Series (BCS) titles going to the Louisiana State University Tigers (2003 and 2005), the Florida Gators (2006 and 2008), and the Alabama Crimson Tide (2009). The Gators, in particular, had an outstanding decade, with three conference championship game wins (2000, 2006, and 2008) and two near-perfect seasons (2006 and 2008), during each of which they recorded only one loss. Florida superstar quarterback Tim Tebow, who had propelled his team to unprecedented success, was honored with the Heisman Trophy in 2007, becoming the first college sophomore to earn it. During his career with Florida, Tebow set the SEC records for total yards earned (11,699) and total touchdowns (141).

Tebow was not the only college football player to set records during the decade, nor was he even the most remarkable. Kicker Billy Bennett of Georgia set an NCAA record when he ended his college career, which spanned from 2000 to 2003, with a 79.1 percent field goal success rate, having hit 87 of his 110 attempts. In 2002, Division II Grand Valley State wide receiver David Kircus had a record 35 touchdown receptions. Bryan James "B.J." Simmons, a quarterback for Texas Tech, set a new record for single-season yardage with 5,976 in 2003. Quarterback Timmy Chang of the University of Hawaii set the NCAA all-time career yardage record in 2004 by finishing his college football career with 16,910 total yards earned. In 2008, wide receiver Nate Kmic of Division III Mount Union set a new NCAA career rushing yardage record of 8,074. The following season saw receiver Freddie Barnes of Bowling Green catch a record 155 passes in 13 games, as well as Eastern New Mexico receiver J.J. Harp's feat of making 66 receptions in a single game.

❖ HOCKEY

One of the most significant events in professional hockey during the 2000s decade was the National Hockey League (NHL) lockout of 2004–2005. The lockout came about when a ten-year collective bargaining agreement between the NHL and the NHL players' union expired in early 2004, at which point the two parties began negotiations to reach a new agreement so that play could be resumed. The NHL officials wanted to establish a salary cap for players within the league. The players' union predictably rejected this notion, and, with neither side willing to cede to the demands of the other, no satisfactory agreement could be reached, forcing an indefinite delay in play. The negotiations ultimately took 310 days, effectively resulting in the cancellation of an entire season of North American professional hockey. This marked the first time in almost a century that the Stanley Cup, the NHL's top honor, was not awarded to any team, as well as the first time an American professional sports organization was forced to cancel an entire season because of a labor dispute. NHL activity resumed on July 21, 2005, but only after significant damage had been done to the league's reputation and the enthusiasm of American hockey fans.

❖ TENNIS

American tennis during the 2000s centered on one family name: Williams. Over the course of the decade, sisters Venus and Serena Williams established themselves as a dominant presence in the world of professional tennis by consistently racking up wins on both the U.S. and global circuits. Venus, the older of the two, claimed five singles wins at the prestigious Wimbledon Championship (2000, 2001, 2005, 2007, 2008); two singles wins at the U.S. Open (2000, 2001); and a gold medal in women's singles at the 2000 Summer Olympics. Little sister Serena earned a career Grand Slam (winning all four Majors tournaments at some point in one's career) by claiming five singles titles at the Australia Open (2003, 2005, 2007, 2009, and 2010); one French Open singles title (2002); three singles wins at Wimbledon (2002, 2003, 2009); and two singles wins at the U.S. Open (2002, 2008). She was also ranked number one in the world in singles tennis by the Women's Tennis Association on five separate occasions, while Venus achieved the title three different times. As a team, the dynamic duo managed to claim titles in women's doubles three times at the Australia Open (2001, 2003, 2009); four times at Wimbledon (2000, 2002, 2008, 2009); one doubles win at the U.S. Open (2009); and gold medals in women's doubles at both the 2000 and 2008 Summer Olympics.

In men's tennis, American athletes performed proficiently, although none managed to command the level of control exhibited by the Williams sisters. A particularly surprising development was the rise of a second sibling pair, Bob and Mike Bryan, who claimed more than fifty men's doubles titles during the decade. Most notable among such titles were the pair's three Australia Open wins (2006, 2007, 2009); a win at the French Open in 2003; a Wimbledon title in 2006; two wins at the U.S. Open (2005, 2008); and a bronze medal in men's doubles at the 2008 Summer Olympics. Andre Agassi, widely considered one of the best male tennis players in the history of the sport, won three Australia Open singles titles (2000, 2001, 2003) before announcing his retirement from professional tennis in 2006. Esteemed tennis legend Pete Sampras also ended his career during the decade at a special ceremony during the 2003 U.S. Open.

❖ GOLF

Professional golf was increasingly popular with American audiences during the 2000s, owing primarily to the remarkable talent of Tiger Woods. Woods's photogenic smile and prowess on the links quickly garnered him an adoring public. Over the course of the decade Woods charted fifty-six tournament wins and twelve majors (professional golf's most prestigious tournaments, consisting of the Masters Tournament, the U.S. Open Championship, the Open Championship, and the Professional Golfers' Association Championship). He also became the youngest golfer ever to achieve a career Grand Slam (winning all four of the majors in one's career), and the second person ever to earn three Grand Slams. Woods was highly marketable as well, gaining lucrative endorsements and sponsorship deals, causing him to become one of the decade's most recognizable and publicly visible athletes, and in 2009 to become the first athlete in history to earn $1 billion in his career. His public image was marred, however, when in late 2009 news broke that he had engaged in several extramarital affairs. On December 11 of that year Woods issued a public apology for cheating on his wife and announced an indefinite withdrawal from professional golf.

Top Earners

Although professional athletes had long been among the most generously paid people in the United States, the salaries awarded to top sportspeople during the 2000s were nothing short of astronomical. The average yearly salary of an NFL player rose from $79,000 in 1980 to $1.75 million, while NBA players saw a tenfold increase in compensation, from an average of $500,000 per year to $5 million. In 2009 *Forbes* magazine released a list of the year's highest-paid athletes, which was unsurprisingly topped by Tiger Woods, whose golf career had by that year netted him $1 billion. Below is a list of the top-earning American athletes at the end of the decade, along with their earnings for the 2009 season:

1. Tiger Woods, golfer: $110 million in prize money and endorsements
2. Kobe Bryant (tie), basketball player: $45 million in salary from the Lakers and endorsements
3. Michael Jordan (tie), retired basketball player: $45 million in endorsements and brand sales
4. LeBron James (tie), basketball player: $40 million in salary from the Cavaliers and endorsements
5. Phil Mickelson (tie), golfer: $40 million in prize money and endorsements
6. Dale Earnhardt Jr., race car driver: $34 million in prize money, endorsements, and merchandise sales
7. Shaquille O'Neal, basketball player: $33 million in salary from the Phoenix Suns and endorsements
8. Oscar De La Hoya (tie), boxer: $32 million in prize money and endorsements
9. Alex Rodriguez (tie), baseball player: $32 million in salary from the New York Yankees and endorsements
10. Kevin Garnett (tie), basketball player: $30 million in salary from the Boston Celtics and endorsements
11. Jeff Gordon (tie), race car driver: $30 million in prize money and endorsements
12. Derek Jeter (tie), baseball player: $30 million in salary from the New York Yankees and endorsements

❖ AUTO RACING

The image of National Association for Stock Car Auto Racing (NASCAR)–sanctioned stock car racing underwent a dramatic and rapid change during the 2000s, resulting in increased public interest from audiences both in the United States and abroad. Traditionally the sport was more popular in the rural South; however, modifications made to its marketing schemes and title sponsorships made NASCAR racing appeal to a broader demographic than ever before. Consequentially, race attendance and television viewing increased sharply, as did the profitability of the sport. In 2004 NASCAR introduced a new championship format known as the Chase for the Cup, in which the top ten (later expanded to twelve) point-earning drivers out of twenty-six races earned a chance to compete in ten "race-within-a-race" competitions that took place during regularly scheduled competitions, with the overall winner earning the championship title. Jimmie Johnson, already a dominant force in the NASCAR circuit, was the most frequent winner of the Chase for the Cup championship, with four consecutive titles from 2006 to 2009. In 2009 he became the first racecar driver to be named AP Male Athlete of the Year, further indicating the elevated public profile of NASCAR competition.

Not everything that occurred for NASCAR during the decade was cause for celebration, however. On February 18, 2001, celebrated driver Dale Earnhardt was killed when, during the final lap of the Daytona 500 race, a competitor clipped the rear of his car and sent it careening into a concrete wall. The tragedy prompted an investigation into the safety of the sport, the findings of which resulted in stricter seatbelt and head protection regulations for drivers and a redesign of the safety barriers on racetracks.

❖ SOCCER

Never a particularly popular sport in the United States, soccer was mostly ignored by many American sports enthusiasts throughout the 2000s, although Major League Soccer (MLS) did manage to attract more attention than it had in the past. The MLS saw record growth during the decade, expanding its original ten-team roster significantly with the addition of five clubs: the Houston Dynamo, the Toronto Football Club, Club Deportivo Chivas USA, Real Salt Lake, and the Seattle Sounders Football Club, with three more teams projected to join the league in the near future.

The biggest story in MLS was the acquisition of famed British midfielder David Beckham by the Los Angeles Galaxy in 2007, which caused a significant stir in the media and helped raise public awareness of the sport's presence in the United States. The team was already one of the most successful in the league, having won the U.S. Open Cup in 2001 and 2005 and the MLS Championship in 2002 and 2005, but it floundered later in the decade despite the addition of Beckham. D.C. United became the most decorated club in the league, claiming its fourth MLS Cup in 2004, its second U.S. Open Cup in 2008, and its third and fourth MLS Supporters' Shield (awarded for having the league's best regular season record) in 2006 and 2007.

Internationally, the U.S. national team performed better than ever before (albeit by only a slight margin), claiming the Confederation of North, Central American and Caribbean Association Football (CONCACAF) Gold Cup (the conference's main competition) title in 2002, 2005, and 2007. Despite those accomplishments, the national team continued its longstanding custom of performing poorly at the international level.

❖ COMBAT SPORTS

Boxing, traditionally a favorite U.S. spectator sport, continued the steady decline in popularity during the 2000s that began in the early 1990s. This trend was likely attributable to a decrease in the number of high-caliber American boxers and to the astounding rise of mixed martial arts (MMA) fighting. The most noteworthy boxer to hail from the United States during the 2000s was Floyd Mayweather Jr., who had recorded forty career wins (twenty-five by knockout) by the end of the decade without a single loss. By the end of the decade, the technically skilled fighter had earned nine world titles in five different weight classes. Other Americans to find success as boxers during the decade were Bernard Hopkins, who was named Undisputed World Middleweight Champion in 2001, and Shane Mosley, who made a name for himself as a top contender in the lightweight class with a record of thirteen wins and five losses.

As boxing promoters grew increasingly dismayed at their steadily dwindling audiences, MMA organizers prospered like never before. What had once been considered a barbaric exercise was transformed, primarily under the guidance and marketeering of the Ultimate Fighting Championship (UFC, the major U.S. MMA governing body and promoter), into an extraordinarily popular, highly disciplined competition that attracted some of the world's top athletes with the tantalizing prospect of huge victory purses and profitable endorsement deals. Audiences crowded to fights (and paid enormous sums for pay-per-view televised events), enthralled by the notion of trained fighters grappling and striking one another—with techniques borrowed from

Randy Couture (right) fights Antonio Nogueira in a UFC (Ultimate Fighting Championship) match in 2009. Randy Couture was one of the more famous fighters on the circuit in the first decade of the twenty-first century. © *Jon Kopaloff/Getty Images*

wrestling, Muy Thai, boxing, Karate, Jui-Jitsu, and other combat disciplines—in hopes of either forcing an opponent's submission or earning a knockout. Legitimized by strict regulations that barred unsafe moves, required the use of gloves, and established time limits and refereeing guidelines, MMA quickly rose to the forefront of the American sports psyche as one of its more popular sports. Although many of the top competitors in the sport were foreign, many Americans made names for themselves in the ring. Some of the most famous American competitors to emerge during the decade were Randy Couture, Clay Guida, Brock Lesnar, Tito Ortiz, Tim Sylvia, Urijah Faber, and Forrest Griffin.

❖ EXTREME SPORTS

Also known as action sports or freesport, extreme sports are any type of athletic activity with a higher-than-average level of danger for its participants. Although no exact definition had ever been decided upon, general public sentiment regarding what sports get classified as "extreme" usually has more to do with the age of their participants than anything else. Such sports are primarily youth-oriented, involve a higher level of individual creativity and risk than more traditional team sports, and are often part of a larger countercultural movement. The 2000s brought with them an increase in the mainstream acceptance and profitability of extreme sports, chief among them skateboarding, snowboarding, BMX biking, mountain biking, surfing, and freestyle skiing. The increased popularity of extreme sports was largely due to the proliferation of the X Games, a made-for-television sporting event, organized and hosted by U.S. sports broadcaster ESPN, which provided a much larger audience for the sports. Extreme sports fans were further vindicated when the 2006 Winter Olympics added snowboard cross and parallel giant slalom to the scheduled events and again in 2008 with the addition of BMX to the Summer Olympic itinerary.

Of the newest generation of extreme sports athletes, several garnered attention for pushing the boundaries of their respective sports and disregarding their own bodily safety. Shaun White, one of snowboarding's most respected and consistent champions, made a name for himself as the first athlete to compete and medal in both the Summer and Winter X Games in different events (he was also an acclaimed skateboarder). Motocross racer Travis Pastrana became a fan favorite for his charisma and ability on motorbikes, winning gold medals in supercross and freestyle motocross. Andy Macdonald, a vert (meaning vertical) skateboarder, earned his fifteenth X Games skateboarding medal in 2009, breaking the performance record of Tony Hawk.

 For More Information

....

BOOKS

Boyles, Bob, and Paul Guido. *Fifty Years of College Football: A Modern History of America's Most Colorful Sport*. New York: Skyhorse, 2007.

Browne, David. *Amped: How Big Air, Big Dollars, and a New Generation Took Sports to the Extreme*. New York: Bloomsbury, 2004.

Canseco, Jose. *Juiced: Wild Times, Rampant 'Roids, Smash Hits, and How Baseball Got Big*. New York: HarperCollins, 2005.

Dure, Beau. *Long-Range Goals: The Success Story of Major League Soccer.* Washington, DC: Potomac Books, 2010.

Dyreson, Mark, and J.A. Mangan. *Sport and American Society: Exceptionalism, Insularity, and "Imperialism."* New York: Routledge, 2007.

Edmondson, Jacqueline. *Venus and Serena Williams: A Biography.* Westport, CT: Greenwood, 2005.

Kluck, Ted A. *Game Time: Inside College Football.* Guilford, CT: Lyons Press, 2007.

Woods, Tiger. *How I Play Golf.* New York: ETW/Warner Books, 2001.

Yaeger, Don, and Jim Henry. *Tarnished Heisman: Did Reggie Bush Turn His Final College Season into a Six-Figure Job?* New York: Pocket Books/Simon & Schuster, 2008.

WEB SITES

ATP World Tour. http://www.atpworldtour.com (accessed on August 22, 2011).

MLB.com. http://www.MLB.com (accessed on August 22, 2011).

NASCAR.com. http://www.nascar.com (accessed on August 22, 2011).

NBA.com. http://www.NBA.com (accessed on August 22, 2011).

National Collegiate Athletic Association. http://www.NCAA.org (accessed on August 22, 2011).

NFL. http://www.NFL.com (accessed on August 22, 2011).

NHL. http://www.NHL.com (accessed on August 22, 2011).

Official Site of the Olympic Movement. http://www.olympic.org (accessed on August 22, 2011).

PGA. http://www.PGA.com (accessed on August 22, 2011).

WTA. http://www.wtatennis.com (accessed on August 22, 2011).

Where to Learn More

BOOKS

Bennett, Andy and Keith Kahn-Harris, eds. *After Subculture: Critical Studies in Contemporary Youth Culture*. Hampshire, England: Palgrave MacMillan, 2004.

Bush, George W. *Decision Points*. New York: Broadway, 2011.

Caesar, James W. and Andrew E. Busch. *The Perfect Tie: The True Story of the 2000 Presidential Election*. Lanham, MD: Roman & Littlefield, 2001.

Callero, Peter. *The Myth of Individualism: How Social Forces Shape Our Lives*. New York: Rowman & Littlefield Publishers, 2009.

Christensen, Kathleen and Barbara Schneider. *Workplace Flexibility: Realigning 20th-Century Jobs for a 21st-Century Workforce*. Ithaca: ILR Press, 2010.

Clark, Chap. *Hurt: Inside the World of Today's Teenagers (Youth, Family, and Culture)*. Ada, MI: Baker Book House, 2005.

Collins, Allan and Richard Halverson. *Rethinking Education in the Age of Technology: The Digital Revolution and Schooling in America*. New York: Teachers College Press, 2009.

Combs, Cynthia C. *Terrorism in the Twenty-First Century*. Upper Saddle River, NJ: Prentice Hall, 2010.

Corrigan, Jim. *The 2000s Decade in Photos: A New Millennium*. Berkeley Heights, NJ: Enslow Publishers, 2010.

Drew, David E. *STEM the Tide: Reforming Science, Technology, Engineering, and Math Education in America*. Baltimore, MD: The Johns Hopkins University Press, 2011.

Fainaru-Wada, Mark and Lance Williams. *Game of Shadows: Barry Bonds, BALCO, and the Steroids Scandal that Rocked Professional Sports*. New York: Gotham, 2007.

Filkins, Dexter. *The Forever War.* New York: Vintage, 2009.

Gordon, Michael R. and Bernard E. Trainor. *Cobra II: The Inside Story of the Invasion and Occupation of Iraq.* New York: Vintage, 2007.

Grazian, David. *Mix It Up; Popular Culture, Mass Media, and Society.* New York: W.W. Norton & Company, 2010.

Horne, Jed. *Breach of Faith: Hurricane Katrina and the Near Death of a Great American City.* New York: Random House Trade Paperbacks, 2008.

Jenkins, Henry. *Convergence Culture: Where Old and New Media Collide.* New York: NYU Press, 2008.

Jones, Seth G. *In the Graveyard of Empires.* New York: W.W. Norton & Company, 2010.

Lusetich, Robert. *Unplayable: An Inside Account of Tiger's Most Tumultuous Season.* New York: Atria Books, 2010.

Mingst, Karen A and Margaret P. Karns. *The United Nations in the 21st Century.* Boulder, CO: Westview Press, 2011.

Muller, Jurgen. *Movies of the 2000s.* Germany: Taschen, 2011.

National Geographic. *The Knowledge Book: Everything You Need to Know to Get By in the 21st Century.* Margate, FL: National Geographic, 2010.

The New York Times, Jill Abramson and Bill Keller. *Obama: The Historic Journey.* New York: Callaway Editions, 2009.

Norman, James R. *The Oil Card: Global Economic Warfare in the 21st Century.* Walterville, OR: Trine Day, 2008.

Obama, Barack. *The Audacity of Hope.* New York: Vintage, 2008.

Poole, David and Jim McLaurin. *"Then Junior Said to Jeff . . .": The Best NASCAR Stories Ever Told.* Chicago, IL: Triumph Books, 2006.

Radomski, Kirk. *Bases Loaded: The Inside Story of the Steroid Era in Baseball by the Central Figure in the Mitchell Report.* New York: Hudson Street Press, 2009.

Reich, Robert B. *Aftershock: The Next Economy and America's Future.* New York: Vintage, 2011.

Schiff, Peter D. and Andrew J. Schiff. *How an Economy Grows and Why It Crashes.* Hoboken, NJ: Wiley, 2010.

Sinnreich, Aram. *Mashed Up: Music, Technology, and the Rise of Configurable Culture.* Amherst: University of Massachusetts Press, 2010.

Thelin, John R. *A History of American Higher Education.* Baltimore, MD: The Johns Hopkins University Press, 2011.

Tomsen, Peter. *The Wars of Afghanistan: Messianic Terrorism, Tribal Conflicts, and the Failure of Great Powers.* New York: PublicAffairs Books, 2011.

Wallechinsky, David. *The Complete Book of the Olympics: 2008 Edition.* London: Aurum Press, 2008.

White, Jonathan R. *Terrorism and Homeland Security.* Belmont, CA: Wadsworth Publishing, 2011.

Willman, David. *The Mirage Man: Bruce Ivins, the Anthrax Attacks, and America's Rush to War*. New York: Bantam, 2011.

Woods, Mark and Ruth Owen. *Xtreme!: Extreme Sports Facts and Stats*. New York: Gareth Stevens, 2011.

Zafran, Larry. *America's (Math) Education Crisis: Why We Have It and Why We Can('t) Fix It*. Charleston, SC: CreateSpace, 2010.

WEB SITES

"Apple Update." *Computer World*. http://www.computerworld.com/s/article/9137163/Apple_Update (accessed on December 1, 2011).

"Business Day." *The New York Times*. http://www.nytimes.com/pages/business/index.html (accessed on December 1, 2011).

Businessweek. http://www.businessweek.com/ (accessed on December 1, 2011).

Center for Economic and Policy Research. http://www.cepr.net/ (accessed on December 1, 2011).

"CNN Money: Business 2.0." *CNN*. http://money.cnn.com/magazines/business2/ (accessed on December 1, 2011).

"Defining a 21st Century Education: At a Glance." *Center for Public Education*. http://www.centerforpubliceducation.org/Learn-About/21st-Century (accessed on December 1, 2011).

"Economy at a Glance." *Bureau of Labor Statistics*. http://www.bls.gov/eag/eag.us.htm (accessed on December 1, 2011).

"Education." *The World Bank*. http://web.worldbank.org/WBSITE/EXTERNAL/TOPICS/EXTEDUCATION/0,,menuPK:282391~pagePK:149018~piPK:149093~theSitePK:282386,00.html (accessed on December 2011).

Entrepreneur. http://www.entrepreneur.com/ (accessed on December 1, 2011).

"Factbox: Largest U.S. Bankruptcies." *Reuters*. http://www.reuters.com/article/2011/10/31/us-mfglobal-bankruptcies-idUSTRE79U4J520111031 (accessed on December 1, 2011).

"Fast Facts." *National Center for Education Statistics*. http://nces.ed.gov/fastfacts/ (accessed on December 1, 2011).

Glaser, Mark. "Your Guide to Social Networking Online." *PBS: Mediashift*. http://www.pbs.org/mediashift/2007/08/your-guide-to-social-networking-online241.html (accessed on December 1, 2011).

"The History of US Government Corporate Bailouts." *Credit Loan*. http://www.creditloan.com/infographics/the-history-of-us-government-corporate-bailouts/ (accessed on December 1, 2011).

"History of U.S. Gov't Bailouts." *ProPublica*. http://www.propublica.org/special/government-bailouts (accessed on December 1, 2011).

Honan, Mathew and Steven Leckart. "10 Years After: A Look Back at the Dotcom Boom and Bust." *Wired Magazine*. http://www.wired.com/magazine/2010/02/10yearsafter/all/1 (accessed on December 1, 2011).

Madden, Mary and Kathryn Zickuhr. "Social Networking." *Pew Internet*. http://pewinternet.org/topics/Social-Networking.aspx (accessed on December 1, 2011).

Mann, Thomas E. "Reflections on the 2000 U.S. Presidential Election." *Brookings Institution*. http://www.brookings.edu/articles/2001/01elections_mann.aspx (accessed on December 1, 2011).

"Money." *U.S. News*. http://money.usnews.com/money/business-economy (accessed on December 1, 2011).

National Science and Technology Council. "Science for the 21st Century." *White House*. http://www.whitehouse.gov/files/documents/ostp/NSTC%20Reports/Science21Century.pdf (accessed on December 1, 2011).

Padgett, Tim. "Gay Family Values." *Time Magazine,* July 5, 2007. http://www.time.com/time/magazine/article/0,9171,1640411,00.html (accessed on December 1, 2011).

Richebacher, Dr. Kurt. "US Recession." *The Daily Reckoning*. http://dailyreckoning.com/us-recession/ (accessed on December 1, 2011).

Sanneh, Kelefa. "The Reality Principle." *The New Yorker,* May 9, 2011. http://www.newyorker.com/arts/critics/atlarge/2011/05/09/110509crat_atlarge_sanneh (accessed on December 1, 2011).

"Stem Cell Research." *AAAS*. http://www.aaas.org/spp/cstc/briefs/stemcells/ (accessed on December 1, 2011).

Streeter, Leslie Gray. "2000–2010: The Top 10 Pop Culture Trends." *Palm Beach Pulse,* December 12, 2009. http://www.pbpulse.com/movies/2009/12/12/2000-2010-the-top-10-pop-culture-trends/ (accessed on December 1, 2011).

"Top 20 of the 2000s in Pop Culture." *Lounging Pass,* April 20, 2010. http://loungingpass.blogspot.com/2010/04/top-20-of-2000s-in-pop-culture.html (accessed on December 1, 2011).

"2000s: The Decade in Sports." *Sports Illustrated*. http://sportsillustrated.cnn.com/2009/magazine/specials/2000s/12/20/decade.index/index.html (accessed on December 1, 2011).

Wang, Jonathan. "Real Causes for US Financial Meltdown and Global Recession." *Business Week*. http://bx.businessweek.com/the-great-recession/view?url=http%3A%2F%2Fwww.amlinkint.com%2FEnglish%2Fglobal_recession_cause.html (accessed on December 1, 2011).

Woolley, John and Gergard Peters. "The American Presidency Project." *University of California at Santa Barbara*. http://www.presidency.ucsb.edu/elections.php (accessed on December 1, 2011).

"World Conference on Science: Science for the Twenty-First Century." *UNESCO*. http://unesdoc.unesco.org/images/0012/001207/120706e.pdf (accessed on December 1, 2011).

Xtreme Sports Exchange. http://www.xtremesportsxchange.com/ (accessed on December 1, 2011).

Index